CRITICAL MINERALS, SUSTAINABILITY, AND THE ENERGY TRANSITION IN THE GLOBAL SOUTH

This book addresses the relationship between efficient management of critical minerals and sustainability in the Global South, including Sub-Saharan Africa.

Critical minerals are essential raw materials for the technologies that are pivotal in today's energy transition. However, critical mineral host states and communities face social, economic, ecological, political, technological, and governance injustices. The book contends that the criteria currently used in assessing criticality and critical mineral development do not fulfil the sustainable development ambitions of developing countries and that broader considerations must be taken into account to include the stakeholders involved as well as the spatial dimension of the critical mineral value chain.

In particular, the book argues that the law must consider the broader context in which minerals become critical to particular processes. It positions this argument within the current context of climate change, the just energy transition, the minerals-energy nexus, and geopolitical tensions.

By analysing the copper-cobalt value chain through case studies on DRC, Zambia, China, and the EU, the book provides new avenues for critical mineral development and acknowledges the necessity for sustainability amidst the exacerbated impacts of climate change.

Addressing a key challenge of the global energy transition, the book argues for a just holistic framework, which includes parameters such as domestic value addition, human rights in business development, environmental sensitivity, the development of communication channels from remote marginalised communities to international policymakers, and the re-designing of criticality considerations beyond supply and economic aspects.

Global Energy Law and Policy: Volume 9

Global Energy Law and Policy

Series Editors
Peter D Cameron
Pieter Bekker
Volker Roeben
Leonie Reins
Crina Baltag

Energy policy and energy law are undergoing rapid global transformation, characterised by the push in favour of decarbonisation. The 2015 Sustainable Development Goals and the 2015 Paris Agreement on international climate action have forged a consensus for a pathway to a universal just transition towards a low-carbon economy for all states and all societies.

This series publishes conceptual works that help academics, legal practitioners and decision-makers to make sense of these transformational changes. The perspective of the series is global. It welcomes contributions on international law, regional law (for example, from the EU, US and ASEAN regions), and the domestic law of all states with emphasis on comparative works that identify horizontal trends, and including transnational law. The series' scope is comprehensive, embracing both public and commercial law on energy in all forms and sources and throughout the energy life-cycle from extraction, production, operation, consumption and waste management/decommissioning. The series is a forum for innovative interdisciplinary work that uses the insights of cognate disciplines to achieve a better understanding of energy law and policy in the 21st century.

Recent titles in this series:

Decarbonisation and the Energy Industry
edited by Tade Oyewumni, Penelope Crossley, Frédéric Gilles Sourgens and Kim Talus

The Global Energy Transition: Law, Policy and Economics for Energy in the 21st Century
edited by Peter D Cameron, Xiaoyi Mu and Volker Roeben

The Law and Governance of Mining and Minerals: A Global Perspective
by Ana Elizabeth Bastida

National Climate Change Acts: The Emergence, Form and Nature of National Framework Climate Legislation
edited by Thomas L Muinzer

Governing the Extractive Sector: Regulating the Foreign Conduct of International Mining Firms
by Jeffrey Bone

Stability and Legitimate Expectations in International Energy Investments
by Rahmi Kopar

Land Law and the Extractive Industries: Challenges and Opportunities in Africa
by Victoria R Nalule

China's Global Energy Expansion: A Regulatory Assessent
by Xiaohan Gong

Critical Minerals, Sustainability, and the Energy Transition in the Global South: A Justice Perspective
by Susan Nakanwagi

Critical Minerals, Sustainability, and the Energy Transition in the Global South

A Justice Perspective

Susan Nakanwagi

• HART •
OXFORD • LONDON • NEW YORK • NEW DELHI • SYDNEY

HART PUBLISHING

Bloomsbury Publishing Plc

Kemp House, Chawley Park, Cumnor Hill, Oxford, OX2 9PH, UK

1385 Broadway, New York, NY 10018, USA

29 Earlsfort Terrace, Dublin 2, Ireland

First published in Great Britain 2024

A catalogue record for this book is available from the British Library.

A catalogue record for this book is available from the Library of Congress.

Library of Congress Control Number: 2024944063

ISBN: HB: 978-1-50997-670-6
ePDF: 978-1-50997-672-0
ePub: 978-1-50997-671-3

Typeset by Compuscript Ltd, Shannon

To my dear husband, Mr Ismael Ssemakula, for pushing me to embark on personal growth and for the unwavering financial support.

To my loving father, Mr Vincent Mugumya, and Uncle Dan Lwanga, for being my greatest cheerleaders and pushing me to be the best version of myself.

To my wonderful mother, Ms Mary Nakasagga, for her steadfast love and care for my children.

To my support team – Mary, Joseph, Kevin, Frank, Arnold, Martin and Eva.

To my lovely daughters, Ariana and Ayra, for the time spent without a mother's presence as I immersed myself in research.

To the Global South, in its pursuit of justice and meaningful growth and development.

ACKNOWLEDGEMENTS

This book would not have been achieved without the direct and indirect input of so many people along the way, which persons I wish to acknowledge.

Words cannot express my gratitude to Dr Ana Elizabeth Bastida, who has made immeasurable input throughout my research. Her guidance, support and excellent mentorship have helped me produce this piece of work; she did this with a gentle, friendly and engaging approach. I am also grateful to Raphael J Heffron, whose research on energy justice helped me develop justice as a concept in this book.

Special thanks also go out to Professor Hanri Mostert and Professor Peter Cameron, who offered fresh insight towards my research. Professor Mostert's guidance was particularly important in the appraisal and fine-tuning of the final version of this book. I would also like to thank colleagues at the Office of Legal Affairs at the International Energy Agency in Paris KC Micheals, Tomás de Oliveira Bredariol and Sakeena Moeena, with whom I worked on the sustainability chapter in the 2021 report on 'Role of Critical Minerals in Clean Energy Transition', which also shaped my research. Many thanks too to the management and colleagues at Regenerate Africa, who have accorded me with the time and support to complete this book.

Lastly, I would be thoughtless in not mentioning my family, especially my spouse, parents, siblings and children, whose belief in me has kept my spirits and motivation high during this process. Most importantly, this endeavour would not have been possible without the generous support from my dear husband, Mr Ismael Ssemakula, who financed my research and study. Kevin, my brother, thank you for your help, especially in making some of my illustrations come to life and listening to my lamentations about research life. My entire family and friends, thank you for your continuous prayers, support and understanding when undertaking my research and writing my project.

To God be the Glory.

CONTENTS

ABBREVIATIONS

AMV	African Union's Africa Mining Vision
ASM	artisanal and small-scale mining
BRI	Belt and Road Initiative
BRICS	Brazil, Russia, India, China, South Africa
CAP	Cobalt Action Partnership
CBO	Congressional Budget Office
CEAP	circular economy action plan
CEC	Commission of the European Communities
CEE	climate, environment and energy
CMC	Chinalco Mining Corp
COP	Conference of the Parties
CRBC	China Road and Bridge Corporation
CRMs	critical raw materials
CSD	Commission on Sustainable Development
CSR	corporate social responsibility
DA	development agreement
DOE	Department of Energy
DRC	Democratic Republic of Congo
EC	European Commission
EBA	European Battery Alliance
EBITDA	Earnings before interest, taxes, depreciation, and amortisation
EI	economic importance
EIA	environmental impact assessment
EITI	Extractive Industries Transparency Initiative
ESG	environmental, social and governance

FCA	Fair Cobalt Alliance
FPIC	free, prior and informed consent
GDP	gross domestic product
GVCs	global value chains
HDI	Human Development Index
ICMM	International Council on Mining and Metals
ICPD	International Conference on Population and Development
IEA	International Energy Agency
IFC	International Financial Corporation
ILO	International Labour Organization
IPCC	International Panel for Climate Change
IRENA	International Renewable Energy Agency
IRP	International Resource Panel
JPOI	Johannesburg Plan of Implementation
LCSA	life cycle sustainability assessments
LDCs	least developed countries
LME	London Metals Exchange
LSM	large-scale mining
MDGs	Millennium Development Goals
NDCs	nationally determined contributions
NGOs	non-governmental organisations
OECD	Organisation for Economic Co-operation and Development
OXFAM	Oxford Committee for Famine Relief
PGMs	platinum group metals
PSNR	permanent sovereignty over natural resources
REE	rare earth elements
SADC	Southern African Development Community
SDGs	Sustainable Development Goals
SDLO	sustainable development licence to operate

SED	sustainable energy development
SSA	sub-Saharan Africa
TWAIL	Third World Approaches to International Law
UNCSD	United Nations Conference on Sustainable Development
UNDRIP	United Nations Declaration of the Rights of Indigenous Peoples
UNECE	United Nations Economic Commission for Europe
UNFCCC	United Nations Framework Convention for Climate Change
UNICEF	United Nations Children's Fund
WB	World Bank
WBCSD	World Business Council for Sustainable Development
WGI	World Bank Worldwide Governance Indicators
WGI-PV	Worldwide Governance Indicators – Political Stability and Absence of Violence
WSSD	World Summit on Sustainable Development
ZEA	Zone d'Exploration Artisanal

LIST OF FIGURES

LIST OF TABLES

TABLE OF CASES

TABLE OF LEGISLATION

Instruments

Soft Law Standards, Initiatives and Guidelines

1

Overview of the Critical Minerals Industry from a Justice Perspective

1.1. The Argument of this Book: The Premise of the Just Holistic Framework

This book provides insight into the critical mining industry in sub-Saharan Africa and its intricate relationship with sustainable development, as well as the growing demand for these minerals in the Global North. For many years, the demand for minerals and other natural resources from sub-Saharan Africa has been a key driver of the global economy. However, the development fallacy given to the Global South countries is adopting an export-led development strategy, rather than developing local consumption capacity that would improve the delivery of social services and promote the development of the world's most impoverished regions. Mineral resources have always been crucial to the global economy due to their wide application in day-to-day aspects like industries, security, fashion and construction.[1] Moreover, their use today is more pronounced – they are vital in driving the energy transition, as renewables will probably make up over 91 per cent of the energy mix by 2050.[2] As a result, policymakers in various nations and regions, especially in technologically advanced countries (such as China, the USA, the UK and the EU), have produced assessments evaluating their economies' vulnerability to disruptions in the supply of minerals.[3] Most of these studies have one common agenda – to compile a list of what is known as 'critical minerals'.

Critical mineral assessments have often considered only two parameters – supply risk and economic importance.[4] That is, (i) minerals for which the risk of

[1] RG Eggert, 'Critical Minerals and Emerging Technologies' (2010) 26(4) *Issues in Science and Technology* 49.

[2] IEA, 'The Role of Critical Minerals in Clean Energy Transitions. World Energy Outlook Special Report' (International Energy Agency, 2021).

[3] R Coulomb, S Dietz, M Godunova and TB Nielsen, 'Critical Minerals Today and in 2030: An Analysis for OECD Countries' (OECD Publishing, 2015) OECD Environment Working Papers No 91.

[4] D Schrijvers, A Hool, GA Blengini, WQ Chen, J Dewulf, R Eggert, L van Ellen, R Gauss, J Goddin, K Habib and C Hagelüken, 'A Review of Methods and Data to Determine Raw Material Criticality' (2020) 155 *Resources, Conservation and Recycling* 104617.

supply disruption is relatively high and (ii) minerals for which supply disruptions will have significant economic consequences. However, this is a construct mainly concerned with the minerals' availability. Critical minerals might be spatially concentrated, posing a threat to supply security. The Global North increasingly relies on supplies from the mineral-rich Global South,[5] which is prone to political instability and state fragility. According to the Organisation for Economic Cooperation and Development (OECD), many Sub-Saharan and Latin American states are fragile.[6] These are states that cannot fully utilise their natural resources and meet the basic requirements of their citizens due to institutional flaws, governance issues and corruption. Consequently, the governments fail to legitimise their programmes both within the state and in the international community, with far-reaching ramifications for achieving the United Nations' Sustainable Development Goals (SDGs).[7] Simultaneously, increasing demand from the

[5] The concept of Global North and South is gaining traction and usage as the world moves away from the normative nation classification of developed *vis-à-vis* developing countries. See D Hammett and KV Gough, 'IDPR in 2016 and Beyond' (2016) 38(4) *International Development Planning Review* 347. There is now a decreasing relevance of the distinction between developing and developed countries. See D Lewis, 'Contesting Parallel Worlds: Time to Abandon the Distinction between the "International" and "Domestic" Contexts of Third Sector Scholarship?' (2015) 26(5) *VOLUNTAS: International Journal of Voluntary and Nonprofit Organizations* 2084. In 2015, the World Bank stated that the 'developing/developed world' dichotomy was losing relevance and would phase out its use. See T Khokhar and U Serajuddin, 'Should We Continue to Use the Term "Developing World"?' (World Bank, 2015) https://blogs.worldbank.org/opendata/should-we-continue-use-term-developing-world. In a global context, the term 'North–South divide' is frequently used to refer to the grouping of countries based on their socio-economic and political features. The Global South countries share a common history of colonialism, neo-imperialism and divergent economic and social transformation, all of which contribute to the maintenance of huge disparities in life expectancy, living standards and access to resources. N Dados and R Connell, 2012. 'The Global South' (2012) 11(1) *Contexts* 12. On the other hand, the phrase 'Global South' is frequently used to refer to low-income countries and the term 'Global North' refers to the more developed countries. See R Horner and P Carmody, 'Global North/South' in A Kobayashi (ed) *International Encyclopedia of Human Geography* (Elsevier BV, 2019) 181–87. A body of literature is also emerging advocating for a 'Global East' categorisation for those countries which are too rich to fall into the Global South category and too poor to fall into the Global North. See M Müller, 'In Search of the Global East: Thinking Between North and South' (2020) 25(3) *Geopolitics* 734. Take the example of China, which, although falling under the Global South, is now considered a model for developing countries. The country has lifted nearly 700 million people out of poverty, gained more influence than the majority of Western countries and developed into one of the world's leading economic powers. See X Lin, 'China Takes Extraordinary Initiatives in South–South Cooperation' (United Nations Office for South–South Cooperation, 2019) www.unsouthsouth.org/2019/04/30/china-takes-extraordinary-initiatives-in-south-south-cooperation/#:~:text=China%20is%20a%20model%20for,said%20in%20Beijing%20last%20Tuesday. Schmitz explored the growing role of China in the global arena and in development studies basing on its rapid economic development: HB Schmitz, 'The Rise of the East: What Does It Mean for Development Studies?' in O Kenichi and O Izumi (eds), *Eastern and Western Ideas for African Growth* (Routledge, 2013) 84–96.

[6] OECD, 'The Changing Face of Fragility and Its Implications Post-2015' in *States of Fragility 2015: Meeting Post-2015 Ambitions* (OECD Publishing, 2015) 29–54.

[7] On the world-systems theory, a sociological and economic theory proposed in 1974 by sociologist Immanuel Wallerstein which also partly explains the resource dependence between the traditional 'developed and developing countries', see I Wallerstein, 'The Rise and Future Demise of the World Capitalist System: Concepts for Comparative Analysis' (1974) 16(4) *Comparative Studies in Society and History* 387.

Global North's expanding markets, new technologies requiring vast quantities of rare minerals, low application substitutability and low recycling rates have increased the economies' vulnerability to supply disruptions.[8] However, several countries in the Global South are not end users of these critical minerals. Hence, criticality assessments ignore a myriad of considerations that are pertinent to the development of the critical mineral industry in the Global South. These are what we call in this book 'Just considerations', which will be elaborated through the Just Holistic Framework.

Critical minerals today are closely linked to their role in climate-change mitigation, and the book briefly explores that relationship and its impact on the Global South. The climate change legal regime primarily drives the current rise in the demand for critical minerals. This is due to the mitigation commitments under the 1992 United Nations Framework Convention for Climate Change (UNFCCC), the 2015 Paris Agreement and the 2030 Agenda for Sustainable Development, which call for concerted efforts to mitigate climate change.

The growth of nations has led to massive greenhouse gas emissions into the atmosphere. The development and growth of nations, particularly in the Global North (the USA, the UK, EU, Canada), moved from human labour to the use of machines driven by the First Industrial Revolution in the eighteenth century.[9] This saw the rise of companies such as Ford Motor Company, General Electric, DuPont and Slate Mill,[10] which used fossil fuels that consequently released pollutants that have contributed to the current climate crisis.[11] The Industrial Revolution has now reached its fourth stage with the rise of digital currencies, social networks, low-carbon energy systems and artificial intelligence. Climate change today seriously impacts several aspects of society, the economy and the environment.[12]

The exacerbated impacts of climate change have led to a new scramble for minerals, mostly those considered critical for the economies of the Global North and China. The scramble has social, economic and geopolitical implications for all those countries in the global value chain, both in the Global North and the Global South.[13] Countries have devised legal, technological and political tools

[8] Coulomb et al (n 3).

[9] J Taskinsoy, 'No Brainer, Tackle Climate Change by 2030 or Await the Doomsday by 2100: Tackle Climate Change by, 2030' [2020] *SSRN Electronic Journal* DOI: 10.2139/ssrn.3532709.

[10] A Petrillo, F De Felice, R Cioffi and F Zomparelli, 'Fourth Industrial Revolution: Current Practices, Challenges, and Opportunities' [2018] *Digital Transformation in Smart Manufacturing* 1.

[11] P Erickson, M Lazarus and G Piggot, 'Limiting Fossil Fuel Production as the Next Big Step in Climate Policy' (2018) 8(12) *Nature Climate Change* 1037.

[12] H Lee, K Calvin, D Dasgupta, G Krinner, A Mukherji, P Thorne, C Trisos, J Romero, P Aldunce, K Barret and G Blanco, 'IPCC, 2023: Climate Change 2023: Synthesis Report, Summary for Policymakers' (Contribution of Working Groups I, II and III to the Sixth Assessment Report of the Intergovernmental Panel on Climate Change, 2023).

[13] The Global North is limited to countries that process and import large quantities of critical minerals, like the EU, the UK, Canada. The Global South is limited to countries that have critical minerals for the purposes of this book, mainly Zambia and the DRC. Even though China is in the Global South, it enjoys a big processing and importing capacity.

to pool resources and address the current climate crisis for current and future generations. Hence, ratifying the 2015 Paris Agreement has accelerated the need to develop low-carbon technologies for global sustainability,[14] which has led to an explosive demand for critical minerals such as rare earth metals, cobalt, coltan, copper, nickel and aluminium.[15]

This book builds on established literature and research in mineral supply chain management that utilises justice as a core issue and extends to critical mineral development.[16] Using a case study analysis of selected production, processing and consumption of critical minerals in countries and regions, the book inquires how far critical minerals have been considered beyond scientific, economic and technological issues to encompass socio-political aspects in the assessments and development criteria.

Furthermore, the book, through the Just Holistic Framework that engineers the tenets of justice – namely, distributive, procedural, recognition, restorative and cosmopolitan justice – creates a framework for criticality assessments while incorporating the social, ecological, spatial, policy, political, technological and economic considerations of the Global South. The ambit of the study is limited to the copper and cobalt supply chains originating in Zambia and the Democratic Republic of Congo (DRC), while in the Global North the book limits its study to the USA, the EU, the UK and China.

This book makes two core arguments; firstly, criticality assessments should consider parameters beyond economic importance and the security of supply of critical minerals to address the concerns of the marginalised resource-rich countries. Secondly, a Just Holistic Framework for the entire critical minerals value chain is necessary for achieving sustainable development and sustainability in the Global South.

1.2. The Relationship between Critical Minerals, Sustainable Development and the Energy Transition

The concepts of critical minerals, sustainable development and the energy transition are interdependent. Sustainable development cannot be achieved

[14] YX Zhang, QC Chao, QH Zheng and L Huang, 'The Withdrawal of the US from the Paris Agreement and Its Impact on Global Climate Change Governance. (2017) 8(4) *Advances in Climate Change Research* 213.

[15] Z Vrontisi, I Charalampidis and L Paroussos, 'What Are the Impacts of Climate Policies on Trade? A Quantified Assessment of the Paris Agreement for the G20 Economies' (2020) 139 *Energy Policy* 111376.

[16] RJ Heffron, 'The Role of Justice in Developing Critical Minerals' (2020) 7(3) *The Extractive Industries and Society* 855.

without an energy transition because of the increased emissions and the need for clean technology. However, clean technology cannot exist without critical minerals, essential raw materials for developing clean energy. Therefore, these key aspects need to be balanced, but the question remains: who benefits from this balance? Sustainable development has different meanings in different regions. For example, Zambia and the DRC are struggling to meet basic needs, while the USA and the UK are trying to avoid dependence on Chinese critical minerals. Therefore, the world needs to ensure a fair and just perspective that considers the needs and wants of each region according to their realities, rather than adopting a one-size-fits-all approach.

The role of critical minerals in the energy transition must be discussed hand in hand with the just sustainable development aspect of mineral development in resource-rich countries. Resource-rich regions like South America, sub-Saharan Africa and South-East Asia are the potential hotspots for critical mineral development. The main hurdle to attaining just sustainable development in the critical mineral value chain is that when resource-rich countries attempt to add value to these minerals within their national borders, this threatens the global supply of those minerals needed to drive the transition.[17] Retaining local value addition threatens the supply of these minerals and can be considered a powerful argument against the methodology deployed to assess criticality.[18] The justice discourse is essential in developing the critical minerals industry in the Global South. Critical minerals have a complex global supply chain, with the highest degree of monopoly of the downstream segment of the critical mineral value chain, taking in parts other than the Global South.[19] The current criticality studies limit the essence of critical minerals to their economic importance as well as the risk of disruption of their supply in global markets.[20]

Critical minerals are key and integral to the energy transition and sustainable development. However, there must be mechanisms put in place through policy and practice at all levels of critical minerals governance that garner responsible sourcing and management but that do not minimise the livelihoods of host countries for the development of consumer countries, thus creating a polarised conception of sustainable development.

[17] S van den Brink, R Kleijn, B Sprecher and A Tukker, 'Identifying Supply Risks by Mapping the Cobalt Supply Chain' (2020) 156 *Resources, Conservation and Recycling* 104743.

[18] TE Graedel, R Barr, C Chandler, T Chase, J Choi, L Christoffersen, E Friedlander, C Henly, C Jun, NT Nassar and D Schechner, 'Methodology of Metal Criticality Determination' (2012) 46(2) *Environmental Science & Technology* 1063.

[19] AL Gulley, NT Nassar and S Xun, 'China, the United States, and Competition for Resources that Enable Emerging Technologies' (2018) 115(16) *Proceedings of the National Academy of Sciences* 4111.

[20] SM Hayes and EA McCullough, 'Critical Minerals: A Review of Elemental Trends in Comprehensive Criticality Studies' (2018) 59 *Resources Policy* 192.

1.3. Towards a Justice Perspective

The current energy transition should be grounded on justice principles.[21] Already, parties to the 2015 Paris Agreement incorporate 'just transition' objectives in their Nationally Determined Contributions (NDCs).[22] The EU, for instance, committed to developing a just transition mechanism, in particular for a green economic recovery after the COVID-19 pandemic.[23] The book argues for and leads to the conceptualisation of justice in the criticality aspect of critical minerals to create a just criticality paradigm. Assessing criticality is intended to be a tool that facilitates the identification of concerns and tensions that might arise over access to resources.

However, the procedural, recognition and distributive elements go beyond supply risk and the economic importance of those metals essential to the energy transition. They examine how legal processes and decisions are reached, if all affected groups of people are considered and if the ills and benefits of the energy transition (in this case, critical minerals) are equitably distributed. This is because the principles of sustainable development advocate for a just energy transition that can only be materialised with a unifying and holistic collection of principles, processes and practices for generating economic and political outcomes that depict equality and equity in addressing the climate crisis. Justice avails a new approach to the energy, mining and extractive life cycle. The transition must be reasonable and equitable, with reparations redressing past wrongs and establishing new power arrangements for the future. If the transition process is not just, the end will never be just, leading to weak sustainability.

The key elements of justice that are needed in the mining life cycle briefly include: (i) distributive justice; (ii) procedural justice; (iii) recognition justice; (iv) restorative justice; and (v) cosmopolitan justice. The above elements will be elaborated in chapter five of the book. Using these key elements of justice, the book advocates for 'the just criticality concept' in criticality assessments. The just criticality concept will go beyond the supply risk and economic importance of the critical aspect of critical metals and incorporate the environmental, social and governance issues. Most importantly, it will highlight the justice concerns that are

[21] S Carley and DM Konisky, 'The Justice and Equity Implications of the Clean Energy Transition' (2020) 5(8) *Nature Energy* 569.

[22] NDCs are national publicly outlined plans highlighting climate actions, including climate related targets, policies and measures governments aim to implement in response to climate change and as a contribution to global climate action. They are actions in the 2015 Paris Agreement to contribute to international efforts to keep increases in global temperature below 2°C with respect to pre-industrial levels, preferably within a limit of 1.5°C. See Art 4 of the 2015 Paris Agreement, which requires parties to prepare, communicate and maintain successive NDCs.

[23] European Commission, 'The Update of the Nationally Determined Contribution of the European Union and Its Member States' (2020) www4.unfccc.int/sites/ndcstaging/PublishedDocuments/European%20Union%20First/EU_NDC_Submission_December%202020.pdf.

particularly acute in places with weak institutional structures and are more prone to adverse impacts on the people.

1.4. The Role of Critical Minerals in the Energy Transition

Critical minerals have been essential and significant mainly for military, climate and environmental uses, and social service delivery such as hospitals. Nevertheless, in this book, I deduce the importance and significance of critical minerals to their role in the global energy transition and how this process drives or hinders sustainable development in resource-rich countries of the Global South. Minerals such as hafnium, rhenium, tantalum and uranium are key for the energy sector, while germanium, indium, gallium and rare earth minerals are critical for the technology sector.[24] Beryllium, zirconium, tungsten, aluminium, the platinum group of metals (PGMs), barite, fluorspar, arsenic, scandium, strontium, titanium and potash are essential for the industrial sector. At the same time, magnesium, chromium, tin, tellurium, manganese, vanadium and niobium are vital to the steel industry.[25] Lithium, cobalt, antimony and graphite are essential to specific batteries for electric vehicles and the research and development sector using helium, rubidium, caesium and bismuth.[26]

The new renewable future hastened by the energy transition is not only caused by the need for cleaner energy sources; other factors, such as the increased scarcity of economically viable oil and gas fields, the negative environmental impacts of the extractive sector and the impact of the COVID-19 pandemic, along with the declining costs of renewable power, have heightened the need for a green future.[27] Though clean energy sources are needed to address the climate crisis, a substantial percentage of the critical minerals powering this green revolution and the energy transition are in countries with high degrees of fragility, corruption, weak governance and instability.[28] For instance, studies show that most countries in sub-Saharan Africa are categorised as fragile states.[29] Due to deficiencies in

[24] T Watari, K Nansai and K Nakajima, 'Review of Critical Metal Dynamics to 2050 for 48 Elements Resources' (2020) 155 *Conservation and Recycling* 104669.

[25] ibid.

[26] Y Yuan, M Yellishetty, MA, Muñoz and SA Northey, 'Toward a Dynamic Evaluation of Mineral Criticality: Introducing the Framework of Criticality Systems' (2019) 23(5) *Journal of Industrial Ecology* 1264.

[27] R Chadha, 'Skewed Critical Minerals Global Supply Chains Post COVID-19: Reforms for Making India Self-reliant (Brookings, 10 June 2020) www.brookings.edu/research/skewed-critical-minerals-global-supply-chains-post-covid-19/.

[28] MD Bah, 'Mining for Peace: Diamonds, Bauxite, Iron Ore and Political Stability in Guinea' (2014) 41(142) *Review of African Political Economy* 500.

[29] ME Gelbard and R Xu, *Building Resilience in Sub-Saharan Africa's Fragile States* (International Monetary Fund, 2015).

institutional structures, governance challenges and corruption, fragile states have been identified as being unable to effectively use their natural resources and cater to their people's basic needs.[30] Consequently, this leads to its citizens and the international community failing to legitimise government policies, with far-reaching implications for achieving the SDGs.[31]

Nevertheless, for resource-rich countries to attain justice, they must take advantage of the evolving commodities market responding to the low-carbon energy transition. The Latin American region (primarily Chile, Brazil, Peru, Argentina and Bolivia) is in an excellent position to supply the global energy transition.[32] Africa should also serve as a growing resource market, with its platinum, manganese, cobalt, copper and bauxite reserves.[33] In Asia, there is a global Chinese monopoly on both production and reserve levels of many minerals like antimony and rare earth elements. India is dominant in iron and steel, while Indonesia has opportunities with bauxite and nickel, as do Malaysia and the Philippines to a lesser extent.[34] On the other hand, the Global North is the most industrialised region in the world, with significant greenhouse gas emissions, and is a big consumer of the critical minerals for the energy transition.

The location of the critical minerals shows the need for attaching and addressing transition requirements and attaining justice by emphasising environmental, social, trade and other governance-related matters. Managing governance and just sustainability in resource-rich countries has a probable impact on the reliability of the supply of the materials critical to the energy transition.[35] Critical metal supply is contingent on whether the deposits are economically viable for extraction using current or future technology in a post-COVID-19 volatile market. Moreover, the degree of critical mineral reliance is subject to what services and products countries produce and their position along the supply chain.[36] Hence, as countries that produce renewable energy technologies have sophisticated expertise and financial muscle to add value to these metals, they are closer to the refining stage in the supply chain. As a result, this leaves resource-rich countries with depleted reserves and no technology, thus failing to propel their economies to prosperity.

[30] OECD (n 6) 29–54.

[31] ibid.

[32] M Koengkan and JA Fuinhas, 'Exploring the Effect of the Renewable Energy Transition on CO_2 Emissions of Latin American & Caribbean Countries (2020) 39(6) *International Journal of Sustainable Energy* 515.

[33] MO Dioha and A Kumar, 'Exploring Sustainable Energy Transitions in Sub-Saharan Africa Residential Sector: The Case of Nigeria' (2020) 117 *Renewable and Sustainable Energy Reviews* 109510.

[34] M Murshed and MM Tanha, 'Oil Price Shocks and Renewable Energy Transition: Empirical Evidence from Net Oil-Importing South Asian Economies' [2020] *Energy, Ecology & Environment* 1.

[35] C Church and A Crawford, 'Minerals and the Metals for the Energy Transition: Exploring the Conflict Implications for Mineral-Rich, Fragile States' in M Hafner and S Tagliapietra (eds), *The Geopolitics of the Global Energy Transition* (Springer International Publishing, 2020) 279–304.

[36] J Lee, M Bazilian, B Sovacool, K Hund, SM Jowitt, TP Nguyen, A Månberger, M Kah, S Greene, C Galeazzi and K Awuah-Offei, 'Reviewing the Material and Metal Security of Low-Carbon Energy Transitions' (2020) 124 *Renewable and Sustainable Energy Reviews* 109789.

1.5. Geopolitics of the Critical Mineral Value Chain

The global energy transition is currently driving a high demand for critical metals, bringing about analogies to the gold rushes of the nineteenth century. Still, the transition also facilitates an international multipolar system. The current and expected technological advancement in the Global North creates options for these economies to replace and substitute these minerals over time, leaving the Global South impoverished because of their mineral resources. The green revolution that brings about the energy transition is a double-edged sword for host economies worldwide. As these countries fuelled industrialisation through fossil fuels, they are now fuelling the energy transition and having their minerals extracted at the expense of their socio-economic development.

Geopolitical risks can threaten the supply of critical minerals, with economic, social and political factors such as external shocks like the COVID-19 pandemic affecting the mining industry, as seen in Peru's mine shutdown between March and June of 2020.[37] Resource nationalism, like Chile's move to nationalise the lithium industry, and export restrictions, like Zimbabwe's lithium export ban in December 2022, can also impact critical mineral supply.[38] Mineral cartels may manipulate prices and production, leading to instability. Political unrest and social upheaval, such as the Angolan civil war and the Myanmar protests, can also significantly impact export earnings, with a decline of over 80 per cent seen in the case of Angola.[39] Minerals are usually found in the interior of any resource-rich country. The major benefits these communities could derive from the resources are public goods, yet even the value of these resources has been quantified in other regions.[40] In critical mineral development, justice must be the central question since critical mineral mining takes place at the expense of either a population or a marginalised host community.[41] Justice in mineral development and the extractive industry has explicitly been advocated in legal and regulatory frameworks using local content and social licence-to-operate provisions or corporate practice using corporate social responsibility provisions.[42] Nevertheless, in critical mineral development, we do not discuss the integration of a community into the value chain to make a living or escape the poverty trap. Justice can thus play a significant

[37] A Smith-Roberts, KD Bruckner, VM Bellido, HF Ossandón, M Nayak, NM Smith and LJ Urrego, 'All That Glitters Is Not Gold': The Effects of the COVID-19 Pandemic on Artisanal and Small-Scale Gold Mining and Supply Chains in Peru. (2021) 39(4) *Journal of Energy & Natural Resources Law* 489.

[38] O Hailes, 'Lithium in International Law: Trade, Investment, and the Pursuit of Supply Chain Justice' (2022) 25(1) *Journal of International Economic Law* 148.

[39] Church and Crawford (n 35).

[40] ibid.

[41] CBL Nkulu, L Casas, V Haufroid, T De Putter, ND Saenen, T Kayembe-Kitenge, PM Obadia, DKW Mukoma, JML Ilunga, TS Nawrot and OL Numbi, 'Sustainability of Artisanal Mining of Cobalt in DR Congo' (2018) 1(9) *Nature Sustainability* 495.

[42] BK Sovacool and MH Dworkin, 'Energy Justice: Conceptual Insights and Practical Applications' (2015) 142 *Applied Energy* 435.

role in achieving sustainable development and the socio-economic well-being of a community based on its natural resource wealth.

The rise of Tesla and other tech giants has increased the demand for products such as lithium-ion batteries, which power electric vehicles.[43] These elements are produced by a handful of countries, enhancing tensions in the geopolitical sphere of critical minerals due to the distribution of ills and benefits. The Global South has the means to win the global geopolitical struggle of the race towards decarbonising economies. The domination of China in the critical mineral global supply chain, using China's Belt and Road Initiative (BRI), a transnational infrastructure investment scheme with participants from all over the world, strengthens China's position in the global supply chain of critical minerals. Though China is notably classified as a Global South country, its position in the critical mineral supply chain creates an imbalance in deriving benefits and ills of the critical mineral supply chain.[44] The US, the EU and Japan have all attempted to control the critical mineral global supply chain. However, China still has the dominant global position as the critical minerals global supply chain epicentre. Chile and Bolivia, two of the countries creating the 'lithium triangle' in Latin America, are members of the BRI (the third country, Argentina, has yet to join), reinforcing China's global dominant position in the critical mineral supply chain.[45] The DRC is the world's biggest producer of cobalt, producing more than 70 per cent of the world's cobalt, and China is its most prominent investor.[46] China's dominance makes the country the most significant stakeholder in the critical minerals value chain. The country's domination shows that for the Global South to gain sustainable development from their minerals, there must be a sufficient sense of justice to create a level playing field for all stakeholders in the energy transition.

Critical minerals usually have complex global supply chains, with production subject to a high degree of monopoly.[47] The International Energy Agency noted that China produces 63 per cent of the world's output of rare earth elements, while 70 per cent of cobalt is mined in the DRC. Further, Australia produces 55 per cent of the world's lithium and South Africa mines 72 per cent of the world's platinum output, while Chile and Peru account for over 20 per cent of the global copper supply.[48] The scramble to control these elements' supply chains is intensifying. For example, electric vehicles made by Tesla and other automotive firms run on

[43] B Jones, RJ Elliott and V Nguyen-Tien, 'The EV Revolution: The Road Ahead for Critical Raw Materials Demand' (2020) 280 *Applied Energy* 115072.

[44] S Kalantzakos, 'The Race for Critical Minerals in an Era of Geopolitical Realignments' (2020) 55(3) *The International Spectator* 1.

[45] K Bersch and RI Koivumaeki, 'Making Inroads: Infrastructure, State Capacity, and Chinese Dominance in Latin American Development' (2019) 54(3) *Studies in Comparative International Development* 323.

[46] C Kabemba, 'China–Democratic Republic of Congo Relations: From a Beneficial to a Developmental Cooperation' [2016] *African Studies Quarterly* 16.

[47] Kalantzakos (n 44).

[48] IEA, 'Global Energy Review 2020' (International Energy Agency, 2020) www.iea.org/reports/global-energy-review-2020.

lithium-ion batteries, but only a handful of countries produce most of the world's lithium. The tension between the geographic concentration of critical resources and the increasing global competition for supply will further unsettle geopolitics in the twenty-first century.

The International Renewable Energy Agency (IRENA) states that critical mineral development has three geopolitical dynamics: physical constraint, disruptive innovation and a circular economy.[49] The dynamics mentioned above pose a threat to the development of a mineral downstream industry in the Global South. For example, Norge Mining has recently discovered vast deposits of phosphate, titanium and vanadium in Norway.[50] These geological findings challenge the idea that these minerals are exclusive to the Global South, especially when coupled with circular economy-supported recycling technology. In the end, the Global South will be at a disadvantage in achieving sustainable development and a low-carbon economy.

Critical minerals are spatially distributed across the globe, even though injustice issues manifest more in the Global South. Countries like Chile, Peru, the DRC, Zambia and Russia export copper (Cu) to China, Germany, the USA, Italy and Korea.[51] Lithium (Li) producing countries like Australia, Portugal, the Czech Republic and Zimbabwe export these resources to Indonesia, Hong Kong, Germany and France.[52] Nickel (Ni) is produced mainly in Indonesia, the Philippines, Cuba, Brazil and Tanzania, and is exported to South Korea, India, Malaysia and Turkey.[53] Cobalt (Co) is found mostly in the Copper Belt of the DRC and Zambia, Papua New Guinea and Australia, chiefly exporting resources to China, the Netherlands, Finland, India and South Africa.[54] China is the top producer of rare earth elements and holds the world's largest reserves.[55] Other countries with large reserves include Brazil, Vietnam, Russia, India, the USA, Australia, Madagascar and Myanmar. The minerals include dysprosium, neodymium and praseodymium, which are essential in clean energy applications. PGMs are produced mainly by South Africa, which accounts for over 80 per cent of the global production and exports these minerals to the USA, Germany, the UK, Japan and Hong Kong.[56]

[49] IRENA, 'Geopolitics of the Energy Transition: Critical Materials' (International Renewable Energy Agency, 2023).

[50] ibid.

[51] X Hu, C Wang, MK Lim and WQ Chen, 'Characteristics of the Global Copper Raw Materials and Scrap Trade Systems and the Policy Impacts of China's Import Ban' (2020) 172 *Ecological Economics* 106626.

[52] J Lunde Seefeldt, 'Lessons from the Lithium Triangle: Considering Policy Explanations for the Variation in Lithium Industry Development in the "Lithium Triangle" Countries of Chile, Argentina, and Bolivia' (2020) 48(4) *Politics & Policy* 727.

[53] X Dong, F An, Z Dong, Z Wang, M Jiang, P Yang and H An, 'Optimization of the International Nickel Ore Trade Network' (2021) 70 *Resources Policy* 101978.

[54] Van den Brink et al (n 17).

[55] SN Kamenopoulos and Z Agioutantis, 'Geopolitical Risk Assessment of Countries with Rare Earth Element Deposits' (2020) 37(1) *Mining, Metallurgy & Exploration* 51.

[56] C Saguru, S Ndlovu and D Moropeng, 'A Review of Recent Studies into Hydrometallurgical Methods for Recovering PGMs from Used Catalytic Converters' (2018) 182 *Hydrometallurgy* 44.

This book, however, focuses on the copper–cobalt value chain from the DRC and Zambia (producing), through China (processing and refining) to the EU (consumers). The value chain approach allows for a 'holistic' view of the entire life cycle of the critical minerals. There is no concise definition of the term 'value chain'. However, the World Business Council for Sustainable Development (WBCSD) defined a value chain as the 'full life cycle of a product or process, including material sourcing, production, consumption and disposal/recycling processes', further noting that value chains form an integral part of the strategic planning process for many business operations today.[57] It is essential to differentiate between the supply and value chains for clarity. The term 'value chain' refers to the process in which companies receive raw materials, then add value to them through production, manufacturing and other processes to create a finished product, which it then sells to consumers; a supply chain, on the other hand, represents the steps it takes to get the product or service to the customer.[58] The WBSCD thus defines value chain as 'the full life cycle of a product or process, including material sourcing, production, consumption and disposal/recycling processes'.[59] For the purposes of this book, the critical mineral value chain studied is that of copper and cobalt originating from the DRC and Zambia, from the investment stage, through production, refining and processing, to consumption, mine closure and waste management.

The concerns of the Global South have largely been left unattended. Little attention has been paid to developing complementary qualitative indicators to ensure justice in criticality studies, hence the outcry for reform to what constitutes 'just criticality' within the critical mineral value chain.[60] Some studies have investigated the motivations for pursuing a particular social, environmental and governance agenda within the realm of justice.[61] There have also been studies around supply chain justice. Hailes, for example, recognises that there may be laws governing aspects of environmental protection, human rights and the rights of Indigenous peoples that might be pertinent in interpreting investment obligations and should act as a benchmark in states' exercise of sovereignty over natural resources.[62] However, he argues that there is a need for legal reform to ensure supply chain justice and guarantee that the concerns of affected communities are addressed.[63] The just criticality concept provides both a theoretical and conceptual

[57] WBCSD, 'Collaboration, Innovation, Transformation: Ideas and Inspiration to Accelerate Sustainable Growth – a Value Chain Approach' (World Business Council for Sustainable Development, 2011).

[58] J Fessehaie and M Morris, 'Value Chain Dynamics of Chinese Copper Mining in Zambia: Enclave or Linkage Development?' (2013) 25(4) *European Journal of Development Research* 537.

[59] WBCSD (n 57).

[60] ID Qurbani, RJ Heffron and ATS Rifano, 'Justice and Critical Mineral Development in Indonesia and Across ASEAN' (2020) 8(1) *The Extractive Industries and Society* 355.

[61] ibid.

[62] Hailes (n 38).

[63] ibid.

lens for evaluating and understanding environmental, social and governance outcomes in the critical mineral industry, which, in this case, is linked to the Global South.

1.6. Purpose of the Book

Studies conducted by Oxfam in 2015 disclosed that, globally, the world's richest 10 per cent (mainly in the Global North) were responsible for more than 50 per cent of total carbon emissions, while the poorest half of the population (mainly in the Global South) – the 3.5 billion who are the most climate-vulnerable – contributed only 10 per cent.[64] Moreover, the critical minerals needed to feed the decarbonisation process to foster the achievement of the international climate change mitigation goals, for instance, under the 2015 Paris Agreement[65] and the SDGs,[66] are primarily located in the same vulnerable Global South. The growing demand for clean energy technologies is expected to increase the demand for the production of minerals like cobalt, lithium and graphite by nearly 500 per cent by 2050.[67] Further, over three billion tons of minerals will be needed to generate solar, wind and geothermal power and energy storage technology to achieve the global goal of reducing emissions sufficiently to keep the increase in global temperature to below 2°C.[68]

Fossil fuels were needed to propel economic development, fight wars and advance the development of technology during the first industrialisation era. Now, advanced economies source critical minerals to fuel the energy transition. These resources are largely sourced from the Global South, leaving the region with a resource curse and an 'everlasting' socio-economic and political instability. The same utilitarian argument for global economic development is synonymous with the current utilitarian argument for addressing climate change.

The current critical mineral discourse has largely been limited to supply disruption, thus limiting criticality studies and methodologies to two components: supply risk and economic importance. It makes the argument that criticality is an evolving phenomenon. What makes minerals critical in the post-COVID-19 world, the Russia/Ukraine conflict and the formation of the BRICS era, for

[64] T Gore, 'Extreme Carbon Inequality: Why the Paris Climate Deal Must Put the Poorest, Lowest Emitting and Most Vulnerable People First' (Oxfam, 2 December 2015) Oxfam Media Briefing.

[65] The United Nations Paris Agreement, 2015, https://unfccc.int/files/essential_background/convention/application/pdf/english_paris_agreement.pdf.

[66] 'Transforming Our World: The 2030 Agenda for Sustainable Development, 2015 (Goals 7 and 13, on clean energy and climate change respectively) www.un.org/ga/search/view_doc.asp?symbol=A/RES/70/1&Lang=E.

[67] World Bank, *Minerals for Climate Action: The Mineral Intensity of the Clean Energy Transition* (2020) http://pubdocs.worldbank.org/en/961711588875536384/Minerals-for-Climate-Action-The-Mineral-Intensity-of-the-Clean-Energy-Transition.pdf.

[68] ibid. See also the Paris Agreement; SDG Goals 7 and 13.

example, is not what made minerals critical during the Cold War era. However, justice is a 'static' concept deriving its importance from basic human rights. Justice is essentially about human rights and the leverage of the Global South against the powerful Global North. Thus, Heffron observes that the primary motivation for justice is to ensure fairness and equality in society.[69] Further, he notes that since many countries have committed to supporting a low-carbon economy through the 2015 Paris Agreement, and given the critical role that critical minerals play in the transition, it is necessary to have a comprehensive view of justice that encompasses this global industry with global implications.[70]

This book aims to bridge the gap between high-level concepts of justice and the pressing contemporary issues. This will help in the development and formulation of policies. The book expands on the critical variables and invites researchers from various fields, such as physics, geology and economics, to join the conversation about evaluating critical minerals and their value chains.

The book's expansion of criticality assessments creates a holistic approach that enables an integrated assessment of the critical mineral supply chain. The Just Holistic Framework creates a balance between trade-offs and just considerations. This will hopefully provide a better framework for the Global South to negotiate more favourable extractive deals with global consumers. Additionally, it will guide the Global South countries and regions in defining and formulating their strategies for critical minerals. The book also emphasises the importance of international collaboration. Lastly, it explores new avenues for research on how the elements of justice, such as procedural, recognition, cosmopolitan, distributive and restorative, can be integrated into the critical minerals industry using a case study of the copper and cobalt value chains.

1.7. Book Overview

The book is divided into six chapters, which essentially discuss the critical minerals, sustainable development and justice, and the copper and cobalt value chains.

This chapter has provided an overview of the critical minerals industry. It has established the foundation for the argument for justice by demonstrating the interdependent relationship between critical minerals, sustainable development and the energy transition. These aspects raise awareness of the need for a justice perspective, which should be analysed considering the geopolitical aspects of the critical mineral value chain.

Chapter two provides an overview of criticality in the history of the critical mineral industry and its impact. It explains the critical aspects of critical minerals,

[69] RJ Heffron, 'The Just Framework' in RJ Heffron (ed), *Achieving a Just Transition to a Low-Carbon Economy* (Palgrave Macmillan, 2021) 21–42.

[70] ibid.

starting with the definition of criticality and the indicators of criticality assessments. The chapter further discusses the impact of supply risk and a just criticality analysis. It also explains the importance of a contextual perspective of justice in critical mineral development, emphasising the need for sustainable development and a holistic approach to criteria in critical minerals.

Chapter three discusses the sustainability roadmap for critical minerals. The chapter explores the idea of achieving sustainable development in the Global South and the challenges arising from human nature. It also highlights the shortcomings of current sustainable development measures in the Global South. The chapter emphasises the need for a Just Holistic Framework by examining the imbalanced relationship between the Global North and the Global South, as well as the polycentric interests of the extractive industry. Furthermore, the chapter focuses on sustainable energy and mineral development, the transition to a low-carbon economy and justice in critical mineral development. It also delves into the reconstruction of justice and sustainable development, particularly emphasising African prospects in critical mineral development.

Chapter four provides an insight into the development of critical minerals within the copper–cobalt value chain in sub-Saharan Africa. The chapter delves deeper into this value chain, discussing the relationships between the DRC, Zambia, China and the EU. It also investigates the different segments of the critical mineral value chain and highlights any gaps within it. In addition, the chapter outlines measures that can be taken to mitigate risks associated with the copper–cobalt value chain.

Chapter five introduces the holistic framework to achieve fairness and justice in the critical mineral industry. The chapter discusses the critical mineral evaluation process and the importance of the Just Holistic Framework for the critical mineral supply chain. It also highlights the need and significance for a just framework in the critical mineral industry to address the critical mineral supply and value chain issues.

Chapter six concludes and suggests further research considerations.

2

Understanding the Criticality Aspect in Critical Minerals Development

2.1. Introduction

There is a synergy between development, climate change and the demand for critical minerals. The technology age has brought about rapid development and growth of economies worldwide. The rise of global economies initially came about due to the accelerated industrialisation in the Global North and the increasing demand for sophisticated goods and services, which increased greenhouse gas emissions. Does economic growth directly correlate to greenhouse gas emissions and, if so, how? Bill Gates points out in his book that China alone installed more concrete in the first 16 years of the twenty-first century than the United States did in the entire twentieth century.[1] The increased demand for concrete and steel to build skyscrapers, the concrete used to construct the dams to power our industries and transportation, and the fertiliser used in growing food and feeding livestock all lead to increased greenhouse gas emissions. Furthermore, critical minerals have been used for non-energy transition uses; for example, 90 per cent of nickel is used in iron and steel production; 80 per cent of graphite is used for steel, aluminium and ceramics; and over 80 per cent of manganese is used in steel and chemical production, foundry and welding.[2] Smil emphasises that we need to mitigate and adapt, or else we will face a global climate disaster.[3] Climate change adaptation and mitigation can only be brought about by using specific technology and changing our day-to-day lives. Hence, the world can only realise the global move to a low-carbon economy by developing and manufacturing clean energy sources.

Critical minerals are becoming more important today, especially as the world transitions to cleaner energy fuels and technologies. Different authors believe the shift to low-carbon economies is metal-intensive and entails a shift from

[1] B Gates, *How to Avoid a Climate Disaster: The Solutions We Have and the Breakthroughs We Need* (Allen Lane, 2021).

[2] IRENA, *Geopolitics of the Energy Transition: Critical Materials* (International Renewable Energy Agency, Abu Dhabi, 2023).

[3] V Smil, *Energy Myths and Realities* (AEI Press, 2010).

hydrocarbons to metals.[4] Metals have been pivotal in everyday life from the Stone Age to the new technology age.[5] Critical minerals have always been crucial for society.[6] They are unevenly distributed in the earth's crust, making their importance vary from region to region according to a given area's pressing demands and issues. However, one would assume that climate change is a global problem and should have a 'general' consensus.[7] Historically, the mining industry has driven economies out of poverty.[8] Since the Gold Rush of the 1800s, developing countries (the Global South) have seen minimal material development even with the presence of traditional mineral resources in their part of the earth's crust.[9] Today, the same countries are rich in metals enabling a low-carbon economy and have different perspectives on what 'critical' should be in critical minerals.

The perspectives on the role of critical metals are divided between the tripartite contextual reality of poverty, sustainable development and justice. Sub-Saharan African countries like the Democratic Republic of Congo (DRC), Zambia, South Africa, Namibia, Ghana, Zimbabwe and Tanzania have supplied Western countries with minerals like uranium, nickel, platinum, gold, copper, cobalt and manganese. The role of these metals in sub-Saharan African countries has always been to change the realities and propel these societies to economic prosperity. In contrast, consuming countries such as the EU, the USA and China have different definitions and perspectives on these metals' roles. Essentially, they would deduce that role to be in enabling climate-friendly technology that could sustainably develop their economies. The different roles and expectations of critical mineral development across the globe also dictate the diverse perspectives and reflections of principles pertinent to critical mineral development, such as justice, sustainability and sustainable development.

2.2. A Brief History of Critical Minerals

Numerous factors in the mining industry have affected the 'criticality' of minerals. Gold, tin and copper were carried from the British Isles to mainland Europe

[4] D Humphreys, 'The Mining Industry and the Supply of Critical Minerals' in G Gunn (ed), *Critical Metals Handbook* (John Wiley & Sons, 2014) 20–40; M Hafner and S Tagliapietra, 'The Global Energy Transition: A Review of the Existing Literature' in M Hafner and S Tagliapietra (eds), *The Geopolitics of the Global Energy Transition. Lecture Notes in Energy*, vol 73 (Springer, 2020).

[5] AE Bastida, *The Law and Governance of Mining and Minerals: A Global Perspective* (Bloomsbury Publishing, 2020).

[6] RJ Heffron, 'The Role of Justice in Developing Critical Minerals' (2020) 7(3) *The Extractive Industries and Society* 855.

[7] SD Benegal and LA Scruggs, 'Correcting Misinformation About Climate Change: The Impact of Partisanship in an Experimental Setting' (2018) 148(1) *Climatic Change* 61.

[8] AE Bastida, 'From Extractive to Transformative Industries: Paths for Linkages and Diversification for Resource-Driven Development' (2014) 27(2–3) *Mineral Economics* 73.

[9] K Werthmann, 'Gold Rush in West Africa: The Appropriation of "Natural" Resources: Non-industrial Gold Mining in South-Western Burkina Faso' [2000] *Sociologus* 90.

in the Bronze Age, rendering other regions dependent on foreign resources. Critical minerals date back to World War I (the War), when numerous states rushed for supplies to support their war efforts (eg the Shell Crisis of 1915).[10] The War was another geopolitical stage for the identification of the 'criticality' of these rare elements, such as when Germany took control of most of the world's tungsten production, forcing other countries to seek alternative sources. Tungsten was an essential component of high-speed steel tools used to make weapons and ammunition quickly and efficiently, giving monopolists an advantage over their enemies.[11] The War doubled tungsten demand, and other critical mineral concentrates rose tenfold, causing many mining booms in western USA and other countries.

The USSR State Committee for Reserves (established in 1931) and other countries' comparable organisations followed the US War Department's Army and Navy Munitions Board (1922) in procuring and stockpiling war materials.[12] Subsequently, the conflict from 1939 proved these tactics were appropriate. Later, President Nixon of the USA introduced a list of Critical Imported Materials, which identified 19 essential industrial raw materials.[13] The official paper examined mineral prices and supply interruptions, and followed national, security and economic concerns about 'critical' minerals such as bauxite, platinum and chromium. Expert qualitative evaluations have dominated historical criticality research. The Human Development Index (HDI) and the World Bank Worldwide Governance Indicators (WGI) are strong indicators of supply threats. Zambia and the DRC are mineral-rich but destitute, according to the HDI. The WGI also reveals that these countries' low living standards are due to a lack of internal national concerns in criticality assessments.

2.3. The Critical Mineral Industry

The critical mineral industry is driven mainly by the multiple criticality studies that dictate global demand and supply. Various experts and researchers maintain that the industry will grow exponentially because of the current energy transition

[10] The Shell Crisis of 1915 resulted from a scarcity of artillery shells on the front lines during World War I, resulting in a political crisis in the UK. This is because the rapid rate of fire over an extended period was not anticipated, and the shell stock dwindled. See D French, 'The Military Background to the "Shell Crisis" of May 1915' (1979) 2(2) *Journal of Strategic Studies* 192.

[11] RH Limbaugh, *Tungsten in Peace and War, 1918–1946* (University of Nevada Press, 2010).

[12] R Dumett, 'Africa's Strategic Minerals During the Second World War' (1985) 26(4) *Journal of African History* 381.

[13] Office of the Historian, '260. Study Prepared by the Ad Hoc Inter-Agency Group on Critical Imported Materials' (Foreign Relations of the United States, 1969–1976, Volume XXXI, Foreign Economic Policy, 1973–1976) https://history.state.gov/historicaldocuments/frus1969-76v31/d260#fn:1.7.4.12.64.146.4?.

and the climate change crisis.[14] The demand for clean energy is increasing, leading to clean transportation, technology and manufacturing. However, critical minerals are spatially distributed across the globe. Geological distribution of the minerals is not universal, making some regions susceptible to demand and supply instabilities. More than half of the world's population relies on the critical mineral industry, accounting for over one-quarter of the world's GDP.[15] The British Geological Survey data shows the significant demand for some resources; between 2017 and 2018, they highlight the growth in lithium (an increase of 25 per cent), cobalt (up 18 per cent), graphite and nickel (both increased by about 13 per cent).[16] Indeed, the Organisation for Economic Co-operation and Development (OECD) states that the use of extracted critical metals will more than double by 2060, irrespective of technological change or efficiency improvements.

Nonetheless, some studies have expressed fear for resource availability; these sentiments and misconceptions revolve around the global resource markets' functionality, complexity and diversity.[17] The simplified highlight of the critical mineral industry is also based on concerns about resource availability in a post-COVID-19 Russia/Ukraine war market. As noted in chapter one, critical minerals in developing countries are situated in fragile countries. The Global South, for instance, has a considerable amount of minerals, but the mining industry faces challenges ranging from corruption to pollution, human rights issues and civil wars. Sovacool et al note that mining has become a catalyst for negative impacts.[18]

Furthermore, populism, global trade protectionism, COVID-19 and the Russia/Ukraine conflict have all impacted the global critical mining industry. The disruption of supply value chains and the increased demand for certain low-carbon technologies provide a 'niche'-like mineral market related to the demand for emerging technology functions.[19] Developed critical mineral-rich countries, such as Australia, plan to increase the export of lithium and base metals to match the value of coal exports by 2027–28.[20] Several countries in the Global North are exploring ways to diversify processing towards nations with abundant renewable

[14] BK Sovacool, SH Ali, M Bazilian, B Radley, B Nemery, J Okatz and D Mulvaney, 'Sustainable Minerals and Metals for a Low-Carbon Future' (2020) 367(6473) *Science* 30. Heffron, 'The Role of Justice (n 6).

[15] World Bank, *The Growing Role of Minerals and Metals for a Low Carbon Future* (World Bank, 2017) http://documents.worldbank.org/curated/en/207371500386458722/pdf/117581-WP-P159838PUBLIC-ClimateSmartMiningJuly.pdf.

[16] British Geological Survey World Mineral Production 2014–2018, www2.bgs.ac.uk/mineralsuk/download/world_statistics/2010s/WMP_2014_2018.pdf.

[17] R Coulomb, S Dietz, M Godunova and TB Nielsen, 'Critical Minerals Today and in 2030: An Analysis for OECD Countries' (OECD Publishing, 2015) OECD Environment Working Papers No 91, www.lse.ac.uk/GranthamInstitute/wpcontent/uploads/2015/11/OECD_minerals_paper_Coulomb_et_al.pdf.

[18] Sovacool et al (n 14).

[19] R Chadha, 'Skewed Critical Minerals Global Supply Chains Post COVID-19: Reforms for Making India Self-reliant (Brookings, 10 June 2020) www.brookings.edu/research/skewed-critical-minerals-global-supply-chains-post-covid-19/.

[20] CC Mavhunga, 'Africa's Move from Raw Material Exports Toward Mineral Value Addition: Historical Background and Implications' (2023) 48(4) *Materials Research Society Bulletin* 395.

energy resources to reduce their emission footprint. For instance, Chile is considering using solar power to decarbonise copper refining since it has plentiful solar energy resources.[21] Western Australia, known for its renewable energy resources, is attracting new investments in midstream critical mineral projects, including three rare earth and three lithium processing facilities. Unfortunately, the critical mineral industry is leaving the Global South, particularly sub-Saharan Africa, behind.

The critical mineral industry is threatened by international geopolitical conflicts that are exacerbating challenges such as individual welfare loss, community stability and equitable country development. The determination of the prices, volumes and producer and supplier dominance varies according to the criticality studies and the demand for high-tech companies such as Apple, Tesla, Dell and Microsoft. Finally, problems due to the dependency on certain materials might not be caused by issues related to the mining phase of the critical minerals but rather by bottlenecks or dependencies further up in the value chain, eg in the refining stage or manufacturing of semi-products.[22] However, several industries may be dictated by the natural causes of demand and supply. The critical mineral industry has been volatile due to specific historical events; for example, tungsten was needed in World War I. On the other hand, the current rise of the energy transition to mitigate the climate change crisis gives rise to the demand for minerals like cobalt, lithium and platinum-group metals (PGMs).[23] During the colonial regime and the Cold War era of the 1800s to 1990s, critical minerals were needed to develop weapons and gain advantage by the scrambling socio-economic blocs of the Global North.

2.4. Influences of the 'Criticality Aspect' of Critical Minerals

This section examines what 'criticality' means in criticality assessments and studies. Since critical metals are significant beyond the energy transition, these metals were first defined and assessed as early as 1947, mainly related to strategy and defence.[24] Criticality studies have evolved beyond strategy and defence, but these aspects are still pivotal in defining criticality today. From the start of the new millennium, a new shift emerged in what aspects of critical metals were regarded as critical. Scholars and researchers started to consider critical natural

[21] SH Boccas, 'Integration of Green Hydrogen in the Chilean Industry: The Case Study of Copper Mining CAEX Hauling Trucks' (Doctoral Dissertation, Politecnico di Torino, 2022).

[22] SM Hayes and EA McCullough, 'Critical Minerals: A Review of Elemental Trends in Comprehensive Criticality Studies' (2018) 59 *Resources Policy* 192.

[23] Y He, 'The Trade–Security Nexus and US Policy Making in Critical Minerals Resources Policy' (2028) 59 *Resources Policy* 238.

[24] DG Haglund, 'Strategic Minerals: A Conceptual Analysis' (1984) 10(3) *Resources Policy* 146.

capital, where environmental concerns emerged in the criticality debate.[25] The evolution of the criticality concept in critical metals has not been limited to environmental aspects. Other notions of technology, politics, physical availability, and strategic and economic aspects have recently become mainstream in research and critical assessment studies. However, there is minimal literature on justice as a criticality aspect in critical metals.

The international perspective of what should be critical in criticality assessments has largely influenced criticality determination. For example, the Brundtland Report focused on sustainable exploitation and the use of natural resources.[26] The Kyoto Protocol was first published in 1998,[27] and the United Nations Millennium Declaration came out in 2000, stressing the importance of sustainable development and protecting our shared environment.[28] This indicates that these events, and a widespread global environmental consciousness, may have influenced the criticality debate. Furthermore, the 2008 financial crisis was another international phenomenon linked to a rise in publications and research focusing more on the criticality idea. Further, the European Commission's 2010 and 2020 reports on critical raw materials linked to the EU's Circular Economy Action Plan may have helped raise awareness of the problem.[29]

Nonetheless, the topic of criticality concerning the environment has not disappeared entirely from the debate. The UN's 2030 Agenda for Sustainable Development came out in 2015.[30] The Agenda emphasised environmental issues, enflaming the global environmental consciousness. Most publications and research on defining and assessing criticality emerge mainly from the UK, Germany, the Netherlands, Canada and the USA.[31] These assessments and criticality definitions have taken the concerns of resource-consuming countries in the Global North, leaving the concerns of the locality of these metals in the Global South to the wind.

Recently, research has proposed to 'provincialise' critical mineral assessments. Gilbert states that

> provincialising critical raw materials assessments means recognising that … by starting with the concerns about critical or 'strategic' minerals expressed by the DRC or

[25] DV MacDonald, N Hanley and I Moffatt, 'Applying the Concept of Natural Capital Criticality to Regional Resource Management' (1999) 29 *Ecological Economics* 73.

[26] United Nations, 'Report of the World Commission on Environment and Development: Our Common Future' (1987) www.un-documents.net/our-common-future.Pdf.

[27] United Nations, 'United Nations Millennium Declaration' (2000) www.un.org/millennium/declaration/ares552e.pdf.

[28] United Nations, 'Kyoto Protocol to the United Nations Framework Convention on Climate Change' (1998) https://unfccc.int/resource/docs/convkp/kpeng.pdf.

[29] European Commission, 'Closing the Loop – An EU Action Plan for the Circular Economy' (2015) https://eur-lex.europa.eu/resource.html.

[30] United Nations, 'Transforming Our World: The 2030 Agenda for Sustainable Development' (2015) www.un.org/ga/search/view_doc.

[31] MK Schellens and J Gisladottir, 'Critical Natural Resources: Challenging the Current Discourse and Proposal for a Holistic Definition' (2018) 7(4) *Resources* 79.

> South Africa, we can question the taken-for-granted ideas that currently underpin criticality assessments, broadening their scope, and situating them in relation to the concerns of resource-rich postcolonial countries.[32]

The recent findings on criticality and critical assessments have followed a Western narrative on what should be regarded as critical in critical assessment studies and definitions of criticality. Schellens and Gisladottir state that 'the plausible over-representation of Western perspectives could influence the understanding of natural resources' criticality since other parts of the world are not considered to the same extent'.[33] Hence, this book follows a nascent perspective towards understanding the criticality of natural resources – in this case, critical metals – and incorporating the tenets of justice throughout the critical mineral value chain, as justice is not determined by geographical boundaries or scholarly interpretation considering the concept's inherent virtue.

2.5. Defining Criticality

This section explores the meaning of 'criticality' as far as it relates to minerals, especially in light of the utility of the minerals over time. According to a variety of researchers, the adjectives 'critical,' 'strategic' and 'scarce' have been used interchangeably since they are not clearly distinguished from one another.[34] Haglund describes the historical development and use of the term 'strategic' in the context of critical metals.[35] In a nutshell, conceptualising criticality came soon after World War I, when the scarcity of some natural resources exposed the need for industrial capability and input to win wars.[36] The term 'sensitive' was first used in the 1930s as a separate category, but was later merged into the term 'strategic and critical materials', which was still in use in the 1980s.[37] Usually, the words 'critical' and 'strategic' are used interchangeably, with 'strategic' referring to threats to national security and 'critical' referring to threats to the national economy.[38]

As shown in Table 1, Schellen and Gisladottir analysed the criticality studies conducted between 1947 and 2017, showing a pattern of development in the definition of 'critical' in natural resources from initially strategic minerals required

[32] PR Gilbert, 'Making Critical Materials Valuable: Decarbonization, Investment, and "Political Risk" in A Bleicher and A Pehlken (eds), *The Material Basis of Energy Transitions* (Academic Press, 2020) 91–108.

[33] Schellens and Gisladottir (n 31).

[34] DM Jacobson, RK Turner and AAL Challis, 'A Reassessment of the Strategic Materials Question' (1988) 14 *Resource Policy* 74.

[35] Haglund (n 24).

[36] P Le Billon, 'The Political Ecology of War: Natural Resources and Armed Conflicts' (2001) 20(5) *Political Geography* 561.

[37] S Glöser, LT Espinoza, C Gandenberger and M Faulstich, 'Raw Material Criticality in the Context of Classical Risk Assessment' (2015) 44 *Resources Policy* 35.

[38] ibid.

for military use to the criticality of raw materials. What stands out are the security of supply and economic importance as significant considerations.

Table 1 The evolving definitions of the concept 'critical' as related to natural resources in literature

Definitions tied to the concept of 'critical'	**Scope of the definition**	**Overriding considerations of 'critical'**
Strategic and critical minerals (1947, 1979)	War emergency materials The procurement of which in adequate quantities, quality, and time is sufficiently uncertain for any reason to require prior provision for the supply thereof Military, industrial, essential civilian needs	Security of supply and economic importance
Critical natural capital (1993, 1994)	Parts of environment supporting life, health, systems, biodiversity Assets that are highly valued, or irreplaceable or unsubstitutable for all practical purposes Irreversibility of environmental processes or stock changes has implications for intergenerational equity	
Critical natural capital (2003)	Parts of the environment with irreplaceable functions and cannot be substituted by human, manufactured or other natural capital Ecosystem services are crucial for survival and cannot be substituted (anthropocentric perspective) Ecosystems most important to maintaining environmental health/ integrity (ecocentric perspective)	
Critical materials (2008)	Those materials for which a threat to supply from abroad could involve harm to the nation's economy (National Research Council)	
Raw material criticality (2010, 2012)	To qualify as critical, a raw material must face high risks with regard to access to it, ie high supply risks or high environmental risks, and be of high economic importance (European Commission)	

(continued)

Table 1 ***(Continued)***

Definitions tied to the concept of 'critical'	**Scope of the definition**	**Overriding considerations of 'critical'**
	The systemic risk of damages to an economy due to disturbances in raw material supply (general risk matrix)	
Strategic or critical minerals (2012)	Supply is concentrated in one country or could be restricted by a few corporate interests, or because they are important economically or for national security	
Criticality of metals (2013, 2014)	Extent of current and future risks associated with a certain metal The quality, state or degree of being of the highest importance	
Criticality (2014, 2015)	The combination of the potential for supply disruption and the exposure of a system of interest to that disruption An evaluation of the holistic importance of a resource, which can be interpreted as an assessment of the risks connected with resource production, use and end-of-life A dynamic, multidimensional characteristic of materials, eg something vital, absolutely essential and on the verge on the state of emergency	
Criticality of ecosystem services (2015)	Depends on their essentiality to human well-being, non-substitutability and risk of becoming irreversibly extinct if degraded beyond critical thresholds	
Criticality of a raw material (2017)	A measure of the (economic) risk arising from its utilisation (including production, use and end-of-life) for a specific consumer over a certain period	

Source: Author's own elaboration, adapted from MK Schellens and J Gisladottir, 'Critical Natural Resources: Challenging the Current Discourse and Proposal for a Holistic Definition' (2018) 7(4) *Resources* 79.

The definitions shown in Table 1 include keywords such as 'threat' and 'emergency' ('risk') related to the importance of the natural resource. Furthermore, the illustrations vary depending on the resource's essentiality, substitutability or irreplaceable nature. Frenzel et al believe that the 'true meaning of risk' has fundamental links to criticality, dictating several conceptual and methodological issues in research for critical minerals.[39] On the other hand, De Groot et al argue that the importance and significance of the resource should be the point of consideration in the conceptualisation of critical metals.[40] Critical metals are to be assessed according to their economic and risk importance. However, assessing their importance and criticality is also essential, considering these resources' direct benefit to human society. The importance of critical metals should not be reduced to only their essence in creating a carbon-free society. Technology could evolve and find other ways to reach this goal without critical minerals, diminishing the demand for and value of these minerals. De Groot et al state that 'although human inventions can replace many functions of natural resources, it might be undesirable because it is often technically difficult and usually imperfect, it is often socially undesirable and economically not very sensible'.[41]

Furthermore, the criticality and various developed definitions vary depending on the resource's essentiality, substitutability or irreplaceable nature. Frenzel et al believe that the 'true meaning of risk' has fundamental links to criticality, dictating several conceptual and methodological issues in research for critical minerals.[42] On the other hand, De Groot et al argue that the importance and significance of the resource should be the point of consideration in the conceptualisation of critical metals.[43] Critical metals are to be assessed according to their economic and risk importance. However, assessing their importance and criticality is also essential, considering these resources' direct benefit to human society. The importance of critical metals should not be reduced to only their essence in creating a carbon-free society. Technology could evolve and find other ways to reach this goal without critical minerals, diminishing the demand for and value for these minerals. De Groot et al further argue that while human inventions can potentially substitute many functions of natural resources, such substitution is generally technically challenging, often imperfect, socially undesired and economically impractical.[44]

Many researchers and authors who have defined the criticality of natural resources have limited their definition to the importance of these natural resources being a catalyst to an end, such as technological innovation, the creation of green

[39] M Frenzel, J Kullik, MA Reuter and J Gutzmer, 'Raw Material "Criticality" – Sense or Nonsense?' (2017) 50(12) *Journal of Physics D: Applied Physics* 123002.

[40] R De Groot, J Van der Perk, A Chiesura and A Van Vliet, 'Importance and Threat as Determining Factors for Criticality of Natural Capital' (2003) 44(2–3) *Ecological Economics* 187.

[41] ibid.

[42] Frenzel et al (n 39).

[43] De Groot et al (n 40).

[44] ibid.

energy and the Tesla boom in the automotive industry. Here, I pose the question, if the importance of criticality studies were reviewed, to whom would they be significant? This is where the concept of just criticality becomes pertinent to critical mineral development.

Among other researchers, Purnell et al hold that non-anthropocentric perspectives consider parts of the natural environment as resources or critical resources to species other than humans. They argue that within the dominant anthropocentric perspective, the criticality concept is guided by different interest groups, such as those critical to the global human society (or humanity), a region, a country, a corporation, an economic or industrial sector, or a specific product or technology.[45] The interpretation of what is critical is neither inherent nor 'actual'; the resource is 'critical', but a natural resource being critical depends on the needs of the time. Hence, the international sphere of perspectives in international energy law and international mineral law are the drivers behind what will be regarded as critical from a geopolitical, climate change, security and technological advancement point of view.

2.6. Evolution and Considerations of Criticality Assessments

According to Frenzel et al, the most frequently used approach for assessing raw material criticality includes integrating plausible sets of various defined indicators to shape aggregate scores for vulnerable and supply risk indicators and mapping their dimensions against each other to assess the area of critical raw materials.[46] Glöser et al state that the strategy 'is a subset of conventional risk matrix methodology'.[47] As stated in the previous section, some scholars have taken a single-dimension approach, while others have included other factors, such as socio-environmental and political aspects, in their system.[48] Economic value and supply risk indicators are two widely used indicators for assessing criticality. Below is a discussion of the economic importance and supply risk included in many evaluations.

[45] P Purnell, D Dawson, KE Roelich, JK Steinberger and J Busch, 'Critical Materials for Infrastructure: Local vs Global Properties' (2013) 166(5) *Proceedings of the Institution of Civil Engineers-Engineering Sustainability* 272; Thomas Telford Ltd, SI Hallstedt and O Isaksson, 'Material Criticality Assessment in Early Phases of Sustainable Product Development' (2017) 161 *Journal of Cleaner Production* 40; TE Graedel and BK Reck, 'Six Years of Criticality Assessments: What Have We Learned So Far?' (2016) 20(4) *Journal of Industrial Ecology* 692.

[46] Frenzel et al (n 39).

[47] Glöser et al (n 37).

[48] TE Graedel, R Barr, C Chandler, T Chase, J Choi, L Christoffersen, E Friedlander, C Henly, C Jun, NT Nassar and D Schechner, 'Methodology of Metal Criticality Determination' (2012) 46(2) *Environmental Science & Technology* 1063.

2.6.1. Economic Vulnerability Indicators

Helbig et al state that 'economic impact is an extra cost which arises from an imbalance in supply or demand'.[49] Besides, scholars have significantly differed on the scope of vulnerability evaluation. The economic importance (EI) variable is the significance of raw materials to the EU economy.[50] Also, the economic indicator relates to the possibility of disrupting the supply of critical raw material situations. The indicators widely adopted in many studies, including other indicators of economic importance employed in a few assessments, are discussed below.

2.6.1.1. Substitutability

Substitution is challenging to realise without any deterioration in the economic viability, performance or quality of a product. Helbig et al show that substitutability signifies the most applied indicator for both vulnerability impact and supply indicators. In the interpretation of supply risk, for instance, a shortage in supply is less likely if manufacturers can employ substitutes, thereby reducing the materials' overall demand.[51] Regarding the vulnerability dimension, substitution possibilities show a diminished significance when compared to a mineral without a suitable substitute. Furthermore, metals' substitutability can be interpreted on multiple levels of the development of a product, such as technological substitution, functional substitution, material substitution, non-material substitution and quality substitution.[52] Frenzel et al showed that substitutability is inversely linked to the economic importance indicator.[53]

2.6.1.2. Value of the Product

The value of the product is the second most significant indicator for EI.[54] Furthermore, the product's value shows the interwoven relationship with EI. Graedel et al ranked critical metals to be critical when the revenue was dependent on the raw material by more than 5 per cent. The product value indicator estimates the probable damage to the resource supply disruption.[55] Beylot and

[49] C Helbig, L Wietschel, A Thorenz and A Tuma, 'How to Evaluate Raw Material Vulnerability- An Overview' (2016) 48 *Resources Policy* 13.

[50] GA Blengini, P Nuss, J Dewulf, V Nita, LT Peirò, B Vidal-Legaz, C Latunussa, L Mancini, D Blagoeva, D Pennington and M Pellegrini, 'EU Methodology for Critical Raw Materials Assessment: Policy Needs and Proposed Solutions for Incremental Improvements' (2017) 53 *Resources Policy* 12.

[51] Helbig et al (n 49).

[52] ibid.

[53] Frenzel et al (n 39).

[54] ibid.

[55] Graedel et al (n 48).

Villeneuve supposed that this indicator measures the possible damage of a raw material supply disruption by considering each resource's occurrence rather than its quantity.[56] The study found that the affected product's value is the second most adopted indicator for assessing economic importance.

2.6.1.3. Future Demand

Helbig et al found that five of the 16 identified studies used the ratio between the recent supply and potential demand for the raw material, with all the studies assessing at either the technological or national level.[57] This metric is distinct from the others in that it has a value dependent on future data rather than historical or current data. The general view of the indicator is that 'ramp-up' raw materials are vital for technologies intended to be deployed on a large scale or for a regional or national economy, such as resource technological innovations or low-carbon energy. According to Kavlak et al, a shortage in the development of necessary critical raw materials could prove to be a considerable challenge.[58] Future demand has also been used to calculate supply risk indicators. It is inversely linked in the sense that too much reliance on future technology is harmful. The same technology is threatened by capital, while emerging technologies with a fast-growing demand rate may negatively affect the continuous availability of resources. In other words, increased potential demand has a negative impact on the goods.

2.6.1.4. Strategic Importance

Another factor that influences vulnerability is strategic importance. The term 'strategic importance' describes how a resource's potential requirements for securing a nation's economic status or the needs that emerge because of future strategic technologies are assessed.[59] According to a report by Roelich et al, the market for renewable energy is strategic.[60] Parthemore looked at the dangers of the US government's dependence on mineral resources, which the report referred to as 'vital raw materials'.[61]

[56] A Beylot and J Villeneuve, 'Assessing the National Economic Importance of Metals: An Input–Output Approach to the Case of Copper in France' (2015) 44 *Resources Policy* 161.

[57] Helbig et al (n 49).

[58] G Kavlak, J McNerney, RL Jaffe and JE Trancik, 'Metal Production Requirements for Rapid Photovoltaics Deployment' (2015) 8(6) *Energy & Environmental Science* 1651.

[59] Helbig et al (n 49).

[60] K Roelich, DA Dawson, P Purnell, C Knoeri, R Revell, J Busch and JK Steinberger, 'Assessing the Dynamic Material Criticality of Infrastructure Transitions: A Case of Low Carbon Electricity' (2014) 123 *Applied Energy* 378.

[61] C Parthemore, 'Elements of Security: Mitigating the Risks of US Dependence on Critical Minerals' (Center for a New American Security, 2011).

2.6.1.5. *Material Value*

Many studies have used material value as a measure of resource vulnerability.[62] For example, Helbig stated that mineral resources' value is easier to measure than other previously used metrics because data can be derived directly from economic and corporate statistics.[63] Furthermore, this measure is inversely linked to vulnerability since a supply shortage leads to a rise in price volatility rather than a disruption in supply. This means that by limiting production, the risk is considered to raise the cost of raw materials rather than lower revenue. Instead of using commodity value as an indicator for assessing the vulnerability of resources, Duclos et al used it as a bottleneck to prioritise the raw material of interest.[64]

2.6.1.6. *Diversified Utilisation*

This measure considers the fact that raw materials may have a higher value in some countries than in others,[65] implying that resources may not be of equal significance in all societies. Erdmann and Graedel coined the phrase 'value chain sensitivity' to describe how the raw material crisis affected Germany's economy.[66] On the other hand, Achzet and Helbig asserted that the rare use of an indicator does not mean lower quality because it is likely to have been introduced recently or has a limited emphasis.[67]

Market share of the target group, shift in demand share, willingness to pass on cost increases and import dependency are some of the measures found to have been used in several studies. Duclos et al introduced the ability to pass through cost increases.[68] The metric assesses a company's ability to pass on increased resource costs to its customers. Erdmann et al and Hatayama and Tahara used the market share transition metric to measure the change in raw material demand in relation to global resource demand over time.[69] Parthemore used the dependence on minerals importation predictor to assess the critical minerals economic risks on countries.[70] The study calculated the country's net dependence on imports by

[62] Helbig et al (n 49).

[63] ibid.

[64] SJ Duclos, JP Otto and DG Konitzer, 'Design in an Era of Constrained Resources' (2010) 132(9) *Mechanical Engineering* 36.

[65] Graedel et al (n 48).

[66] L Erdmann and TE Graedel, 'Criticality of Non-Fuel Minerals: A Review of Major Approaches and Analyses' (2011) 45 *Environmental Science Technology* 7620.

[67] B Achzet and C Helbig, 'How to Evaluate Raw Material Supply Risks – An Overview' (2013) 38(4) *Resources Policy* 435.

[68] Duclos et al (n 64).

[69] L Erdmann, S Behrendt and M Feil, 'Critical Raw Materials for Germany (short version)' (Institute for Future Studies and Technology Assessment, 2011); H Hatayama and K Tahara, 'Adopting an Objective Approach to Criticality Assessment: Learning from the Past' (2018) 55 *Resources Policy* 96.

[70] Parthemore (n 61).

comparing the rate of consumption to the flow of capital. The target group's share demand indicator was used in studies that claimed that a resource's high share demand compared to global demand indicated the country's raw material value. Scholars also use recyclability, price sensitivity and primary resource prices as measures of economic effect.[71]

2.6.2. Indicators of Supply Risk

Supply risk measures are used to assess the probability of supply constraints. In addition, much like the economic impact dimension, measures of supply risk vary from one study to the next. These risks impact companies that rely on critical minerals as raw materials and exporting countries. The supply risk assessment below is not exhaustive and does not include all risk factors since risk factors can range from a single or a group of countries, companies, products and economic sectors. According to Blengini et al, the supply risk measure assesses the risk of insufficient raw material supply to satisfy technical industry demand.[72] The metrics, weightings, calculation formulas, measurements and selected studies are all mentioned below.

2.6.2.1. Depletion Time

The depletion cycle indicator is an indicator that assumes an inverse relationship with supply risk. The longer it takes for conventional raw materials to deplete, the less likely a supply interruption may occur in each time frame.[73] In addition, the depletion time denotes a complex scope that considers demand patterns, reserve levels and recycling rates.

2.6.2.2. Dependence on By-products

Company production is closely linked to the predictor of by-product dependence. Many raw materials, especially useful in modern technology, are mined as a by-product of the metal extraction process. Nassar et al argued that certain metals are critical for technological advancement but are subject to supply disruptions,

[71] ibid.

[72] GA Blengini, D Blagoeva, J Dewulf, C Torres de Matos, V Nita, B Vidal-Legaz, C Latunussa, Y Kayam, L Talens Peirò, CEL Baranzelli and S Manfredi, 'Assessment of the Methodology for Establishing the EU List of Critical Raw Materials: Background Report' (JRC Technical Reports, 2017).

[73] H Ohno, K Matsubae, K Nakajima, S Nakamura and T Nagasaka, 'Development of Efficient Recycling System for Steel Alloying Elements in End-of-Life Vehicles' in A Kvithyld et al (eds), *REWAS 2013: Enabling Materials Resource Sustainability* (Springer, 2013) 414–22.

and demonstrated that this is due to the host metal's annual extraction limiting the by-product supply, which may fail to adapt to rapid increases in demand, resulting in shortages.[74] Other indicators that affect supply are import dependency and demand growth. According to Frenzel et al, greater dependence on imports increases the risk of supply disruption due to conflicts in other parts of the world.[75]

2.6.2.3. *The Opportunity to Recycle*

With regard to the demand for products that can be recycled, supply risk is influenced by substitutability in the same way that vulnerability is. Critical mineral supply is determined by the availability not only primary, but also of secondary raw materials. As a result, raw material recyclability is also a significant predictor. Although most critical minerals' recyclability rate appears to be zero or poor, many resources are recovered indirectly, according to the EU Commission study. Feldspar, for example, cannot be recycled in its naturally occurring form; however, it is used in many recycled glasses.

2.6.2.4. *Other Risks*

Different critical minerals are found in different parts of the world, with some minerals concentrated in a single or few countries, making some countries more prominent exporters and others large consumers of natural resources. However, the various host countries with critical minerals have environmental and political factors that also raise risks in criticality assessments. For example, the DRC is the world's largest cobalt exporter (approximately 88 per cent of global exports).[76] The World Bank finds that the DRC has the lowest World Governance Indicators – Political Stability and Absence of Violence (WGI-PV) ranking of all mining countries regarding political stability.[77] Van den Brink et al state that the DRC ratings are the WGI-PV's lowest possible score (–2.5).[78] The global average WGI-PV on mining country political stability is weighted to cobalt output. The average suggests a relatively poor governance performance on a scale of –2.5 (weak governance performance) to 2.5 (strong governance

[74] NT Nassar, TE Graedel and EM Harper, 'By-Product Metals Are Technologically Essential but Have Problematic Supply' (2015) 1(3) *Science Advances* 1400180.

[75] Frenzel et al (n 39).

[76] D Krummel and P Siegfried, 'The Dark Side of Samsung's Value Chain: The Human Costs of Cobalt Mining "BLOOD, SWEAT AND COBALT"' (2021) 90(2) *Journal of Geoscience and Environment Protection* 182.

[77] World Bank, 'Worldwide Governance Indicators' (2019) https://info.worldbank.org/governance/wgi/#home.

[78] S van den Brink, R Kleijn, B Sprecher and A Tukker, 'Identifying Supply Risks by Mapping the Cobalt Supply Chain' (2020) 156 *Resources, Conservation and Recycling* 104743.

performance).[79] Graedel et al show that environmental damage leads to supply risks in addition to political supply risks, especially when cobalt is extracted and processed at a degree unacceptable to host communities.[80] Certain deposit forms can pose greater environmental risks than others. For example, deposits vary in the stripping ratio, the generation of metal-ridge sludge or the generation of highly reactive waste, resulting in higher concentrations of dissolved metals or acid mine drainage.[81] These differences suggest that criticality studies should be included in environmental life cycle sustainability assessment frameworks.

2.7. Just Criticality: A Conceptual Analysis

This section makes a case for the concept of 'just criticality'. Critical metals are regarded as 'critical' for two major reasons: these minerals' resource security and economic importance.[82] Hence, the criticality aspect of critical minerals has been reduced to the risk of supply disruption and the disruption's probable economic impact. The two aspects are the combined overall measure of what is regarded as 'critical' when assessing and measuring criticality in critical minerals. However, such an aggregate concept of criticality does not address the possible assessment of other strategic risks towards critical mineral-exporting countries and other significant factors like environmental and health concerns that might appear.[83] According to Hayes and McCullough, the criticality evaluations made accessible to the public only reflect the viewpoints of a small portion of the world's population – mostly industrialised countries that have significant technology and information industries. The economic interests of these regions are likely to be significantly distinct from those in less-developed states that have not been involved in this discussion so far.[84] Defining and grouping the different significant concerns into one overall 'criticality' value concept confuses and fails to address other values that can be distinguished from the economic importance and supply risk factors. Nevertheless, criticality can be divided into several categories for analysis, as illustrated in Figure 1 and elaborated below.

[79] P Amoah, G Eweje and R Bathurst, 'Understanding Grand Challenges in Sustainability Implementation Within Mining in Developing Countries' (2020) 10(2) *Social Business* 123.

[80] Graedel et al (n 48).

[81] KJ Schulz, JH DeYoung Jr, RR Seal II and DC Bradley (eds), *US Geological Survey, 'Critical Mineral Resources of the United States – Economic and Environmental Geology and Prospects for Future Supply'* (2017) US Geological Survey Professional Paper 1802, F1–F40, https://doi.org/10.3133/pp1802.

[82] Heffron, 'The Role of Justice (n 6).

[83] BK Sovacool, M Martiskainen, A Hook and L Baker, 'Decarbonization and Its Discontents: A Critical Energy Justice Perspective on Four Low-Carbon Transitions' (2019) 155(4) *Climatic Change* 581.

[84] Hayes and McCullough (n 22).

Figure 1 The conceptual development of justice

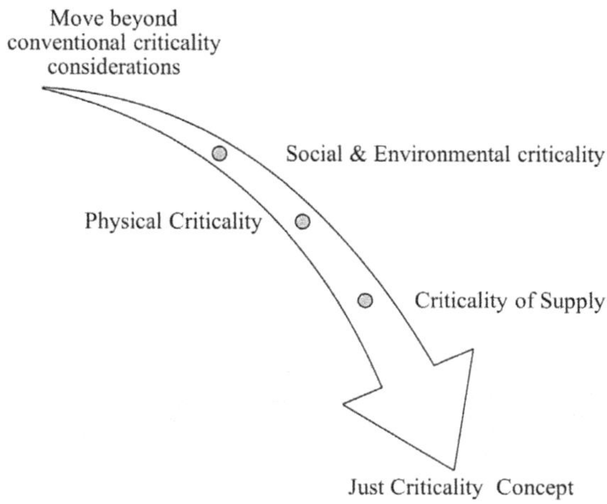

Source: Author's illustration.

The criticality of supply is a fundamental part of all studies and assessments on critical mineral security.[85] This includes the import dependence of consumer countries such as those in the Global North. Consumer countries have the means of production and the companies to finance the industrialisation of these minerals. They possess the technology to provide substitutes in volatile price markets that may be caused by global emergencies such as the COVID-19 pandemic. However, the substitutability of minerals does not guarantee supply. This criticality aspect includes the geopolitical risks associated with the concentrated production in unstable countries.[86] This is also known as 'political criticality'.

With regard to social and environmental risks, the socio-environmental concerns of critical mineral production could be called 'environmental and social criticality'.[87] The literature shows that this criticality can be found in the manner, means and ways in which critical minerals are sourced in developing countries.[88] The cobalt found in the DRC has been stained with child labour, while occurrences like the Marikana massacre have marred the PGMs found in South Africa and the environmental degradation of copper mining in Chile. These issues are becoming paramount globally. For instance, the UN includes environmental and social issues that may affect the development of a project in the classification of projects under the United Nations Framework Classification for Resources.[89]

[85] Coulomb et al (n 17).

[86] RG Eggert, 'Minerals Go Critical' (2011) 3(9) *Nature Chemistry* 688.

[87] R Motoori, BC McLellan and T Tezuka, 'Environmental Implications of Resource Security Strategies for Critical Minerals: A Case Study of Copper in Japan' (2018) 8(12) *Minerals* 558.

[88] JX Kasperson, RE Kasperson and BL Turner, 'Regions at Risk: Exploring Environmental Criticality' (1996) 38(10) *Environment: Science and Policy for Sustainable Development* 4.

[89] UNECE, *United Nations Framework Classification for Resources Update 2019*, ECE Energy Series No 61 (United Nations, 2020). This is an update of the United Nations Framework Classification for Fossil Energy and Mineral Reserves and Resources 2009.

Physical criticality concerns whether the earth can provide the resources for future global demand.[90] Criticality studies cannot be limited to the perspective of developed nations as the frames and perspective of criticality are strategic to the development of several countries. This is central to the question of whether it might not be better to examine the crucial concerns which underlie the various aspects of criticality. These concerns may not be specified or limited to a specific critical mineral but are more general or 'generic'.[91]

Concepts such as just criticality have neither been associated with mineral criticality nor applied in other industries or resources. This is primarily attributed to the criticality criteria being assessed by consumer countries relegated to import dependency because the multinational tech companies are not found in areas with mineral reserves.[92] Fear of the availability of technology-advancing metals such as rare earth minerals, cobalt and PGMs is one of the major concerns about minerals.[93]

This book introduces the concept of 'just criticality' in mineral development. Developing just criticality ensures that the criticality aspect of critical metals considers both inter- and intragenerational aspects, resulting in sustainability.[94] Through just criticality considerations, the Global South can secure more substantial rights and a fair distribution that increases the socio-economic and political significance of critical minerals that 'could' fulfil the UN's Sustainable Development Goals. It also fosters the recognition of marginalised host communities who simultaneously suffer the adverse effects and the ills resulting from possessing these natural resources. The equal distribution following the right and fair procedures of critical mineral development must be ascertained under a just criticality framework. Therefore, studying the fundamental concerns beyond critical minerals' supply risk and economic importance is crucial. Since criticality is an ever-evolving concept, it is impossible to quantify and assess what will be critical in the future. Still, it is crucial to ensure that the justice framework is upheld in all criticality determinants and incorporated in all critical minerals decision-making processes.

[90] J Wang, L Yang, J Lin and Y Bentley, 'The Availability of Critical Minerals for China's Renewable Energy Development: An Analysis of Physical Supply' [2020] *Natural Resources Research* 1.

[91] ibid.

[92] Y Yu, 'Assessing the Criticality of Minerals Used in Emerging Technologies in China' [2020] *Gospodarka Surowcami Mineralnymi-Mineral Resources Management* 5.

[93] He (n 23).

[94] Sustainability is a long-term goal – it encourages activities whose design is defined by social, economic and environmental dimensions for the long-term, rather than short-term gains. Sustainable development, on the other hand, is the development that meets the need of the present generation without compromising the ability of the future generation to meet their own needs, ie the pathways and processes needed to achieve the sustainability goal. See UNESCO, 'Sustainable Development' (nd) https://en.unesco.org/themes/education-sustainable-development/what-is-esd/sd. For a definition of sustainable development, see World Commission on Environment and Development, *Our Common Future* (Oxford University Press, 1987).

2.8. The Contextual Perspective of Justice in Critical Mineral Development

Justice can be traced back to earlier studies such as John Rawls's 1971 work, *A Theory of Justice*.[95] An American philosopher, Rawls aimed to create a non-utilitarian justification for a democratic political order marked by fairness, equality and individual rights. His view of justice as fairness envisions a community of free citizens with equal fundamental rights cooperating within a just economic system.[96] Rawls modified and developed the concept of justice. However, he made two distinctions between justice and the individual sense of being based on equal liberties compatible with the principles of liberty for all. Secondly, he acknowledged the social and economic inequalities as the most significant challenge to marginalised communities and advocated for fair equality of opportunity conditions. Indirectly, Rawls understood and highlighted the dichotomy of distributional, recognition and procedural justice. To Plato, justice is a soul trait that enables persons to set aside their irrational urge to enjoy every pleasure and to derive selfish satisfaction from every object in favour of performing a particular role for the greater good;[97] this was more in line with distributional justice.

More contemporarily, justice was reflected in the environmental justice movement, which began in the late 1970s in the USA when residents of a Black, middle-class area in Houston, Texas learned that the state intended to allow the establishment of a solid waste facility in their neighbourhood. Given the state of facts, Schlosberg states that 'the concept of environmental justice was used to illustrate that some communities received more environmental risks than others'.[98] The environmental justice phenomenon has seen a spatial and conceptual expansion into food and energy security at the epicentre of the current environmental justice discourse.[99] Furthermore, many scholars have argued for a pluralistic understanding of the concept of justice.[100] Carrillo and Pellow have argued for multiple frames and contexts of injustice.[101] The criticality assessments and methodologies employed in determining the criticality aspect of these metals cause injustice to several critical metal exporting countries by not considering their need for technology, spatial, social, economic, policy and political aspects in determining the strategic utility of these critical metals.

[95] J Rawls, *A Theory of Justice* (Harvard University Press, 1971).

[96] MY Said and Y Nurhayati, 'A Review on Rawls Theory of Justice' (2021) 1(1) *International Journal of Law, Environment, and Natural Resources* 29.

[97] MD Udoudom and SA Bassey, 'Plato and John Rawls on Social Justice' (2018) 9(3) *Researchers World* 110.

[98] D Schlosberg, 'Theorising Environmental Justice: The Expanding Sphere of a Discourse' (2013) 22(1) *Environmental Politics* 37.

[99] G Walker, 'Globalizing Environmental Justice: The Geography and Politics of Frame Contextualization and Evolution' (2009) 9(3) *Global Social Policy* 355.

[100] J Sze and JK London, 'Environmental Justice at the Crossroads' (2008) 2(4) *Sociology Compass* 1331.

[101] I Carrillo and D Pellow, 'Critical Environmental Justice and the Nature of the Firm' [2021] *Agriculture and Human Values* 1.

Justice is an integral part of society. Carrillo and Pellow state that

> justice research has established those environmental inequities such as exposure to toxic hazards are systemic and that they can amplify or reinforce, moreover, other social inequities and divisions such as those between racial or ethnic groups or different socio-economic classes.[102]

The different contexts of justice in critical minerals are dictated by the social inequities, socio-economic classes and divisions of racial or ethnic groups in the places where it occurs. There is little conceptual or empirical analysis of justice and mineral development or the different perspectives of resource dependence across polar socio-economic realities.[103] Conceptually, justice hinges on different kinds of justice – distributive, procedural, recognition and restorative.[104] Distributive justice refers to the distribution of environmental goods and ills among populations and focuses on the inequitable distribution of hazards and risks in marginalised communities. Procedural justice includes participatory aspects of justice, especially whether members of the public have the opportunity to authentically participate in making decisions about how their resources are developed.[105] Ryder states that having access to sound, transparent information that can be used in the decision-making process is an essential part of this kind of equity.[106] Recognition justice identifies historical and structural patterns of privileging (white, Western, patriarchal) worldviews and cultural systems over others and endeavours to encourage, in their place, the acceptance and inclusion of diverse cultures and worldviews in extractive industry decision-making.[107] Finally, restorative justice focuses on the historical exclusion and displacement of native and indigenous peoples whose relationships with the land have been changed through co-optation, industrialisation and defilement of their ancestral homes.[108]

The above definition and tenets of justice conceptualise what justice is and ought to be in critical mineral development, highlighting the different injustices along the critical mineral value chain while offering avenues to channel possible solutions. The difficulty emanates from the different contextual perspectives of justice and, ultimately, from critical mineral development. The

[102] ibid.

[103] SA Malin, *The Price of Nuclear Power: Uranium Communities and Environmental Justice* (Rutgers University Press, 2015).

[104] M Menton, C Larrea, S Latorre, J Martinez-Alier, M Peck, L Temper and M Walter, 'Environmental Justice and the SDGs: From Synergies to Gaps and Contradictions' (2020) 15(6) *Sustainability Science* 1621.

[105] G Walker, 'Beyond Distribution and Proximity: Exploring the Multiple Spatialities of Environmental Justice' (2009) 41(4) *Antipode* 614.

[106] SS Ryder, 'Developing an Inter-Sectionally-Informed, Multi-Sited, Critical Policy Ethnography to Examine Power and Procedural Justice in Multi-Scalar Energy and Climate Change Decision Making Processes' (2018) 45 *Energy Research & Social Science* 266.

[107] D Schlosberg, *Defining Environmental Justice: Theories, Movements, and Nature* (Oxford University Press, 2019).

[108] ibid.

contextual perspective varies from international to national and local levels of critical mineral development. These competing contexts all advocate for what is regarded as 'just' within their communities. For instance, Shackleton notes that the perspective of justice in critical mineral development in the Paris Agreement (COP21) of December 2015 was determined by stakeholders, such as the regulators implementing policies at a national level and the host communities of Katanga in the DRC and the rich Copperbelt cities of Kitwe, Ndola, Mufulira, Luanshya, Chingola and Chililabombwe.[109]

Energy law and mining law have extended the study of minerals to engage with other disciplines, such as politics, economics, geography, environmental sciences and engineering,[110] as well as the need to promote the goals of energy transitions and sustainability. Aligning the contextual perspectives in critical mineral development does not strictly subscribe to mining law as traditionally understood. It is consistent with the emerging evolution and function of the law and governance of mining and minerals if understood from a global perspective, which should engage with the global challenges of our age. On this point, Bastida argues that contemporary mining law must adopt a global perspective, as

> the study of mining law has … mostly circumscribed to domestic legal systems and generally limited to national boundaries. It has not yet broadened systematically to encompass the international, transnational, regional, national and local levels of normative orderings of social relations concerning mining and minerals.[111]

Bastida argues for the establishment of a framework for studying mining law from a global perspective. She provides insight into the global economy's interaction with environmental sustainability, human rights and social equality. She methodically broadens the area of study to embrace all the various normative levels, with a particular emphasis on the gaps at the local level, which must be filled by acknowledgement of indigenous/local peoples' rights through dissecting issues like land rights and public interest.

[109] RT Shackleton, 'Loss of Land and Livelihoods from Mining Operations: A Case in the Limpopo Province, South Africa' (2020) 99 *Land Use Policy* 104825.

[110] RJ Heffron, *Energy Law: An Introduction* (Springer, 2014); see also DS Olawuyi, 'Can MENA Extractive Industries Support the Global Energy Transition? Current Opportunities and Future Directions' (2021) 8(2) *The Extractive Industries and Society* 100685. TL Humby, 'Redressing Mining Cegacies: The Case of the South African Mining Industry' (2016) 135(4) *Journal of Business Ethics* 653; H Mostert, CL Young and JL Hassman, 'Towards Extractive Justice: Europe, Africa and the Pressures of Resource Dependency' (2019) 26(2) *South African Journal of International Affairs* 233; H Mostert and C Young, 'From Promise to Practice: South Africa's Legal Framework for Mineral Resources and the Sustainable Development Goals' (South African Institute of International Affairs, 2018); C Sbert, *The Lens of Ecological Law: A Look at Mining* (Edward Elgar Publishing, 2020) (on ecological justice); C Sbert Carlsson, 'Mining from the Lens of Ecological Law: Obstacles and Opportunities for Re-formation' (Doctoral Dissertation, Université d'Ottawa/ University of Ottawa, 2019); DS Olawuyi, *Extractives Industry Law in Africa* (Springer International Publishing, 2018).

[111] Bastida, *The Law and Governance* (n 5) chs 3 and 6.

2.8.1. International Perspective of Critical Mineral Development

This part of the research examines the international perspective of critical mineral development. It traces its drivers to international law instruments and guidelines, such as those related to climate change and global trends like the energy transition. It also considers the role of international trade and relations in the industry and the different capacities of players along the critical mineral value chain, hence offering a cosmopolitan perspective.

The international perspective of critical mineral development is driven by both international law treaties and soft law that establish standards and guidelines used by states to govern how they relate among themselves and to develop resources and policy at the international level.[112] This emanates from international economic law being pivotal in managing the global architecture for trade and investment.[113] From this same narrative, the global drivers of change establish climate change adaptation and mitigation mechanisms, dictating global markets on what should be demanded and what should not be demanded, driving the global energy transition.[114] International treaties such as the United Nations Framework Convention on Climate Change, the 1997 Kyoto Protocol and the Paris Agreement have reached a consensus on reducing greenhouse gas emissions by 2050. The COP21 conference, which culminated in the Paris Agreement, led to the submission of nationally determined contributions. Large carbon emitters such as the EU pledged a 40 per cent reduction in emissions by 2030.[115] Such commitments have led to the rise in demand for critical minerals that facilitate carbon reduction technology.

International relations are also vital in driving the perspectives of critical mineral development at the international level. A good example is President Trump's decision to withdraw the USA from the Paris Agreement, which impacted other countries and reduced the USA's financial aid to the Green Climate Fund.[116] Terminating the $3 billion US funding impacted climate change research and decreased society's chance of reaching the Paris Agreement goals that the nationally determined commitments had set.[117] On the other

[112] AE Bastida, 'Mining Law in the Context of Development: An Overview' in P Andrews-Speed (ed), *International Competition for Resources: The Role of Law, State and Markets* (Dundee University Press, 2008) 101–36, https://ssrn.com/abstract=2216635.

[113] ibid.

[114] Heffron, *Energy Law* (n 110). See also Bastida, *The Law and Governance* (n 5) ch 4, where she makes a case for a comprehensive mining and interacts with the developments of energy law.

[115] GP Peters, RM Andrew, JG Canadell, S Fuss, RB Jackson, JI Korsbakken, C Le Quéré and N Nakicenovic, 'Key Indicators to Track Current Progress and Future Ambition of the Paris Agreement' (2017) 7(2) *Nature Climate Change* 118.

[116] HB Zhang, HC Dai, HX Lai and WT Wang, 'US Withdrawal from the Paris Agreement: Reasons, Impacts, and China's Response' (2017) 8(4) *Advances in Climate Change Research* 220.

[117] ibid.

hand, the Biden administration created an Energy Justice Department within the US Department of Justice to advocate for energy justice to address energy poverty issues, to achieve a just energy transition and to address the minority rights impacted by that energy transition.[118] Such developments led to a fluctuation of mineral prices, as well as of criticality considerations due to international policies.

International business also drives the perspective of critical mineral development. For example, copper and cobalt are among the main metals driving the energy transition. The DRC supplies over 70 per cent of the world's cobalt; the country reached an agreement with China and concluded a $9 billion deal to secure a concession for the Sicomines.[119] The deal was struck under the Belt and Road Initiative, with $6 billion for infrastructure and $3 billion invested in mining operations.[120] Such investments linked with international politics drive the perspectives of critical mineral development.

It has been argued that a broader view is required to capture the range of normative legal phenomena on mining and minerals from a global perspective.[121] Like Bastida argues, the international drivers of change in the perspective of critical mineral development must be understood from all geographical levels of relations as they determine what is just in the critical mineral development value chain.[122] Bastida believes that a global perspective helps us better comprehend mineral law as an under-theorised and long-ignored topic of study at the confluence of global economics, environmental sustainability and climate action, human rights and social fairness, and law and development. In chapter seven of her book, Bastida argues that an area in need of further research in this field revolves around the evolving transnational and global institutions and structures to ensure the just distribution of benefits across global value chains.

The determination of criticality aspects must consider the inequities and other established disparities within the critical mineral development global value chain. Hence, there must be an intersection and an explicit synergy between critical mineral development and poverty, disease and ignorance, as these are some of the most prominent challenges facing the Global South today. There must also be consideration of the needs of the Global South, such as diseases, ignorance and poverty, to meet the total threshold of cosmopolitanism in international mineral law and the global value chain for critical mineral development.

[118] J Brady, 'NPR Cookie Consent and Choices' (NPR, 2022) www.npr.org/2021/06/08/1004059950/energy-justice-nominee-brings-activist-voice-to-bidens-climate-plans.

[119] AL Gulley, EA McCullough and KB Shedd, 'China's Domestic and Foreign Influence in The Global Cobalt Supply Chain' (2019) 62 *Resources Policy* 317.

[120] ibid.

[121] Bastida, *The Law and Governance* (n 5).

[122] ibid.

A global perspective of global corporate structures shows the legal and governance infrastructures used to attain these critical minerals for profit. This perspective is engrained in transboundary politics and treaties to attain and exhaust these metals from complex supply chains. Bastida argues that these structures need to be recalibrated around cosmopolitan ethics. As envisaged by Kwame's work reviewed by Witt, cosmopolitanism entails reviewing these structures to work for the poor. Kwame imposes moral obligations on people to help others beyond kinship and citizenship.[123]

2.8.2. National Perspectives of Critical Mineral Development

Four main drivers push the national perspectives on critical mineral development – the government's aim, the availability of finance, technological advancements and societal preferences.[124] The government aims to direct foreign investors' engagement with host communities and society. Some countries in sub-Saharan Africa, such as the DRC and Zambia, have proven over the years that the government aims only to maximise profit at whatever cost. Such an attitude from the government leads to the abuse of human rights and the expulsion of host communities from their traditional lands.[125] On the other hand, technological advancement can help in obtaining national value retention in critical mineral development.[126] Economies like Chile have emphasised R&D initiatives in their mining agreements, unlike critical mineral mining countries like Namibia, DRC, Zambia and Zimbabwe, which have concentrated on rent accumulation without retaining technology through R&D initiatives.[127] Besides, the countries with critical minerals are only involved in the exploration and production phases of the value chain. The availability of finance determines how countries and corporations source investment for critical mineral development. Most resource-rich countries do not have the finances to exploit and process their mineral resources. Furthermore, though critical minerals are found in several countries, different countries have different societal expectations and preferences regarding critical mineral development.[128]

[123] MT Witt, 'Book Review: Kwame Anthony Appiah. Cosmopolitanism: Ethics in a World of Strangers. New York: WW Norton & Company, 2006' (2006) 28(4) *Administrative Theory & Praxis* 646.

[124] RJ Heffron, A Rønne, JP Tomain, A Bradbrook and K Talus, 'A Treatise for Energy Law' (2018) 11(1) *Journal of World Energy Law & Business* 34.

[125] R Perks, 'How Can Public–Private Partnerships Contribute to Security and Human Rights Policy and Practice in the Extractive Industries? A Case Study of The Democratic Republic of Congo (DRC)' (2012) 37(2) *Resources Policy* 251.

[126] G Anzolin and C Pietrobelli, 'Local Content Policies: Why Mining Need Consistent Policy Packages to Support Capabilities Development' (2021) 8(1) *The Extractive Industries and Society* 395.

[127] ibid.

[128] Heffron, 'The Role of Justice' (n 6).

The above expectations bring the discussion around to patriotism in critical mineral development in resource-rich countries. For example, sub-Saharan African countries like Tanzania, Zimbabwe, Zambia and the DRC have new political structures, are more resource nationalistic and promote a nationalised agenda in minerals and metal development.[129] This resource nationalism wave also emerges from regional trends, as set in the Africa Mining Vision (AMV). The AMV is a pathway formulated by African nations and puts the continent's long-term and broad development objectives at the heart of all policy-making concerned with mineral extraction. It presents a compelling case for increased taxation from resource exploitation and shows how and why African states might distribute natural wealth among their citizens.

The nationalist wave in these mineral-rich countries has changed the perspective of justice. Devising laws and policies that are strict on foreign investors whilst promoting local integration into the critical mineral value chain is a form of justice. Most mineral-rich countries have now resorted to building and constructing refineries within their own territory to increase the domestic value chains, with the sole purpose of exporting consumable goods rather than raw materials.[130] As much as critical mineral development requires financing, mining corporations have started implementing environmental and social governance mechanisms to ensure just and sustainable means of sourcing critical minerals across their entire value chain.[131]

The Global North versus Global South perspective emanates from a multipolar worldview. Critical mineral development in the national sphere stems from the resource-dependence aspect of consuming and metal-importing countries, particularly in the Global North and the highly dependent exporting countries of the Global South. Hence, the development of these minerals is determined by the Global North's financial liquidity and sub-Saharan Africa's critical minerals endowment. Western countries often create subsystems of administrative law regulating mining in the public interest across a wide range of values, such as environmental concerns, the value of nature, respect for human rights and climate action.[132] In sub-Saharan African countries, mineral policies are intended to guide actions within their territories and internationally to influence the supply of minerals from their economies.

[129] The African Mining Vision 2030, of 2009; G Hilson, 'The Africa Mining Vision: A Manifesto for More Inclusive Extractive Industry-Led Development?' (2020) 41(3) *Canadian Journal of Development Studies/Revue canadienne d'études du développement* 417; see also J Childs, 'Geography and Resource Nationalism: A Critical Review and Reframing' (2016) 3(2) *The Extractive Industries and Society* 539.

[130] I Ramdoo, 'Making Global Supply Chains Sustainable: The Case of the Gold Sector' (European Centre for Development Policy Management, 2015) Briefing Note 83.

[131] CSDS Lokuwaduge and K Heenetigala, 'Integrating Environmental, Social and Governance (ESG) Disclosure for a Sustainable Development: An Australian Study' (2017) 26(4) *Business Strategy and the Environment* 438.

[132] B Selwyn, 'Poverty Chains and Global Capitalism' (2019) 23(1) *Competition & Change* 71.

2.8.3. Local Perspective of Critical Mineral Development

This subsection delves into the local perspective of critical mineral development; in this case, it explains what the industry means for the locals – the host communities of the mining activities. An individual constructs a local perspective towards critical mineral development based on what they deem to be profitable or detrimental in critical mineral development.[133] The local perspective is mainly from the remote communities that host the mining of critical metals. Scholars believe that the local level of normative legal ordering has been absent in granular regulation and agreements.[134] Critical mineral development should be 'just', with three main tenets: procedural, recognition and distribution.[135] The mining industry often acts as an enclave industry, with governments and mining corporations designing policies such as local content policies, shared value mechanisms and corporate social responsibility strategies, which have all been designed from a national or international perspective of what is regarded to be just, leaving out the local indigenous stakeholder.[136]

Since critical mineral exploitation and development directly affects the local communities by impacting their health, personal finances, infrastructural development and environmental degradation, it has led to nimbyism (not-in-my-backyard syndrome).[137] Most mining host communities do not have access to finance and sophisticated technology to conduct larger mining operations. They often resort to artisanal and small-scale mining (ASM).[138] ASM is largely regarded as 'illegal'. Although traditional customs and land tenure practices might have been met, ASM activities are largely extra-legal,[139] operating outside of the national legal frameworks and mining laws.[140] The lack of recognition of ASM in most mining jurisdictions fails to acknowledge the importance of minerals mined locally and

[133] Y Lei, N Cui and D Pan, 'Economic and Social Effects Analysis of Mineral Development in China and Policy Implications' (2013) 38(4) *Resources Policy* 448.

[134] Bastida, *The Law and Governance* (n 5).

[135] K Jenkins, D McCauley, RJ Heffron, H Stephan and R Rehner, 'Energy Justice: A Conceptual Review' (2016) 11 *Energy Research & Social Science* 174.

[136] AM Esteves, B Coyne and A Moreno, 'Local Content Initiatives: Enhancing the Subnational Benefits of the Oil, Gas and Mining Sectors' (National Resource Governance Institute, 2013).

[137] Nymbism is a characterisation of the opposition of residents to proposed developments in their local area, as well as support for strict land use regulations. It carries the connotation that such residents are only opposing the mining development because it is close to them and that they would tolerate or support it if it the mining operations were conducted elsewhere.

[138] M Menegaki and D Kaliampakos, 'Dealing with NIMBYism in Mining Operations' in C Drebenstedt, R Singhal (eds), *Mine Planning and Equipment Selection: Proceedings of the 22nd MPES Conference, Dresden, Germany, 14th–19th October 2013* (Springer International Publishing, 2014) 1437–46.

[139] S Siegel and MM Veiga, 'Artisanal and Small-Scale Mining as an Extralegal Economy: De Soto and the Redefinition of "Formalization"' (2009) 34(1–2) *Resources Policy* 51.

[140] SN Jennings, 'Towards a Sustainable Role for Artisanal and Small-Scale Mining in Mineral Production' in E Bastida, TW Waelde and J Warden-Fernández (eds), *International and Comparative Mineral Law and Policy: Trends and Prospects* (Kluwer Law International, 2005) 505–16.

their impact on local economies. Siegal and Veiga argue that formalisation is key to the growth of the ASM sector.[141]

2.9. Sustainability of Critical Minerals

The concepts of sustainability and sustainable development in critical minerals have recently become more prominent in global critical mineral sourcing and supply chain management. The greatest challenge in critical mineral development is integrating its economic importance with social and environmental integrity.[142] Barkemeyer et al found that the Brundtland Report of 1987 underscored the need for socio-economic progress which could be sustained without asserting damaging effects on the environment that depleted the natural reserves.[143] The report shifted the focus of sustainable development from a physical concept to one focused on environmental, social and economic concerns. As the world's economies become more energy- and resource-intensive, the sustainable production of essential raw materials becomes increasingly crucial in the private and public sectors.[144]

The manufacturing mechanisms are unsustainable and translate to massive global environmental damage.[145] The significance of sustainability for critical raw materials is to create an equilibrium in environmental, social and economic considerations, thus providing intra-generational equity in the world's resources.[146] Furthermore, sustainable development entails taking an integrated, long-term approach to establishing a sustainable community by jointly addressing social, economic and environmental problems while avoiding the overconsumption of raw materials. The concept of sustainable development regarding critical minerals is significant because it enhances the conservation of metals and minerals by gradually altering technological developments and consumption.

2.10. The Need for Holistic Criteria

This chapter shows commonalities in what is 'critical' in critical metals. These commonalities, or mutual concepts of criticality, revolve around aspects of

[141] Siegel and Veiga (n 139).

[142] International Institute for Environment and Development, 'Breaking New Ground: Mining, Minerals and Sustainable Development' (2002) https://pubs.iied.org/9084iied.

[143] R Barkemeyer, D Holt, L Preuss and S Tsang, 'What Happened to the "Development" in Sustainable Development? Business Guidelines Two Decades after Brundtland' (2014) 22(1) *Sustainable Development* 15.

[144] P Koltun, 'Materials and Sustainable Development' (2010) 20 *Progress in Natural Science: Materials International* 16.

[145] H Salmenperä, K Pitkänen, P Kautto and L Saikku 'Critical Factors for Enhancing the Circular Economy in Waste Management' (2021) 280 *Journal of Cleaner Production* 124339.

[146] ibid.

uncertainty or threat and importance.[147] Some scholars have found a correlation between the criticality studies' importance, threat and vulnerability to the risk theory.[148] Schellens and Gisladottir found that the risk theory brought a fundamental understanding of the concept of criticality.[149] They also defined criticality as a relative and dynamic state of a natural resource of decisive importance: (i) ranked according to a hierarchy of human needs in relation to the issue or interest group specified; and (ii) attended with uncertainty or a threat.[150]

The variables of any criticality assessment are determined or dictated by geopolitical and technological circumstances that evolve, framing criticality in different avenues of assessment over the years. However, scholars such as Schellens and Gisladottir maintain that the importance of these minerals can be ranked according to the hierarchy of human needs.[151] Human needs differ according to national priorities, such as technological industries, defence applications, infrastructural development and food production.[152] Hence, the forces of demand and supply determine criticality, since the major technologically advanced critical mineral-consuming countries will always have criticality assessments according to their importance.

For example, in Australia, a nation rich in mineral resources with a thriving extractive industry, only important agronomic potash and phosphorous are considered essential.[153] Inorganic fertilisers, such as potassium in potash and phosphate, are mined from concentrated geological sources and applied to crops dissipatively. Countries with large populations and few inorganic fertiliser geological resources that have not publicly released criticality lists (for example, some African countries) may also consider agro-commodities critical. Other countries with advanced technology can innovate or substitute these metals. As a result, this influences the demand for and perceived value of specific elements and their criticality. Tellurium, for example, has become oversupplied in China and the USA in recent years as Si-based solar panel growth has outpaced cadmium telluride-based growth.[154] Tellurium prices have fallen during this period, and it has been recognised as a critical component in fewer studies.[155] The percentage of silicon criticality decreased from 42 per cent to 20 per cent over the same time frame.

[147] S Kalantzakos, 'The Race for Critical Minerals in an Era of Geopolitical Realignments' (2020) 55(3) *The International Spectator* 1.

[148] S Roeser (ed), *Handbook of Risk Theory: Epistemology, Decision Theory, Ethics, and Social Implications of Risk* (Springer Science & Business Media, 2012).

[149] Schellens and Gisladottir (n 31).

[150] ibid.

[151] ibid.

[152] Hayes and McCullough (n 22).

[153] RG Skirrow, DL Huston, TP Mernagh, JP Thorne, H Duffer and A Senior, *Critical Commodities for a High-Tech World: Australia's Potential to Supply Global Demand* (Geoscience Australia, 2013).

[154] CS Anderson, 'Selenium and Tellurium Minerals Yearbook: Volume I. Metals and Minerals (US Geological Survey, 2018) https://minerals.usgs.gov/minerals/pubs/commodity/selenium.

[155] Fraunhofer Institute for Solar Energy Systems, 'ISE Photovoltaics Report' (2017) www.ise.fraunhofer.de/de/downloads/pdf-files/aktuelles/photovoltaics-report-in-englischer-sprache.pdf.

Silica (SiO_2) is abundant (approximately 67 per cent of the upper continental crust by mass).[156] High-purity elemental silicon, which is needed for high-tech manufacturing, accounts for a small but crucial portion of elemental silicon use. China is the world's largest silicon metal producer, but it is found worldwide, and supplies have been steadily growing in recent years.[157] The changes in importance of tellurium and silicon also emphasise the interactions between market forces and changing perceptions of criticality over time.

The risk theory only looks at two components: the importance of the resource's function and threat to or uncertainty of its supply. Critical metals cannot be deemed critical due to their rarity in the earth's crust. Customarily, local perspectives are being overridden by global perspectives of what should be considered critical. This is largely due to global market forces driven by global demands, creating a utilitarian effect on what should be regarded as critical when assessing critical minerals. The global urgency to address changing demands during the World War I and II eras, the Cold War era and now climate change and the energy transition era have all washed away the local views and perspectives of what should be regarded as critical when assessing critical minerals. Unfortunately, these washed-away perspectives are those of sub-Saharan African countries such as the DRC and Zambia, which are the host countries of these minerals. This book holds the view that justice as a concept or theory recognises perspectives, values and assessments from any kind of interest group. Following a justice perspective is suitable since justice does not possess a uniform criterion but encompasses all human needs. Using justice as a criterion for critical mineral assessment or assessment of natural resource criticality can be a way to lessen the dominance of economic interests over the sociocultural and life support values of natural resources.[158]

2.11. Summary

The international perspective of critical mineral sourcing from mineral-rich countries like Zambia and the DRC has largely driven the discourse on critical minerals. This discourse overlooks the competing micro-aspects in critical mineral development because of the urgent need for global climate change. The literature shows competing definitions and assessment methodologies on what should be regarded as critical and what methodology should be employed to assess criticality. The particular aspect of analysing and determining criticality is that

[156] RL Rudnick, S Gao, HD Holland and KK Turekian, 'Composition of the Continental Crust' (2003) 3 *The Crust* 1.
[157] EK Schnebele, 'Silicon. Mineral Commodity Summaries' (US Geological Survey, 2018) https://minerals. usgs. gov/minerals/pubs/commodity/silicon.
[158] P Le Billon, *Wars of Plunder: Conflicts, Profits and The Politics of Resources* (Columbia University Press, 2012).

these determinations follow global events. Treaties, agreements and international politics are being determined by Western and some Eastern global influences in decision-making and managing critical minerals. The metals needed for nuclear power would be critical in times of war compared to the photovoltaic solar panels needed in times of the global energy transition. These perspectives leave the sub-Saharan African economies on the periphery of all criticality assessments since the value chains in countries like Zambia and the DRC do not extend beyond mineral sourcing or extraction.

This chapter has identified several trends in the interpretation of criticality. The trends all emanate from an economic concern at the expense of other values that might be significant in other regions, like sub-Saharan Africa and the Latin American region. The book argues that there needs to be a balance in criticality considerations and assessments, moving from an economical and functional point of view to a just view and interpretation in criticality assessments not only of critical metals, but of all natural resources. Hence, the tenets of justice integrate a sociocultural dimension into criticality studies rather than emphasising the supply risk and critical minerals' economic importance. Further, through a just criticality assessment, each community can assess the significance of critical metals according to their prevailing circumstances rather than following a utilitarian approach.

3

Towards Sustainability in Critical Mineral Development

3.1. Introduction

This chapter builds on the book's earlier discussion of sustainable development and the possibility of its materialisation. It examines the shortcomings and challenges of achieving sustainable development – inter- and intra-generational equity – for example, the influence of human nature and corporate practices. It examines why the existing sustainable development measures fail to achieve the desired outcomes, especially in the Global South's critical mineral development. It makes a case for justice in the critical mineral value chain. It analyses the unbalanced dynamics between the Global North and the Global South, and polycentric interests such as the energy transition to a low-carbon economy, resource access, African industrialisation and patriarchy in resource extraction. It finally reconstructs sustainable development and justice in critical mineral development.

The sustainable development pursuit started with the UN Conference on Environment and Development in Rio de Janeiro, Brazil in June 1992 (1992 Rio Earth Summit), when 170 countries committed to protecting biodiversity, mitigating the climate crisis and conserving the environment.[1] However, humanity has yet to achieve the Sustainable Development Goals (SDGs) adopted by all United Nations Member States in 2015, and the unattainability of these goals is clearly visible. Regardless of the international agreements, national and international strategies and policies, municipal plans, and researchers, regulators and scholars engaging in implementing and conceptualising sustainable development, the world is yet to become significantly sustainable.[2]

The major concern is transplanting recommendations and initiatives from an internationally developed platform to developing countries. For example, since the 1970s, humans' ecological footprints have surpassed the earth's capacity,

[1] C Mitcham, 'The Concept of Sustainable Development: Its Origins and Ambivalence' (1995) 17(3) *Technology in Society* 311.

[2] MM Rahman, 'Achieving Sustainable Development Goals of Agenda 2030 in Bangladesh: The Crossroad of the Governance and Performance' (2021) *Public Administration and Policy*.

leaving no room for a sustainable world.[3] The data shows that we are far from achieving the SDGs. The Living Planet Index states that from 1970 to 2016, there was an average decline of 68 per cent in global vertebrate species populations.[4] Climate change-related greenhouse gas emissions have also led to rising sea levels, warmer oceans and more prolonged intense droughts that threaten crops, wildlife and freshwater supplies.[5] Furthermore, the world has lost over 48 per cent of its tropical and sub-tropical forests.[6] The effects of industrialisation and civilisation have led the world and its finite resources to a tipping point. The irreversible changes are difficult to mitigate, and the current human endeavours are challenging to adapt to and change.

We are already halfway to the 2°C above pre-industrial level target, and the projection is that we may exceed it in the coming decades.[7] The biggest question is what is going wrong with our attempt to achieve sustainability? Some scholars and economists claim that economic, political and communication mechanisms and platforms are the predominant reasons for the failure to achieve the SDGs and ultimate sustainability.[8] Pratarelli is of the view that human activity has already exceeded the earth's long-term carrying capacity; moreover, many governments and ordinary citizens alike are focused on creating a new phase of material expansion. Further, humanity is perilously near global collapse. Therefore, academics are committed to exploring humanity's unsustainable condition through an interdisciplinary lens and applying our new understanding to global and local problems before they become irrelevant.[9] The drivers of economic activities are the fundamental issue in seeking financial returns, and some rewards may be environmentally destructive.[10] For example, a forest is economically valuable after being cut down – a problem that exacerbates environmental conservation and sustainability for countries transitioning to a market-based economy.

Sustainable development is not attainable without good governance, and although 'on paper' countries have the political will, they are incapable of implementing effective and explicit policies and strategies.[11] Most economies, especially

[3] MA Destek, 'Deindustrialization, Reindustrialization and Environmental Degradation: Evidence from Ecological Footprint of Turkey' (2021) 296 *Journal of Cleaner Production* 126612.

[4] REA Almond, M Grooten and T Petersen, 'Living Planet Report 2020 – Bending the Curve of Biodiversity Loss' (2021) 35(3) *Natural Resources & Environment* 62.

[5] ME Kahn, K Mohaddes, RN Ng, MH Pesaran, M Raissi and JC Yang, 'Long-Term Macroeconomic Effects of Climate Change: A Cross-Country Analysis' (National Bureau of Economic Research, 2019) No w26167.

[6] ibid.

[7] ME Pratarelli, 'The Failure to Achieve Sustainability May Be in Our Genes' (2016) 27(2–4) *Global Bioethics* 61.

[8] ibid.

[9] ibid.

[10] W Beckerman, 'A Poverty of Reason: Sustainable Development' (Independent Institute, 2002) No 338.9 B393p.

[11] JA van Zanten and R van Tulder, 'Towards Nexus-Based Governance: Defining Interactions Between Economic Activities and Sustainable Development Goals (SDGs)' (2021) 28(3) *International Journal of Sustainable Development & World Ecology* 210.

developing ones, depend mainly on the extractive industry, which makes sustainability unattainable as sustainable activities would negatively impact their economy's socio-economic and political structure. Most policies and strategies of sustainable development and sustainability are discussed and devised by world leaders who rarely understand the context of different economies, communities and structures, and thus lack the subsidiarity principle of sustainability by not having local voices in the decision-making corridors.[12] Nevertheless, subsidiarity is central to sustainability and requires decisions to be taken locally. Bastida argues that mining law has historically been seen as being confined to domestic legal systems – that the confined scope of mining law fails to capture the international instruments and transnational phenomena that have emerged and the greater awareness of local norms.[13] However, mining law exists primarily at the interface with global mining companies. Further, Bastida notes that we need to recognise a global perspective to understand the law applicable to the mining and minerals sector by capturing the multilevel nature of norms and the expansive nexus with other areas of law. This can be done through international human rights law, international investment law, international environmental law, international law of arbitration and international codes of conduct.[14]

3.2. The Global South's Sustainability 'Dream'

The SDG targets are to be met by 2030, but the threats facing the human race demand earlier action. Challenges such as eradication of poverty, producing clean energy, gender equality, survival of marine life and ending hunger must be addressed by society immediately. The challenges and SDGs are intertwined and adopted in a mechanism that is blind to the system's inherent inequalities.[15] The current global order favours the elites, who double as the main drivers of financing sustainability. Researchers claim that achieving sustainable development requires

[12] JM Manjengwa, 'Problems Reconciling Sustainable Development Rhetoric with Reality in Zimbabwe' (2007) 33(2) *Journal of Southern African Studies* 307.

[13] AE Bastida, *The Law and Governance of Mining and Minerals: A Global Perspective* (Bloomsbury Publishing, 2020) ch 4.

[14] ibid. The above perspectives, however, should be exercised within the realms of the applicable sovereign powers in recognition of the principle of permanent sovereignty over natural resources (PSNR) (ibid ch 3). States have the right to PSNR under public international law. This right, however, must be exercised in the interests of national development and the welfare of the entire country's population. See the UNGA Resolution 1803(XVII)14 December 1962. In *ICJ DRC v Uganda*, 2005, 87, www.icj-cij.org/files/case-related/116/116-20051219-JUD-01-00-EN.pdf, PSNR was also recognised as a principle of customary international law.

[15] J Roy, P Tscharket, H Waisman, S Abdul Halim, P Antwi-Agyei, P Dasgupta, B Hayward, M Kanninen, D Liverman, C Okereke, PF Pinho, K Riahi and AG Suarez Rodriguez, 'Sustainable Development, Poverty Eradication and Reducing Inequalities' in V Masson-Delmotte, P Zhai, HO Pörtner, D Roberts, J Skea, PR Shukla, A Pirani, W Moufouma-Okia, C Péan, R Pidcock, S Connors, RBR Matthews, Y Chen, X Zhou, MI Gomis, E Lonnoy, T Maycock, M Tignor and T Waterfield (eds), *Global Warming of 1.5°C: An IPCC Special Report* (Cambridge University Press, 2018).

a systematic reform of our international structures and systems, such as trading frameworks, the rebalancing of global power structures, an overhaul of decision-making processes and inclusivity.[16] In an article by Trinity College Dublin, it is argued that 'ensuring the sustainability of one place, one location, or one country may jeopardise the sustainability of other places'.[17]

Sustainable development mechanisms have been criticised as top-down, tied to endless bureaucracy and ignorant of the local context.[18] Other scholars have thus advanced alternative mechanisms; for instance, Tracy-Lynn Field speaks about the 'post-extractivism' theory, which emphasises the necessity of resource extraction and is one of the numerous transition discourses that seek to elucidate 'alternatives to development rather than development alternatives'.[19] It entails drastically lowering extraction, increasing sustainability through recycling, resolving inequitable material and resource flows, reducing emissions and significantly reducing pressure on ecosystems. Sustainable development is not a one-size-fits-all endeavour. The goals, objectives and global strategies must strike a balance between preserving the local context and reforming global institutions.[20] These challenges, among others (discussed below), make sustainable development objectives a utopia rather than a materialised objective. Secondly, the objectives are not legally binding. They will, however, depend on governance and efficient institutions if they are to come into effect by 2030. Inadvertently, this means that countries cannot be penalised (save for a few components, eg the integration of environmental considerations) for failing to implement them or instead support developing economies to meet the targets.[21]

3.3. The Consequences of Human Nature on Sustainable Development

The sustainable development objectives have been developed without considering that humans are not naturally endowed with the conservation ethic necessary

[16] S Drobyazko, V Okulich-Kazarin, A Rogovyi, O Goltvenko and S Marova, 'Factors of Influence on the Sustainable Development in the Strategy Management of Corporations' (2019) 18 *Academy of Strategic Management Journal* 1.

[17] FutureLearn, 'Are the Sustainable Development Goals the Best Approach to Sustainability?' (Trinity College Dublin, 2021) www.futurelearn.com/info/courses/achieving-sustainable-development/0/steps/35496.

[18] Manjengwa (n 12).

[19] TL Field, *State Governance of Mining, Development and Sustainability* (Edward Elgar Publishing, 2019).

[20] N Blum, J Nazir, S Breiting, KC Goh and E Pedretti, 'Balancing the Tensions and Meeting the Conceptual Challenges of Education for Sustainable Development and Climate Change' (2013) 19(2) *Environmental Education Research* 206.

[21] SA Bekessy, K Samson and RE Clarkson, 'The Failure of Non-Binding Declarations to Achieve University Sustainability: A Need for Accountability' (2007) 8(3) *International Journal of Sustainability in Higher Education* 301.

to maintain ecological balance.[22] LeBlanc and Register state that conservationist behaviour is rare and not an inherent human characteristic.[23] In the last century, the world has developed an addictive need to take advantage of economic markets to expand and grow its society.[24] Inadvertently, the typical social fabric is fundamentally incompatible with the structural dynamics of the ecosystems on which it depends. The predominant fallacy 'driving' sustainable development leaders is that our pre-Neolithic and pre-industrial forefathers lived sustainably; thus, institutions tend to transplant this belief to modern society.[25] On the other hand, the impoverished nature of those times is not taken into account. In their indigenous cultures, our pre-industrial forefathers effortlessly caught prey and harvested fruit due to their environment and nature.

Societal advancement should also be taken into account when discussing sustainable development. The reasons for sustainability in the Neolithic era do not apply to the baby boomer, millennial and Gen Z eras. The advancements in technology increased human capacity to exploit their ecosystems. Technology thus brought over-exploitation of resources, though it is also thought to be the solution to attaining and materialising sustainable development.[26] For example, consider the evolution of the fishing industry, the extractive industry and the fashion industry. Between 7500 and 8000 years ago, man used a gorge hook and line tackle to capture fish. Currently, industrial fishing techniques use blast fishing, bottom trawling and cyanide fishing, which are detrimental to ocean life and sustainability.[27] Though crucial to economic development, the extractive industry is accountable for over 80 per cent of the biodiversity loss through massive carbon emissions.[28]

Nevertheless, such industries maintain that they can sustainably continue their activities. This assumption relies on technological advancement and the belief that it can solve our problems. The increase in demand for electric vehicles, expansion of alternative energy sources such as nuclear and renewable, other greening mechanisms used in product supply and value chains and the geoengineering solutions to global warming all contribute to the argument that technology can achieve sustainable development over time.[29]

[22] SA LeBlanc and KE Register, *Constant Battles: Why We Fight* (Macmillan, 2004).

[23] ibid.

[24] WE Rees, 'Human Nature, Eco-Footprints and Environmental Injustice' (2008) 13(8) *Local Environment* 685.

[25] SM Johnson and ME Pratarelli, 'The Intersection of Evolutionary Principles, Human Behavior and Environmental Sustainability' (2011) 3(2) *Journal of the Evolutionary Studies Consortium* 1.

[26] M Foth, M Mann, L Bedford, W Fieuw and R Walters, 'A Capitalocentric Review of Technology for Sustainable Development: The Case for More-Than-Human Design' in A Finlay (ed), *Global Information Society Watch 2020: Technology, the Environment and a Sustainable World: Responses from the Global South* (Association for Progressive Communications, 2021) 78–82.

[27] JK Yu and HX Wang, 'Evolution of Distant Water Fisheries Policies in China: Overview, Characteristics and Proposals' (2021) 207 *Ocean & Coastal Management* 105592.

[28] AO Jegede, 'The Environmental and Economic Implications of the Climate Change and Extractive Industry Nexus in Africa' (2016) 7(4) *Environmental Economics* 95.

[29] Foth et al (n 26).

These broad assumptions on the relationship between technological advancement and human behaviour do not consider the attitudes towards consumption and growth.[30] There is limited literature and research on issues like planned obsolescence, human overconsumption and sustainable development. There is a need for explicit discussions on the root causes of climate change, desertification, loss of biodiversity and capitalism. The evolution of humanity has developed the intellectual and innovative capacity to temporarily meet the current population's needs. Still, growing population rates necessitate additional adjustments for future generations to avoid socio-economic ruin.[31] Thomas Malthus argued that people are concerned with their own survival.[32] This means that short-term interests outweigh long-term consequences because we risk jeopardising the future's socio-economic, political structures and ecosystem.[33] To concur with Malthus, the current global population is 7.8 billion, whose primary concern is energy and food security. The overproduction of these two life components has led to land degradation, distorted food supply chains, exhausted raw materials and a disastrous extractive industry sourcing critical minerals in developing countries for energy transition.

The interesting assumptions for reconfiguring societies' ecological footprints pay little attention to end users, individual citizens and their families.[34] This shows that society blindly accepts the need to follow policies, strategies and statutes, and the need to satisfy one's personal needs simply disappears. The irony is that human beings do not follow rules and regulations regardless of their benefits to the greater community and future generations. In comparison, the pursuit of sustainable development depends only on public and private institutional transformation and adjustments. Hence, little attention is given to shaky corporate practices and biological and culturally motivated drivers such as patriarchy, leading to weak sustainability.

3.4. Shortfalls of Sustainable Development Measures in the Global South

This section examines the issue of corporate greenwashing and how mining corporations deal with sustainability concerns in their operations to gauge the

[30] AC Marques, JA Fuinhas and DF Pais, 'Economic Growth, Sustainable Development and Food Consumption: Evidence Across Different Income Groups of Countries' (2018) 196 *Journal of Cleaner Production* 245.

[31] W Leal Filho, LO de Sousa and R Pretorius, 'Future Prospects of Sustainable Development in Africa' in W Leal Filho, R Pretorius and LO de Sousa (eds), *Sustainable Development in Africa: Fostering Sustainability in One of the World's Most Promising Continents* (Springer International Publishing, 2021) 733–41.

[32] TR Malthus, D Winch and P James, *Malthus: 'An Essay on the Principle of Population'* (Cambridge University Press, 1992).

[33] ibid.

[34] Pratarelli (n 7).

effect of corporate practices on the general achievement of sustainable development and sustainability.

3.4.1. Corporate Greenwashing

The term 'greenwashing' refers to an unsubstantiated claim made to 'fool' consumers into having confidence in a company's products' environmental sustainability nature.[35] For instance, companies engaging in greenwashing may declare their products recyclable or offer energy-saving benefits.[36] Some of the claims might be true, but corporations engaging in greenwashing frequently exaggerate their claims on sustainable development.

Greenwashing was coined in the 1980s to illustrate a company's disgraceful environmental sustainability claims.[37] The oil giant Chevron ran an advertising campaign in the 1980s to convince the public of its environmental credentials, and the 'People Do' campaign featured Chevron employees protecting wildlife.[38] The campaign won Effie advertising awards in 1990 and was used as a case study at Harvard Business School. Most environmental researchers and scholars named the movement the 'gold standard' of greenwashing that distorts sustainability.[39] Jay Westerveld established what greenwashing entails: with society hooked on media outlets, combined with limited public access to information and seemingly unlimited advertising, corporations can portray themselves as environmentally responsible agents while engaging in environmentally unsustainable practices.[40] For example, the nuclear power division of American electrical behemoth Westinghouse was a leading company in greenwashing.[41] In the 1960s, an anti-nuclear movement raised concerns about the safety and environmental impact of nuclear power. Westinghouse retaliated with a series of advertisements exaggerating nuclear power's safety and cleanliness.[42]

3.4.2. Mining Corporations and Sustainable Development

The mining industry is responsible for 10 per cent of global greenhouse gas emissions. Mining contributes to environmental degradation, such as air

[35] SV de Freitas Netto, MFF Sobral, ARB Ribeiro and GR da Luz Soares, 'Concepts and Forms of Greenwashing: A Systematic Review' (2020) 32(1) *Environmental Sciences Europe* 1.

[36] L Mitchell and W Ramey, 'Look How Green I Am! An Individual-Level Explanation for Greenwashing' (2011) 12(6) *Journal of Applied Business and Economics* 40.

[37] B Watson, 'The Troubling Evolution of Corporate Greenwashing' (2017) 129 *Chain Reaction* 38.

[38] MA Cherry and JF Sneirson, 'Chevron, Greenwashing, and the Myth of "Green Oil Companies"' (2012) 3 *Journal of Energy, Climate, and the Environment*.

[39] ibid.

[40] LP Koh, J Ghazoul, RA Butler, WF Laurance, NS Sodhi, J Mateo-Vega and CJ Bradshaw, 'Wash and Spin Cycle Threats to Tropical Biodiversity' (2010) 42(1) *Biotropica* 67.

[41] Watson (n 37).

[42] ibid.

pollution, soil and water contamination, biodiversity loss, deforestation and soil erosion.[43] As discussed in chapter one, the world is addressing the climate crisis by transitioning from fossil fuels to cleaner energy sources. Inadvertently, the production and consumption of renewable energy on a global scale has led to disastrous environmental problems due to the high carbon footprint from the mining activities for mineral raw materials.[44] This is mainly due to the large-scale requirement for critical minerals to act as raw materials for the energy transition. As noted earlier, critical minerals are required to manufacture renewable energy infrastructures such as wind turbines, solar panels and batteries for electric vehicles.[45] These critical minerals' exploration, extraction and refinement are normally environmentally damaging and carbon-intensive processes.

There is a presumption that ensuring the sustainability of one place, location or country may jeopardise other places' sustainability. The notable question goes back to the assertion by Trinity College Dublin that the sustainability of the Global North can only be enabled by the weak sustainability of the Global South (regions rich in critical minerals).[46] The Global North seeks environmental sustainability by manufacturing green energy hardware and extracting raw materials from the Global South (eg the Democratic Republic of Congo (DRC) and Zambia).[47]

There is international pressure on the extractive sector to improve its environmental performance. Companies are increasingly being pushed to demonstrate how they contribute to the UN's Sustainable Development Goals (SDGs), though mining companies are falling short.[48] Environmental, social and governance (ESG) standards are becoming investment guides and strategy routes in promoting divestment from fossil fuel companies.[49] International financial institutions are also urging the extractive industry to become more environmentally friendly – the World Bank and IFC's Climate Smart Mining programme, for instance, aims to increase the industry's environmental sustainability.[50] Furthermore, there is an urgent need to meet and address the international commitment to keep global temperature increases to 2°C above pre-industrial levels, as specified in the 2015 Paris Climate Agreement.

[43] M Azadi, SA Northey, SH Ali, M and Edraki, 'Transparency on Greenhouse Gas Emissions from Mining to Enable Climate Change Mitigation' (2020) 13(2) *Nature Geoscience* 100.

[44] ibid.

[45] S Kalantzakos, 'The Race for Critical Minerals in an Era of Geopolitical Realignments' (2020) 55(3) *The International Spectator* 1.

[46] FutureLearn (n 17).

[47] ibid.

[48] S Famiyeh, RA Opoku, A Kwarteng and D Asante-Darko, 'Driving Forces of Sustainability in the Mining Industry: Evidence from a Developing Country' (2021) 70 *Resources Policy* 101910.

[49] TW Ahn, HS Lee and JS Yi, 'A Study on the Keyword Extraction for ESG Controversies Through Association Rule Mining' (2021) 30(1) *Journal of Information Systems* 123.

[50] Famiyeh (n 48).

Due to international pressure, mining companies have taken steps to mitigate and adapt to the climate crisis. For example, to reduce carbon emissions by 10 per cent by 2030, Canadian gold giant Barrick Gold's Zaldivar copper mine in Chile is powered by renewable energy sources such as hydro, wind and solar.[51] Anglo American's 2030 goals for climate change include reducing net greenhouse gas emissions by 30 per cent and improving energy efficiency by 30 per cent. These ambitious targets are part of its roadmap for developing a carbon-neutral mine.[52] In December 2020, Newmont Mining – a major gold mining investor in Ghana – committed to investing millions of dollars over the next five years to achieve carbon neutrality by 2050, a goal they expect to accomplish in part through the use of renewable energy.[53] Another Canadian company, B2Gold, operates its mines in Namibia and Mali using off-grid solar and battery power.[54] Much of the energy generated by the upcoming Grand Inga hydropower project on the Congo river in the DRC will be used to power mines in the country's Katanga province.[55] Some of the strategies used to cut down emissions by mining companies include the exploration of electric mining vehicles, drones, environmentally friendly exploration and processing techniques.

While these are admirable examples, and commitments to improve environmental performance appear to be increasing among mining companies, there is currently a scarcity of hard evidence regarding the impact of these initiatives on concrete environmental and climate indicators. The mining industry's accountability for the environment and climate change is a relatively new issue, limiting the amount of data available to quantify the probable impact. Furthermore, as with other corporate responsibility initiatives, it is more likely that larger mining companies with headquarters in the Global North facing international reputational pressures will make an effort to mitigate their environmental impact instead of smaller and government-owned companies.

Sustainable development entails a dual capacity function: each reformist is interwoven with the 1992 Rio Earth Summit's Agenda 21 action plan for sustainable development ideology and radical approaches. It depicts two values. One is the neoliberal emphasis on using market mechanisms and the other is the populist-inspired emphasis on local, participatory and communitarian environmental conservation and management processes.[56] Conventions like the

[51] F Molaei and H Siavoshi, 'The Role of Nanofluids on Enhancing the Solar Energy Performance with Focusing on the Mining Industry' [2021] *International Journal of Energy Research*.

[52] Anglo American, *Climate Change: Our Plans, Policies and Progress. 100 Years, 1917–2017* (2017) www.angloamerican.com/~/media/Files/A/Anglo-American-Group/PLC/sustainability/our-strategy/climate-change-supplement.pdf.

[53] ibid.

[54] ibid.

[55] A Maupin, 'Energy and Regional Integration: The Grand Inga Project in the DR Congo' in S Scholvin (ed), *A New Scramble for Africa? The Rush for Energy Resources in Sub-Saharan Africa* (Routledge, 2015) 53–69.

[56] Manjengwa (n 12).

UNFCCC Framework Convention on Climate Change, Kyoto Protocol, Paris Agreement, Vienna Convention for Protection of the Ozone Layer, Montreal Protocol, Lisbon Agreement and Rio Convention on Biological Diversity represent the latter rhetoric of sustainable development in theory rather than in practice.[57]

The mining industry management in developing sub-Saharan African countries such as Zambia and the DRC is usually technocratic.[58] The 'local' measures retained to achieve sustainable development in countries such as the DRC and Zambia in the mining industry have a traditional top-down technocratic planning, which has yielded no results.[59] Irrespective of the populist rhetoric, sustainable development mechanisms are implemented within a strongly hierarchical top-down framework that fails to bridge the gap between the macro- and micro-levels. The international agreements and conventions that have developed strategies to materialise the SDGs have been disguised to be 'bottom-up', 'participatory' and 'community-based'.[60]

Since the UN Conference on Environment and Development in Rio de Janeiro, Brazil in June 1992, local governments and civil society have attempted to translate Agenda 21 into practice at the local level. More than 6000 local Agenda 21 initiatives in 113 countries have demonstrated local mechanisms to raise awareness, advocate for and practically implement Agenda 21 in their communities.[61] The gathering of information from local people using participatory rural appraisal strategies has yet to yield any significant upward flow of information from local to international level to achieve SDGs.[62] For example, in the DRC, mining reforms had two major components: on the one hand, they involved the liberalisation of the mining sector under the impetus of the World Bank; and on the other hand, they entailed a quest for greater transparency in critical mineral supply chains through traceability schemes.[63] These schemes

[57] D Chirambo, 'Moving Past the Rhetoric: Policy Considerations That Can Make Sino-African Relations to Improve Africa's Climate Change Resilience and the Attainment of the Sustainable Development Goals' (2016) 7(4) *Advances in Climate Change Research* 253.

[58] M Dos Santos, 'Power, Rights, Freedom, Technocracy and Postcolonialism in Sub-Saharan Africa' (2018) 50(3) *Acta Academica*.

[59] A Caramento, 'Cultivating Backward Linkages to Zambia's Copper Mines: Debating the Design of, and Obstacles To, Local Content' (2020) 7(2) *The Extractive Industries and Society* 310.

[60] A Jiménez-Aceituno, GD Peterson, AV Norström, GY Wong and AS Downing, 'Local Lens for SDG Implementation: Lessons from Bottom-Up Approaches in Africa' (2020) 15(3) *Sustainability Science* 729.

[61] C Caruana and P Pace, 'Local Agenda 21 Processes and their Implications for the SDGs' in W Leal Filho, M Mifsud and P Pace (eds), *Handbook of Lifelong Learning for Sustainable Development* (Springer, 2018) 293–305.

[62] B Triatmanto and M Natsir, 'A Descriptive Analysis of Sustainability Development Goals (SDGs), Community Empowerment, and the Participatory Rural Appraisal Approach' in *Proceedings of the 6th International Conference on Community Development* (ICCD, 2019).

[63] CI Wakenge, MRB Nyenyezi, SI Bergh and J Cuvelier, 'From "Conflict Minerals" to Peace? Reviewing Mining Reforms, Gender, and State Performance in Eastern Democratic Republic of Congo' (2021) 8(2) *The Extractive Industries and Society* 100894.

are foreign-devised populist notions superimposed onto a highly technocratic system. This factor makes the materialisation of SDGs in critical mineral extraction countries an empty promise.

Nevertheless, sub-Saharan Africa's populist sustainable development rhetoric has not challenged the status quo quantification and valuation of critical minerals as a dominant paradigm in foreign markets. Hence, these measures implemented to attain SDGs in developing countries have disseminated the existing techno-centrist approach to natural resource management, making critical minerals raw materials for the Global North and minerals for 'nothing' in developing countries. This perpetuity of the dominant technocratic discourse brings about 'Western' conservation philosophies and natural resource management strategies preferred by donors and other foreign stakeholders.[64] Such perpetuity makes sub-Saharan African governments such as those of Zambia and the DRC lose rents with little socio-economic gains in their local communities. The local governments of Zambia and the DRC have only a superficial commitment to attaining SDGs, with little sustainability effect.

Critical minerals are essential in facilitating the energy transition and achieving SDGs 2, 5, 11, 13 and 14. The sustainable development discourse has impressive rhetoric, but the sustainable development initiatives have a low impact on the ground, making the whole process tenuous.[65] Critics point to the impossibility of reconciling economic growth with development. Many criticise the 'development' aspect as it might not necessarily be the goal of most in society – that might rather be well-being. Vandenhole, for instance, argues that 'economic growth does not necessarily lead to economic development, let alone human development'.[66] Sustainable development in the mining industry has been adopted and implemented in the environmental conservation sector without the enabling atmosphere. For example, there is no active involvement of other sectors, and there is a lack of recognition of wider socio-economic, historical and political contexts.

Further, the low level of commitment and lack of ownership at the local level and multiple stakeholder agendas inhibit the efficient achievement of SDGs in critical mineral extraction countries.[67] Sustainable development remains the ideal principle for addressing the gaps and hurdles today. However, to acquire tangible impacts, stakeholders must adopt different institutional, legal and regulatory mechanisms to obtain tangible effects.

[64] PA DeGeorges and BK Reilly, 'The Realities of Community Based Natural Resource Management and Biodiversity Conservation in Sub-Saharan Africa' (2009) 1(3) *Sustainability* 734.

[65] J Hickel, 'The Contradiction of The Sustainable Development Goals: Growth versus Ecology on a Finite Planet' (2019) 27(5) *Sustainable Development* 873.

[66] W Vandenhole, 'De-growth and Sustainable Development: Rethinking Human Rights Law and Poverty Alleviation' (2018) 11(2) *Law and Development Review* 647.

[67] ibid.

3.5. Sustainable Energy and Mineral Development

As the renowned German physicist Max Planck once stated, 'Mining may not be everything, but without mining, everything is nothing'.[68] Optimising energy usage throughout all stages of mining operations, from mineral extraction to product manufacturing, and implementing renewable energy sources and efficient carbon capture methods are essential to decreasing energy consumption and greenhouse gas emissions. The challenge of providing these elements for renewable energy technology is partly due to political instability and environmental concerns regarding the extraction of these metals. Unstable nations play a significant role in producing these minerals, with numerous mines located in rural and agricultural communities. Disseminating sustainable energy among local people can expand agricultural activities and increase employment opportunities, impacting communities and improving social influences and political stability.

These factors ultimately have a positive impact on achieving SDGs. Mining expenses can be reduced by reducing energy costs and enhancing mining towns' competitiveness and economic appeal. This can also encourage mining corporations to conduct mineral processing operations in the countries where they operate. Implementing this plan is crucial and strategic for many mining nations. A significant obstacle to mineral processing in host nations is the lack of cost-effective and reliable energy sources. Several countries export their extracted minerals to nations with more stable energy supplies and lower energy costs, enhancing the efficiency of the processing activities. Consequently, these countries miss out on the benefits that the processed materials provide.

3.6. The Need for a Just Holistic Framework

The differences in aspirations and levels of development, and the unique challenges that underpin critical mineral development give rise to a more holistic framework to meet the needs of the Global South, specifically as discussed below.

3.6.1. The Unbalanced Relationship between the Global South and the Global North

The diverse inter-relationship between the Global South and the Global North has developed over many centuries, with resource dependency at its core.[69] For several

[68] M Pouresmaieli, M Ataei, AN Qarahasanlou and A Barabadi, 'Integration of Renewable Energy and Sustainable Development with Strategic Planning in the Mining Industry' (2023) 20 *Results in Engineering* 101412.

[69] H Mostert, CL Young and JL Hassman, 'Towards Extractive Justice: Europe, Africa and the Pressures of Resource Dependency' (2019) 26(2) *South African Journal of International Affairs* 233.

reasons, the Global South's resources – land, minerals and water – have attracted the Global North's interest. The two regions are linked by historical and cultural overlaps, and economic and political exchanges.[70] For example, sub-Saharan Africa's mineral resources directly affect how the rest of the world interacts with the region.

Further, the Global South has emerged from an isolated, marginalised corner in global politics and socio-political structures that tailor the international agreements and conventions to their resources and well-being.[71] Since the Berlin Conference of 1884–85, the Global North has dictated trade and valuation strategies with the Global South, particularly between sub-Saharan Africa and Europe.[72] Generally, the trading relationship concerning extractive resources creates legal and regulatory framework overlaps. The inception and configuration of these frameworks are created on an unbalanced narrative and infested with unequal relationships between regions.[73] The development of global developmental strategies such as SDGs 'assume' that the world's principles of supply and demand function within defined legal parameters. However, these supply-and-demand principles are multifaceted and complex, and are influenced by political, social, environmental, geographical, religious and cultural factors.[74]

The uneven relationship between the Global South and the Global North can be traced back to the colonial era.[75] For example, when Algeria fought for her independence in the 1950s, the French administration under Mollet called the oil discoveries in the Sahara 'our Saharan oil'.[76] Smith says that the French further created the so-called Organisation Commune des Règions Sahariennes, which aimed to exploit resources from the Sahara with the intent of manoeuvring Algeria's neighbours to support the French efforts in Algeria for the natural resources found at the time.[77] Smith goes on to argue that an independent Algeria would lead to Algeria having the lion's share of its natural resources. It is from such narratives that trade relationships are tailored today. The inherited colonial sentiment creates a vacuum for forging healthier trade partnerships between the Global South and the Global North.

[70] NF Onar and K Nicolaïdis, 'The Decentering Agenda: Europe as a Post-colonial Power' (2013) 48(2) *Cooperation and Conflict* 283.

[71] ibid.

[72] M Craven, 'Between Law and History: The Berlin Conference of 1884–1885 and the Logic of Free Trade' (2015) 3(1) *London Review of International Law* 31.

[73] M Florestal, 'On the Origin of Fear in the World Trade System: Excavating the Roots of the Berlin Conference 2 of 1884–1885' in *Proceedings of the ASIL Annual Meeting* (Cambridge University Press, 2007) 143–46.

[74] AK Smith, *Creating a World Economy: Merchant Capital, Colonialism, and World Trade, 1400–1825* (Routledge, 2019).

[75] ibid.

[76] T Smith, 'The French Economic Stake in Colonial Algeria' (1975) 9(1) *French Historical Studies* 184.

[77] ibid.

Achieving sustainable development may be deepened by the legal and policy initiatives between the Global South and the Global North. Still, there must be a 'value framework' to make the world achieve these SDGs – and this is 'justice'. As Mostert et al state, 'there must be some common understanding of the kind of intercontinental cooperation that is needed to engage in reimagining the relationship between Africa and Europe'.[78] Hence, emphasising justice means creating a balanced relationship between the interests of the Global North and the Global South, particularly between sub-Saharan Africa and Europe, concerning the extraction and sourcing of raw materials such as critical minerals. Such incorporation may reduce the exploitation of vulnerable and marginalised communities and further cooperation and development.[79]

The Global South and Global North paradox creates a multipolar world and a non-hegemonic global world order, leading to rigorous competition. The Global North will compete for strategic access to the finite natural resources of the Global South for various reasons, such as industrialisation, climate change and imperialism. The future of the relationship between the Global North and the Global South is cemented on the pivotal role of justice. Hence, any conceptualisation of the relationship between these multipolar regions will be superficial if justice is not tailored to the interregional relationships. This balance addresses the Global South's needs, mainly eradicating poverty, access to energy, infrastructural development and broad access to equal and credible education. In contrast, the Global North needs to address sustainability and access to clean energy. Once both concerns are addressed equally and with accountability, the world may achieve true justice and achieve SDGs in the process.

3.6.2. Bridging Justice and Resource Extraction

This segment attempts to establish a link between justice and resource extraction in resource-rich countries and host communities. The industrialisation has led to decades of unregulated industrial production that generated a decaying infrastructure and environmental degradation, and exposed low-income marginalised and minority communities to this environmental violation.[80] Several studies have established that environmental and resource inequity exists and that the poor and marginalised indigenous communities are disproportionately impacted by environmental risks and injustices from industrial extractive production modes.[81] These marginalised communities and spaces

[78] Mostert et al (n 69).
[79] ibid.
[80] E Papyrakis and R Gerlagh, 'The Resource Curse Hypothesis and Its Transmission Channels' (2004) 32(1) *Journal of Comparative Economics* 181.
[81] K Ard, 'By All Measures: An Examination of the Relationship Between Segregation and Health Risk from Air Pollution' (2016) 38(1) *Population and Environment* 1.

have predominantly evolved into environmental sacrifice zones, where the extractive industry has been disastrous for landscapes, people and livelihood.[82] Research has examined how extractive industrial production has led to systematic environmental injustices and health disparities. The research has primarily been associated with the extraction of coal, oil and gas, copper, uranium, cobalt and other mineral resources in relation to energy and climate change.[83]

The few studies on justice have been on environmental justice and how environmental issues can be overlooked in the context of corporate or industrial power and influence.[84] Nonetheless, some studies have attempted to establish the link between justice and the extractive industry, and how these justice narratives impact sustainable development. For example, Bell examines economic and cultural influence of corporations in fostering political support for the Appalachian coal industry and the structural barriers to sustained environmental justice activism.[85] Furthermore, Malin et al investigate the ramifications of natural resource dependence and how this leads to persistent poverty, spatial isolation, marginalisation and the cultural and historical ties of the American West region to the uranium industry.[86] The surprising fact is that these American West communities supported the uranium industry regardless of their communities' persistent poverty and marginalisation.[87]

Neo-liberalisation and adjustments of market structures have engendered resource extraction support despite the extractive industry's disastrous legacy in a community's environment and economic structure.[88] Studies have been conducted on societal and environmental inequities brought by resource privatisation, deregulation, corporate self-regulation and free trade agreements that promote the extractive industry, particularly in regions like the Global South.[89] However, there is still a need to conduct further empirical enquiries into neo-liberalisation and its role in perpetuating injustice in marginalised communities and regions brought by the extractive industry. Martinez-Alier has made significant contributions to

[82] S Lerner, *Sacrifice Zones: The Front Lines of Toxic Chemical Exposure in the United States* (MIT Press, 2012).

[83] J Martinez-Alier, L Temper, D Bene and A Scheidel, 'Is There a Global Environmental Justice Movement?' (2016) 43(3) *Journal of Peasant Studies* 731.

[84] D Schlosberg, *Defining Environmental Justice: Theories, Movements, and Nature* (Oxford University Press, 2019).

[85] S Bell, *Fighting King Coal: The Challenges to Micro mobilization in Central Appalachia* (MIT Press, 2016).

[86] SA Malin, T Opsal, T O'Connor Shelley and PM Hall, 'The Right to Resist or a Case of Injustice? Meta-power in the Oil and Gas Fields' (2019) 97(4) *Social Forces* 1811.

[87] ibid.

[88] P Routledge, A Cumbers and KD Derickson, 'States of Just Transition: Realising Climate Justice Through and Against the State' (2018) 88 *Geoforum* 78.

[89] A Bebbington, AG Abdulai, M Hinfelaar, D Humphreys Bebbington and C Sanborn, 'Political Settlements and the Governance of Extractive Industry: A Comparative Analysis of the Longue Durée in Africa and Latin America' (Effective States and Inclusive Development Research Centre, 2017) SID Working Paper No 81; M Obaya, 'The Evolution of Resource Nationalism: The Case of Bolivian Lithium' (2021) 8(3) *The Extractive Industries and Society* 100932.

the field, most notably through his work on the 'environmentalism of the poor', which focuses on the environmentalism of poor or indigenous groups embroiled in resource extraction conflicts worldwide.[90]

Some earlier international agendas attempted to review the inequities and power imbalances between the Global South and the Global North – advocating for equity and solidarity in a New International Economic Order with reference to developing countries.[91] There is also a growing momentum to offset the unbalanced geopolitical power by movements like 'Third World Approaches to International Law' (TWAIL),[92] with leading scholars like Anthony Anghie writing extensively and compiling works on the subject.[93] However, the challenge lies in the lack of political will to address it.[94] Otherwise, no clear conclusion can be drawn between structural dependencies and political–economic inequities, and how they lead to injustice in the Global South. Further, justice considers the extractive industry's structural, procedural and sociocultural dynamics, the crucial disparities in power and equity among polarised stakeholders and institutions involved with the extractive industry, and the impact on meaningful participation.[95] For example, the climate emergency has created a market for critical minerals, leading to the expansion of the extractive industry in remote host communities, particularly in the Global South. Through a 'social licence to operate', the extractive industry has managed to manoeuvre public criticism, inadvertently causing pollution and undesirable socio-economic impacts in host communities.[96] At the same time, several multinational corporations claim to 'adhere' to binding (and non-binding) international standards and agreements to increase transparency and accountability.

[90] J Martinez-Alier, *The Environmentalism of the Poor: A Study of Ecological Conflicts and Valuation* (Edward Elgar Publishing, 2003); J Martinez-Alier, 'Global Environmental Justice and the Environmentalism of the Poor' in T Gabrielson, C Hall, JM Meyer and D Schlosberg (eds), *The Oxford Handbook of Environmental Political Theory* (Oxford University Press, 2016) 563–79; J Martinez-Alier, 'The Environmentalism of the Poor: Its Origins and Spread' in JR McNeill and ES Mauldin (eds), *A Companion to Global Environmental History* (Wiley Blackwell, 2012) 513–29; J Martinez-Alier, 'Mapping Ecological Distribution Conflicts: The EJAtlas' (2021) 8(4) *The Extractive Industries and Society* 100883.

[91] See A/RES/S-6/3201 Resolution adopted by the General Assembly 3201 (S-VI) (1974) Declaration on the Establishment of a New International Economic Order.

[92] TWAIL is a critical school of international legal studies, as well as an intellectual and political movement. The movement believes that international law facilitates the Third World's continued exploitation through subordination to the West. TWAIL scholars strive to alter what they see to be international law's repressive characteristics through a re-examination of international law's colonial underpinnings. See M Mutua, 'What Is TWAIL?' in *Proceedings of the ASIL Annual Meeting* (Cambridge University Press, 2000 94) 31–38.

[93] A Anghie, B Chimni, K Mickelson and OC Okafor (eds), *The Third World and International Order: Law, Politics and Globalization* (Brill, 2021) 45; A Anghie, 'Inequality, Human Rights, and the New International Economic Order' (2019) 10(3) *Humanity: An International Journal of Human Rights, Humanitarianism, and Development* 429.

[94] A Hurrell and S Sengupta, 'Emerging Powers, North–South Relations and Global Climate Politics' (2012) 88(3) *International Affairs* 463.

[95] SA Malin, S Ryder and MG Lyra, 'Environmental Justice and Natural Resource Extraction: Intersections of Power, Equity and Access' (2019) 5(2) *Environmental Sociology* 109.

[96] ibid.

The fundamental point of discussion goes back to achieving sustainable development, but there must be a practical, evidence-based policy framework for this desired outcome to materialise. SDGs can be achieved through justice tenets of procedural equity, and the opportunity is given to marginalised communities to have meaningful participation in issues affecting the extractive industry. Establishing profound channels for unbiased dialogues is challenging, as natural resource competition and conflict prevails in the extractive industry.[97] We can focus on the different non-economic dynamics that affect the extractive industry and arrive at equitable solutions through justice. Justice as an analytical mechanism in the extractive industry can enquire into who makes the decisions, how they are made, when, where and why. Such an inquiry creates channels of contextual understanding into the different perspectives on natural resource extraction, dependence and the prevailing institutional and cultural dynamics, particularly with procedural equity.

3.6.3. Justice and Polycentric Interests of the Extractive Industry

The extractive industry serves polycentric interests, as societies and communities are affected by different issues within their respective contexts. Regardless of the polycentric nature of the extractive industry, the relationship between the richly mineral-endowed countries and the consuming countries must be mutually beneficial, and they must enhance development and cooperation. The values must be supported by principles of good governance, access to information, developing local skills and eliminating socio-economic inequalities. These principles create common values regarding fair and equitable decision-making mechanisms and the recognition of the host communities surrounding extraction sites.[98] The polycentric interests relate to differences in transition to a low-carbon economy needs, the spatial distribution of resources with a concentration of minerals in fragile states, consciousness of African industrialisation, the presence of patriarchy in the extractive industry with gendered implications, and the geopolitics of the extractive industry.

3.6.3.1. Transition to a Low-Carbon Economy

Due to the energy transition, the world expects increased demand for minerals (as mentioned in chapter one). Fossil fuels have predominantly fuelled global energy needs since the eighteenth century.[99] Though fossil fuels have driven global

[97] Malin et al, 'The Right to Resist' (n 86).
[98] Mostert et al (n 69).
[99] M Höök and X Tang, 'Depletion of Fossil Fuels and Anthropogenic Climate Change – a Review' (2013) 52 *Energy Policy* 797.

economies, they are associated with emitting greenhouse gas emissions that are the primary catalyst to the climate crisis.[100] Economies must use decarbonised energy systems to achieve the global energy transition. The transition provides a unique opportunity for the mining industry and inadvertently causes the same environmental degradation, exacerbating the climate crisis.[101] The point of contention is the paradox between energy access and the energy transition.[102] Starting with energy access, sub-Saharan Africa has a population of 1.14 billion, with over 600 million people lacking electricity and almost 890 million people cooking with traditional fuels such as charcoal and firewood.[103]

There is a consensus that human activities must change for a sustainable future, as countries have announced commitments to net-zero energy. Africa, especially sub-Saharan Africa, has been particularly sluggish in making these commitments.[104] Africans have been victims of the climate crisis, in that it is causing mass migration. Still, African economies must address immediate needs and threats if African people are to realise the SDGs. The EU and 44 other countries, which together account for 70 per cent of the global economy, have committed to a net-zero target regarding their carbon emissions.[105] This ambitious commitment should be beneficial to addressing the climate crisis. How does sub-Saharan Africa fit into this equation of achieving net-zero emissions by 2050? Studies show that sub-Saharan Africa will account for over 2 billion people by 2050.[106] As the populations of sub-Saharan African countries grow, there will be increased urbanisation, with almost 500 million people expected to join Africa's urban population.[107] Such demographic and population variations will greatly impact transportation, industrial development and energy demand. The situation is aggravated by the need to address the current 600 million people without access to electricity and the need to shift from traditional and rudimental cooking to cleaner household energy sources.[108]

[100] ibid.

[101] K Svobodova, JR Owen and J Harris, 'The Global Energy Transition and Place Attachment in Coal Mining Communities: Implications for Heavily Industrialized Landscapes' (2021) 71 *Energy Research & Social Science* 101831.

[102] S Nakanwagi and AT Rukundo, 'Covid-19 Pandemic Deranging Energy Transition in Uganda: Challenges and Prospects' (2020) 1(2) *Global Energy Law and Sustainability* 211.

[103] J Gregory and BK Sovacool, 'Rethinking the Governance of Energy Poverty in Sub-Saharan Africa: Reviewing Three Academic Perspectives on Electricity Infrastructure Investment' (2019) 111 *Renewable and Sustainable Energy Reviews* 344.

[104] K Calvin, S Pachauri, E De Cian and I Mouratiadou, 'The Effect of African Growth on Future Global Energy, Emissions, and Regional Development' (2016) 136(1) *Climatic Change* 109.

[105] M Han, J Lao, Q Yao, B Zhang and J Meng, 'Carbon Inequality and Economic Development Across the Belt and Road Regions' (2020) 262 *Journal of Environmental Management* 110250.

[106] Z Bicaba, Z Brixiová and M Ncube, 'Can Extreme Poverty in Sub-Saharan Africa Be Eliminated by 2030?' (2017) 19(2) *Journal of African Development* 93.

[107] G Angelopulo, 'A Comparative Measure of Inclusive Urbanisation in the Cities of Africa' (2021) 22 *World Development Perspectives* 100313.

[108] B Oyalowo and T Lawanson, 'Housing and the SDGs in African Cities: Towards a Sustainable Future' [2021] *Housing and SDGs in Urban Africa* 321.

Furthermore, 33 countries of the world's 47 least-developed countries are in sub-Saharan Africa. The region emits an average of 0.8 metric tons of CO_2 per capita, 10 times less than developed countries, which emit an average of 8 metric tons of CO_2.[109] Chad, Burundi, Niger, Sierra Leone, Somalia, Ethiopia, Malawi, Rwanda and Uganda emit less than 0.1 metric tons of CO_2 per capita.[110] There is a universal need to address the climate crisis. The most pressing question is not whether Africa can use the current technological advancement to achieve global net-zero targets and SDGs; it is rather how the world's poorest region can eradicate poverty in its growing population while navigating a net-zero transition. International organisations and agreements recognise the need for an inclusive energy transition.[111] Global leaders aim to achieve universal access to electricity and change household energy sources by 2030.[112] The commitments and projections are optimistic, while current trends show us heading in the opposite direction. By 2030, there may be 620 million people globally without access to electricity, with 85 per cent of them from sub-Saharan Africa.[113]

3.6.3.2. Resource Access

The sub-Saharan Africa and Europe or Global North dynamics represent a paradox between the resource curse and resource dependence equation. Sub-Saharan Africa (Global South) has significantly been Europe's main source of raw materials for decades. These minerals and metals have been catalysts for fuel and further industrialisation in Global North European countries, making the region resource dependent.[114] Before diving into the dichotomy of the Global South and Global North resource curse and dependence conundrum, we must understand that Europe and the Global North possess the financial liquidity and further investments that sub-Saharan Africa needs. In contrast, sub-Saharan Africa and other Global South countries possess the natural resources the rest of the world requires.[115]

[109] S Ali, S Akter and C Fogarassy, 'The Role of the Key Components of Renewable Energy (Combustible Renewables and Waste) in the Context of CO_2 Emissions and Economic Growth of Selected Countries in Europe' (2021) 14(8) *Energies* 2034.

[110] AJ Njoh, 'Renewable Energy as a Determinant of Inter-Country Differentials in CO_2 Emissions in Africa' (2021) 172 *Renewable Energy* 1225.

[111] A Mengolini and M Masera, 'EU Energy Policy: A Socio-Energy Perspective for an Inclusive Energy Transition' in MPC Weijnen, Z Lukszo and S Farahani (eds), *Shaping an Inclusive Energy Transition* (Springer, 2021) 141–61.

[112] ibid.

[113] G Falchetta, AG Dagnachew, AF Hof and DJ Milne, 'The Role of Regulatory, Market and Governance Risk for Electricity Access Investment in Sub-Saharan Africa' (2021) 62 *Energy for Sustainable Development* 136.

[114] A Mayer and S Malin, 'How Should Unconventional Oil and Gas Be Regulated? The Role of Natural Resource Dependence and Economic Insecurity' (2019) 65 *Journal of Rural Studies* 79.

[115] Mostert et al (n 69).

Resource nationalism also impacts resource access. This is an economic strategy that is often pursued by underdeveloped nations that are rich in natural resources. These countries aim to increase their control over and share of the revenue generated by their natural resources. Critical minerals have become more economically and politically significant due to global climate change measures. Therefore, certain resource-rich countries have increased their influence in the supply chain of these minerals by imposing higher taxes, limiting foreign ownership, raising mining royalties and enforcing environmental protection requirements.

However, resource nationalism can also worsen the instability of the supply of critical minerals while providing opportunities for governments and individuals in underdeveloped nations to capitalise on their natural resource abundance.[116] The Global South can benefit from resource nationalism by having more involvement in the global division of labour and by being held to higher standards of governance and institutional excellence. Nonetheless, chronic rent-seeking behaviour and nepotism in these countries can hinder efforts to achieve national economic autonomy.

Sub-Saharan Africa has fundamental weaknesses in governance, security, poverty, transparency and natural resource management that lead to the resource curse.[117] Additionally, the rules and regulations governing the trading relationship between sub-Saharan Africa and mineral-consuming countries, mainly the Global North and China, are malleable and heavily influenced by money, power and knowledge.[118] Such an unequal relationship on the negotiating table leaves mineral host communities with socio-economic ruin, environmental degradation, displacement, cultural eradication and insecurity.

Multinational mining companies may be enticed to exploit the regulatory and governance loopholes and the extreme need for investment that sub-Saharan African countries need to drive their economies,[119] hence profiting at the expense of people of minority, marginalised communities and the environment. Robinson described it as racial capitalism – whereby capitalism follows a racial identity, and the development of resources is disconnected from social consciousness.[120] There have been movements to balance the means of trade in commodity value chains, but currently sub-Saharan Africa has still not gained much from its natural resources, particularly metals and minerals. The tenets of

[116] E Aspinall, 'The New Nationalism in Indonesia' (2016) 3(1) *Asia & the Pacific Policy Studies* 72.

[117] O Akpan and UE Umoh, '"Resource Curse" and "Resource Wars" and the Proliferation of Small Arms in Africa' in UA Tar and CP Onwurah (eds), *The Palgrave Handbook of Small Arms and Conflicts in Africa* (Palgrave Macmillan, 2021) 245.

[118] T Haastrup, 'Critical Perspectives on Africa's Relationship with the European Union' in D Bigo, T Diez, E Fanoulis, B Rosamond and YA Stivachtis (eds), *The Routledge Handbook of Critical European Studies* (Routledge, 2020) 511.

[119] Mayer and Malin (n 114).

[120] CJ Robinson, *Black Marxism Revised and Updated Third Edition: The Making of the Black Radical Tradition* (University of North Carolina Press Books, 2020).

justice can recognise sub-Saharan African stakeholders by reconfiguring participation in critical mineral and other commodity value chains and promoting equal distribution of the wealth and ills associated with the mining industry.

3.6.3.3. Patriarchy Presence in the Extractive Industry

The extractive industry is a source of living for many host communities, particularly in developing countries like the DRC and Zambia. Men, women and children participate in this industry in hazardous conditions. Throughout history, in different global contexts, the interrelationships of culture and gender have emerged in mining host communities.[121] The pertinent gender roles and relationships associated with mining have drawn the interest of researchers and natural resource scholars. There is a need to pay attention to the contextual analysis of the different roles of men, women and children in recognition of the patriarchy and how it affects the distribution of ills and benefits in host mining communities.[122] In the different contextual perspectives of mining communities, men are regarded as 'reckless drunks' or 'disciplined proletarians',[123] while women are regarded as 'wives' and 'sex workers'.[124] These perspectives vary with context. Justice facilitates recognising the diversity and women's need to navigate the super-patriarchal realities in the mining communities. The norms and systems of power and control within market structures, politics and business are predominantly led by men, and the workforce in heavy industries is also predominantly male.[125] The patriarchal dynamics enhance the interests of global political and business elites, who are mostly male. Several reasons keep women from underneath the earth's crust in mining communities, including superstition, moral outrage, welfare concerns, and concerns for babies and small children.[126]

3.7. Justice in Critical Mineral Development

Critical minerals are a part of the mining industry, which the UN has held to be crucial to achieving SDGs.[127] The mining industry value chain comprises the

[121] ibid.

[122] A Tobalagba and R Vijeyarasa, 'Engendering Regulation of Artisanal and Small-Scale Mining: Participation, Protection and Access to Justice' (2020) 41(10) *Third World Quarterly* 1635.

[123] S Bradshaw, B Linneker and L Overton, 'Extractive Industries as Sites of Supernormal Profits and Supernormal Patriarchy?' (2017) 25(3) *Gender & Development* 439.

[124] ibid.

[125] J Hinton, MM Veiga and C Beinhoff, 'Women and Artisanal Mining: Gender Roles and the Road Ahead' [2003] *The Socio-Economic Impacts of Artisanal and Small-Scale Mining in Developing Countries* 149.

[126] ibid.

[127] United Nations Development Programme, the World Economic Forum, the Columbia Centre on Sustainable Investments and the Sustainable Development Solutions Network United Nations, 'Mapping Mining to the SDGs: An Atlas' (2016); see also United Nations Environment Assembly of the

investment decision, the extraction of the minerals, smelting, refining/processing, transportation and end-use consumption. Much literature is primarily devoted to the business and financing aspects of the mining industry, the political economy of the whole critical mineral value chain and the scarcity of these minerals. The principles of justice have been mentioned in international reports, such as the EU policy report, emphasising 'fairness'. However, they highlight 'fairness' in critical metal pricing as synonymous with critical metals' business and financial aspects.[128] The economic focus of big multinational companies does not address the challenges facing the critical mineral-rich countries. These include restricted access to and militarisation of mining sites, poor demarcation of mining sites, disorganisation of diggers, lack of transparency in the critical metals trade, taxation issues, lack of state accountability towards host mining communities and the precarious inclusion or exclusion of women from mining activities.[129]

There have been tiny droplets of justice research on specific metals such as cobalt, but they are limited to a particular aspect of justice, namely distributive justice.[130] For instance, Mostert et al advocate for a 'value framework' around mineral value chains between Africa and the EU based on justice principles.[131] Furthermore, UN reports have shed light on the role of the law in the context of procedural justice, predominantly in the mining sector.[132] Therefore, this book argues for justice for the entire critical mineral value chain. The current climate crisis has called upon researchers and scholars to investigate the role of critical minerals in enabling and materialising a just energy transition. However, the 'just' aspect of the energy transition has not looked beyond the Global North's supply risk and economic factors. Ali et al state that 'a transition to a low-carbon society will require vast quantities of metals and minerals'.[133] The extraction and sourcing of critical minerals and the emergence of the climate crisis are inseparable because mining consumes a substantial amount of energy and because 'the world cannot address climate change without an adequate supply of raw materials for manufacturing clean technologies'.[134]

United Nations Environment Programme, Nairobi, 11–15 March 2019, UNEP/EA.4/Res.4 (on addressing environmental challenges through sustainable business practices).

[128] European Commission the Raw Materials Initiative, 'Meeting Our Critical Needs for Growth and Jobs in Europe (2008)' COM(2008) 699, https://eur-lex.europa.eu/legal-content/EN/TXT/PDF/?uri=CELEX:52008DC0699&from=EN.

[129] Wakenge et al (n 63).

[130] RJ Heffron, 'The Role of Justice in Developing Critical Minerals' (2020) 7(3) *The Extractive Industries and Society* 855.

[131] Mostert et al (n 69).

[132] United Nations, 'A Guide for Governments and Partners to Integrate Environment and Human Rights into the Governance of the Mining Sector' (2018).

[133] SH Ali, D Giurco, N Arndt, E Nickless, G Brown, A Demetriades, R Durrheim, MA Enriquez, J Kinnaird, A Littleboy and LD Meinert, 'Mineral Supply for Sustainable Development Requires Resource Governance' (2017) 543(7645) *Nature* 367.

[134] BK Sovacool, SH Ali, M Bazilian, B Radley, B Nemery, J Okatz and D Mulvaney, 'Sustainable Minerals and Metals for a Low-Carbon Future' (2020) 367(6473) *Science* 30.

As shown in Table 2, these minerals and metals are used in one way or another for low-carbon technologies, which are now used to leverage the global energy transition geopolitics. They are critical to developing and deploying renewable technologies like solar panels, wind turbines, electric vehicles and energy storage technologies.[135] Multinational companies are also dominant in the industry, which connotes the geopolitical influences and the need to ensure justice across the critical mineral value chain.

Table 2 Role of selected critical minerals in decarbonisation and the producing and importing countries

Mineral	Major producing countries	Major importing countries	Leading mines and mining companies	Role in decarbonisation
Copper (Cu)	Chile, Peru, China, DRC, USA, Australia, Zambia	China, Germany, USA, Italy, Korea	Chile: Escondida Copper Mine, owned by BHP Billiton, Rio Tinto and JECO	Used as a conductor of heat and electricity; used in the production of electric motors
Lithium (Li)	Australia, Chile, China, Argentina, Zimbabwe, Portugal, Czech Republic	USA, Indonesia, Hong Kong, China, Singapore, Japan, Germany, France	Australia: Greenbushes Mine, operated by Talison Lithium Australia Pty Ltd	Used in the production of batteries
Nickle (Ni)	Indonesia, Philippines, Russia, New Caledonia, Australia, Canada, China, Brazil, Cuba, USA	China, Japan, Taiwan, South Korea, India, Singapore, Malaysia, Turkey	Indonesia: PT Vale Indonesia Tbk (PT Vale), operating in areas of Central and Southeast Sulawesi	Used in the manufacture of batteries; electroplating; production of alloys and permanent magnets

(continued)

[135] K Hund, D La Porta, TP Fabregas, T Laing and J Drexhage, *Minerals for Climate Action: The Mineral Intensity of the Clean Energy Transition* (World Bank, 2020) 73; L Grandell, A Lehtilä, M Kivinen, T Koljonen, S Kihlman and LS Lauri, 'Role of Critical Metals in the Future Markets of Clean Energy Technologies' (2016) 95 *Renewable Energy* 53.

Table 2 ***(Continued)***

Mineral	Major producing countries	Major importing countries	Leading mines and mining companies	Role in decarbonisation
Cobalt (Co)	The Copper Belt in DRC, Russia, Cuba, Australia, Philippines, Canada, Madagascar, Papua New Guinea, China, Morocco, Zambia	China, Japan, Netherlands, USA, Germany, Finland, India, South Africa	DRC: Kamoto Copper Company (KCC) mine, owned by Swiss-based Glencore; Tunke Fungurume mine, owned by China Molybdenum	Used in the production of alloys and lithium-ion batteries (from lithium cobalt oxide); manufacture of rechargeable batteries for electric cars
Rare earth elements (neodymium (Nd), dysprosium (Dy))	Most commercial Nd and Dy are mined in China (90 per cent); also Australia, Myanmar	China	China Rare Earth Holdings Ltd, China Minmetals Rare Earth Co Ltd, JL Mag Rare Earth Co Ltd, and China Northern Rare Earth Group High-Tech Co Ltd	Larger Nd and Dy magnets are used in the production of high-power electric motors, eg in hybrid cars, generators, aircraft and wind turbine engine generators
Platinum group of metals (PGM)	South Africa is the biggest producer of PGMs; also Russia, Zimbabwe, Canada, USA	USA, Germany, UK, Japan, Hong Kong	South Africa – Anglo American Platinum; Zimbabwe – Impala Platinum Holdings (implants)	Manufacture of electronics and vehicle; fuel cells of hydrogen-powered vehicles as a chemical catalyst; production of autocatalysis (pollution control devices)

Source: S Nakanwagi, 'Critical Minerals and the Global Energy Transition: Recognising Global South Perspectives' (2023) 4(1–2) *Global Energy Law and Sustainability* 115.

A primary reason for justice is to promote fairness and equality in society, resolving inequalities in the process.[136] While inequality and injustice are pervasive

[136] RJ Heffron, *Energy Law: An Introduction* (Springer, 2021) 75–90.

in developing mining countries,[137] Rawls adheres to the 'difference principle' principle of justice. This principle states that social and economic inequalities are permissible only if the arrangements that generate them benefit the most disadvantaged person (the worst-off position) more than a 'more equal' structure would.[138] The DRC's child labour epidemic and Zambia's low accumulated rents due to mineral and metal transfer pricing violate the difference principle. As a result, the community's less fortunate members face deteriorating conditions, particularly in the mining sector. The adverse effects of the financial crisis of 2007–09 have resulted in the explicit engagement of justice in economic sectors.[139] Piketty criticises the issue, stating that there is a paucity of data on inequality despite living in a data-driven world of public data.[140] Furthermore, he addresses the social, economic and environmental costs of inequality and climate change emissions, especially in developing countries.

Given the critical minerals' role in developing the low-carbon economy, several countries committed to the Paris Agreement.[141] It calls for a broad definition of justice that encompasses this global industry with global implications. In this context, elements of climate, environmental, resource or extractive justice[142] and energy justice[143] must be incorporated. These can be combined to achieve a just transition to a low-carbon economy.[144] This is well articulated in the Just Framework, which applies to the 'Just Transition'. This framework unites scholarship on climate, environmental and energy justice and can increase the likelihood of society reducing inequality and injustice.

There must be a contextual consideration of specified economies' socio-economic and cultural realities to achieve sustainable development. The Just Framework incorporates and operationalises policy and regulations through an interdisciplinary perspective encompassing social, universal justice and geographical considerations since critical minerals are found in global value chains.[145] The Just Framework addresses five crucial aspects of justice that are necessary to ensure the application of justice throughout the critical mineral value chain.[146] Table 3 illustrates the key elements of justice that are needed in the mining life cycle.

[137] BK Sovacool, B Turnheim, A Hook, A Brock and M Martiskainen, 'Dispossessed by Decarbonisation: Reducing Vulnerability, Injustice, and Inequality in the Lived Experience of Low-Carbon Pathways' (2021) 137 *World Development* 105116.

[138] JCY Teng, JTY Wang and CC Yang, 'Justice, What Money Can Buy: A Lab Experiment on Primary Social Goods and The Rawlsian Difference Principle' (2020) 31(1) *Constitutional Political Economy* 45.

[139] Heffron, 'The Role of Justice' (n 130).

[140] T Piketty, *Capital and Ideology* (Harvard University Press, 2020).

[141] Ali et al, 'Mineral Supply for Sustainable Development' (n 133).

[142] Mostert et al (n 69).

[143] Heffron, 'The Role of Justice' (n 130).

[144] ibid.

[145] KE Jenkins, BK Sovacool, A Błachowicz and A Lauer, 'Politicising the Just Transition: Linking Global Climate Policy, Nationally Determined Contributions and Targeted Research Agendas' (2020) 115 *Geoforum* 138.

[146] Heffron, 'The Role of Justice' (n 130).

Table 3 The justice elements and critical mineral development

Distributive justice	This concerns the distribution of benefits and the ills from all segments of the critical mineral value chain (ie are mineral revenues shared sufficiently? Who suffers the environmental damage?)
Procedural justice	The focus here is on the legal and regulatory process undertaken in all critical mineral value chain segments (ie are all the steps for an environmental impact statement observed?)
Recognition justice	This focuses on the concerns and needs of the resource-rich countries and the marginalised host communities. It is about recognition of all marginalised nations and communities and their recognition in powerful decision-making platforms (ie are we recognising the rights of indigenous and marginalised host countries and communities?)
Restorative justice	The negative ramifications of the critical mineral industry must be addressed throughout the mining sector life cycle/value chains. Any injustice caused by the mining and energy sector should be rectified. It focuses on the need to enforce laws (ie mining sites should be returned to their former use; hence, waste management policy and decommissioning should be implemented appropriately)
Cosmopolitan justice	This emanates from globalisation and its impacts, whereby humanity is regarded as a single community. It stems from the belief that we are all citizens of the world. (Have we considered the effects beyond our borders and from a global context?)

Source: Author's own elaboration.

This book argues that economies can efficiently exploit critical minerals for a just transition through these tenets. In the process, economies will also achieve SDGs by considering the contextual realities that would have otherwise been ignored or overlooked.

3.8. The Reconstruction of Justice and Sustainable Development

There is an intricate relationship between justice and sustainable development, as shown in Figure 2. The two concepts are also closely linked to environmental protection. Adekunle notes that 'without a safe environment, man cannot exist to claim other rights, be they political, social, or economic'.[147] The environment and its finite resources call for reconsidering future generations and adequate

[147] AA Adekunle, 'Critical Notes on Environmental Justice and Sustainable Development' (2018) 10(3) *International Journal of Sociology and Anthropology* 21.

equity for all persons currently exploiting those resources.[148] Man enjoys an intricate relationship with the environment – we need natural resources for food and energy to sustain the resources for future generations.[149] However, the exploitation of natural resources for global development has led to the current climate crisis, which, in turn, has led to climate change mitigation and adaptation.[150] Developed countries have had a negative exploitative relationship with their environment, leading to degradation of natural resources and the environment.[151] Though the environment may still be degraded, the communities have gained adequate access to social services, efficient economic structures and stable political structures.[152] Nevertheless, the climate crisis is a global problem – even though most of the problems were caused by developed nations, which were industrialised when developing nations were still colonies with no access to fundamental human rights in certain demographics. Some regions thus took advantage of their economic and political might to exploit other developing regions.[153]

This book argues that the goals and mechanisms tailored to ensure that future generations enjoy the fruits of today's environment conservation must also consider the variations in development. The SDGs advocate for inter- and intra-generational equity, showing the acknowledgement of these variations. The Global North companies have incentives and capabilities to establish zero-carbon companies and industries that will eventually lead the global net-zero economy beyond 2050.[154] As developing regions have just started 'mastering' natural resource management, especially in sub-Saharan Africa, developed countries have the funding, research institutions and infrastructure to lead the way to a low-carbon economy.[155] Such narratives show the dependence between developing and developed countries on global development issues. Since developing countries will be forced to import renewable energy technology just like they imported components of modern industrialisation in the 1980s and 1990s, this enhances a vicious circle between developing and developed countries in terms of global development issues. Normative questions arise: how 'just' are SDGs for developing countries? Do developing countries have room to catch up?

[148] ibid.

[149] AJ Nightingale, T Böhler and B Campbell, 'Introduction and Overview' in AJ Nightingale, T Böhler, B Campbell, L Karlsson (eds), *Environment and Sustainability in a Globalizing World* (Routledge, 2019).

[150] A Sharifi, 'Co-benefits and Synergies Between Urban Climate Change Mitigation and Adaptation Measures: A Literature Review' (2021) 750 *Science of the Total Environment* 141642.

[151] J Huang, G Zhang, Y Zhang, X Guan, Y Wei and R Guo, 'Global Desertification Vulnerability to Climate Change and Human Activities' (2020) 31(11) *Land Degradation & Development* 1380.

[152] E Ikeda, 'Renewable Energy Development, Export-Led Industrialisation, and Its Implications for Climate Strategies in Asian Developing Countries' [2021] *Renewable Energy Transition in Asia: Policies, Markets and Emerging Issues* 89.

[153] FM Collyer, 'Global Patterns in the Publishing of Academic Knowledge: Global North, Global South' (2018) 66(1) *Current Sociology* 56.

[154] J Pinkse and A Kolk, *International Business and Global Climate Change* (Routledge 2009).

[155] ibid.

Figure 2 The interwoven relationship between justice and sustainable development

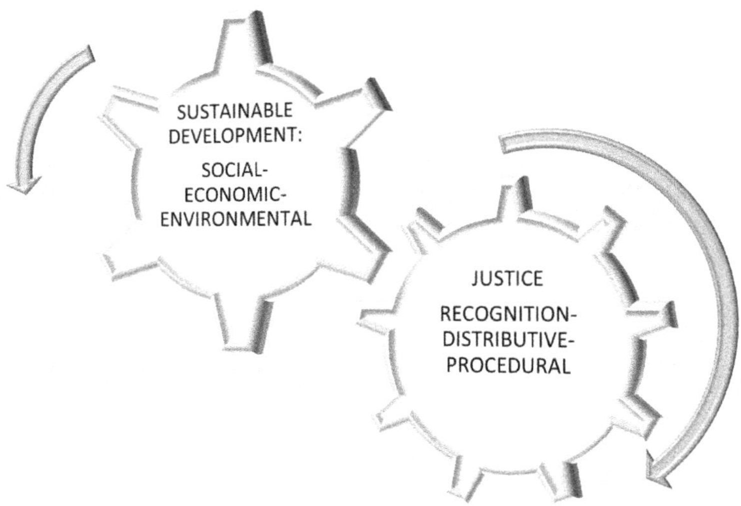

Source: Author's own elaboration.

Justice and sustainable development are the bread and butter of development and sustainability. The relationship between justice and sustainable development originates from the assumption that justice is a *sine qua non* for sustainable development.[156] For example, environmental discrimination breeds environmental inequality, leading to detrimental factors inhibiting development and failure to achieve the SDGs.[157] Hence, justice is a necessity for sustainable development. The social pillar of sustainable development needs to recognise the contextual differences in development and the marginalised communities. The economic pillar of sustainable development needs to adhere to principles of distributive justice whereby the ills and benefits are equally distributed. While the environmental pillar of sustainable development needs to comply with the principles of procedural justice, value chains should follow the law and what the law ought to be in issues of natural resource exploitation and environmental conservation.

It could be argued that sustainable development offers these principles already. However, the adopted policies and regulations do not encompass climate change ramifications in their text, though they promote and address the need for sustainable development. For example, the US Clean Air Act does not mention greenhouse gas emissions from houses.[158] This means that this policy may

[156] ibid.

[157] Adekunle (n 147).

[158] RK Craig, 'Water Law and Climate Change in the United States: A Review of the Legal Scholarship' (2020) 7(3) *Wiley Interdisciplinary Reviews: Water* e1423.

promote the efficient use of natural resources, but it overlooks the issues of justice that carbon emissions might bring. Secondly, when dealing with energy, we must acknowledge its relationship with politics – making energy a volatile issue in every election cycle, with a new administration designing energy policies according to the winning party's manifesto, overlooking the ramifications of justice. However, the changing nature of such policies might still lead to achieving SDGs. Lastly, there is an argument that climate change does not have a unanimous consensus. The lack of a unified consensus leads to different mechanisms being adapted for climate change mitigation and adaptation that might lead to attaining SDGs but could impact justice for marginalised communities and developing countries, particularly in the Global South. Justice is a necessity to fulfilling SDGs.

3.9. The African Prospective Narrative

In recent years, there has been a rise in industrialisation in Africa, driven by various factors. This section examines the factors fuelling industrialisation's growth and advancement challenges. Africa has experienced positive economic growth since the 1990s, attributed to macroeconomic management, increased local demand and higher commodity prices.[159] The contributions attained from GDP growth from industrialisation include increased manufacturing sector, financial and information and communications technology industry growth, and the growth of other linked sectors.[160] Though sub-Saharan African countries aim to foster industrialisation, they are driven predominantly by commodity exports.[161] Africa achieves SDGs by taking advantage of the high commodity prices and transplanting capital, labour and entrepreneurship from subsistence farming and informal sectors to industrialisation.[162] However, the extractive industry is capital-intensive; thus, the industry has lower linkages compared to other economic sectors.[163] It could be argued that commodities could drive an economy to prosperity. Still, the higher rents have often not facilitated growth in sub-Saharan African economies, mainly due to weak and poorly designed fiscal regimes, financial mismanagement and overall poor natural resources governance.[164]

[159] T Moyo, 'Industrialisation in Southern Africa: Towards a Developmental and Strategic Perspective' in S Adejumobi and C Obi (eds), *Developmental Regionalism and Economic Transformation in Southern Africa* (Routledge, 2020) 70–105.

[160] CA Hidalgo, B Klinger, AL Barabási and R Hausmann, 'The Product Space Conditions in the Development of Nations' (2007) 317(5837) *Science* 482.

[161] M Morris and J Fessehaie, 'The Industrialisation Challenge for Africa: Towards a Commodities-Based Industrialisation Path' (2014) 1(1) *Journal of African Trade* 25.

[162] AK Fosu, 'Growth, Inequality, And Poverty Reduction in Developing Countries: Recent Global Evidence' (United Nations University World Institute for Development Economics Research, 2011) Working Paper 2011/01.

[163] WR Freudenburg and R Gramling, 'Linked to What? Economic Linkages in an Extractive Economy' (1998) 11(6) *Society & Natural Resources* 569.

[164] ibid.

Sub-Saharan Africa has a growing population, but one that has already missed the twentieth-century economic boom train. Industrialisation efforts can enhance poverty eradication as well as achieve sustainable development. That will facilitate and boost technology innovation, develop skills and create channels for capital accumulation that will lead to a sustainable African society. However, industrialisation only yields economic progress through linkage development that is linked to global value chains (GVCs).[165] GVCs entail several stages characterised by fluctuating levels of value addition associated with high entry barriers.[166] A lack of skills and technology, poor R&D facilities and weak domestic players in global markets fundamentally create these barriers.[167]

Globalisation has brought about industrialisation opportunities in other regions, such as Asia and Latin America. Africa did not follow the same trajectory and suffered deindustrialisation in the 1980s and 1990s.[168] In contrast to Asian economies, sub-Saharan African countries adopted structural adjustment programmes in the 1980s and 1990s that did not facilitate export-oriented policies designed to enhance industrialisation in domestic economies.[169] This can be seen in sub-Saharan Africa's trade patterns; the region has a high degree of export orientation and import penetration.[170] The imports are predominantly made up of final consumer goods, while the exports are mainly raw materials.[171] The imports to sub-Saharan Africa are capital equipment, with several intermediaries designed for commodity extraction.[172] The region's reintegration has not facilitated sub-Saharan Africa's industrialisation ambitions with regard to GVCs and the world trade order.[173] This is mainly because commodity sectors are characterised by enclaves, offering limited opportunities for linkage development, with weak positive externalities.[174] Investors originating from developed countries, mostly the Global North, invest in developing regions of sub-Saharan Africa with intact linkages from other developed countries, and this acts as a barrier for local stakeholders, especially host communities. Through distributive justice, sub-Saharan African economies can foster technological externalities and provide incentives for investment in supplier industries to foster backwards and forward linkages because there is an equitable share of the profits of the extractive sector.

[165] S Lall, 'Industrial Success and Failure in a Globalizing World' (2004) 3(3) *International Journal of Technology Management & Sustainable Development* 189.

[166] ibid.

[167] Caramento (n 59).

[168] Morris and Fessehaie (n 161).

[169] JB Riddell, 'Things Fall Apart Again: Structural Adjustment Programmes in Sub-Saharan Africa' (1992) 30(1) *Journal of Modern African Studies* 53.

[170] ibid.

[171] M Olabisi and WC Sawyer, 'The Demand for Imports and Exports in Africa: A Survey' (2020) 7(1–2) *Journal of African Trade* 45.

[172] ibid.

[173] H Feyaerts, G Van den Broeck and M Maertens, 'Global and Local Food Value Chains in Africa: A Review' (2020) 51(1) *Agricultural Economics* 143.

[174] FS Weldegiorgis, E Dietsche and DM Franks, 'Building Mining's Economic Linkages: A Critical Review of Local Content Policy Theory' (2021) 74 *Resources Policy* 102312.

3.10. Summary

The climate change crisis has changed international trade and GVCs by dictating what is eco-friendly and what products lead to sustainability. As societies adjust to this new reality, it is important that they also acknowledge the importance of justice. The transition towards a low-carbon economy has made marginalised communities in sub-Saharan Africa's interior famous due to their vast resources in critical minerals. As the availability of these resources promises a decarbonised world, so does the economic potential for these minerals for all stakeholders in the critical mineral value chain. This chapter looked at the conceptual underpinning of a failing sustainable development regime. It holds that there must be an incorporation of the tenets of justice that will lead to the materialisation of SDGs in the process. As much as the disciplines of geology, human geography, economics, science and politics have discussed the depth of critical minerals, this chapter shows a need for an interdisciplinary inquiry into critical minerals, analysing the socio-economic and political issues across the critical mineral value chain.

4

Sub-Saharan Africa's Copper–Cobalt Value Chain

4.1. Introduction

As discussed in chapter one, globally, critical minerals are spatially distributed. However, most of the production occurs in countries relying on resource-based development, for example, lithium production in Chile, Argentina, Peru and Zimbabwe; copper production in Zambia, the Democratic Republic of Congo (DRC), Peru and Mexico; cobalt production in the DRC, Cuba, Australia, the Philippines, Canada, Madagascar and Papua New Guinea; mining of platinum group metals (PGMs) in South Africa and Botswana; nickel in Indonesia, the Philippines and New Caledonia; and rare earth elements in China.[1]

However, these mineral-rich countries rarely enjoy any actual benefits from such resources – a situation commonly referred to as the 'resource curse'.[2] Here, resource-rich nations fail to maximise the benefits from the natural resource wealth, and the concerned governments fail to meet and address the welfare needs of their populations.[3] These countries also suffer from resource conflicts; their economic growth and stability tend to be lower than other nations that are not rich in natural resources.[4] On the other hand, the processing and refining of critical minerals have been dominated by more developed countries with stronger economies like China, the EU, the USA and the UK. These same countries of the Global North are also the foremost consumers of critical minerals.

[1] S Renner and FW Wellmer, 'Volatility Drivers on the Metal Market and Exposure of Producing Countries' (2020) 33(3) *Mineral Economics* 311.

[2] Natural Resources Governance Institute, 'The Resource Curse, The Political and Economic Challenges of Natural Resource Wealth' (NGRI Reader, March 2015) https://resourcegovernance.org/sites/default/files/documents/nrgi_readers_compilation.pdf.

[3] ibid.

[4] ibid.

4.2. Overview of the Case Study Countries

4.2.1. Critical Minerals Development in Sub-Saharan Africa

The sub-Saharan Africa region has a strategic position in the critical mineral industry, especially in the upstream and production stages. The region supplies vanadium, platinum, diamond, cobalt and gold, accounting for more than 60 per cent of the global supply. These minerals have been a significant source of the region's economy, providing employment, bankrolling government coffers and enabling foreign exchange earnings through mineral and metal exports.

The sub-Saharan Africa region holds a key role in the global mineral value chains, and more so for critical minerals. South Africa and Guinea hold more than one key resource and lie in the top 10 of those minerals globally. Other countries, like the DRC, Zambia, Namibia, Mauritania, Morocco, Zimbabwe, Ghana, Niger and Botswana, hold at least one key mineral resource, placing them in the top 10 producers of that particular mineral globally. For instance, the central and southern regions of sub-Saharan Africa supply over 88 per cent of the world's platinum and 84 per cent of chromium. Table 4 further highlights this position. It shows the massive supply reserves of critical minerals held by selected sub-Saharan countries, which places the region in a very precarious position within the value chains of the minerals needed for the energy transition. Table 4 also shows that foreign companies mainly operate the major mining projects; for example, Anglo American Platinum operates platinum-group metal (PGM) mines in both South Africa and Zimbabwe, and China Molybdenum operates the Tenke Fungurume copper–cobalt mine in the DRC.

Environmental mismanagement, social risks, poor governance and weak resource management characterise the extractive sector in sub-Saharan Africa. Countries such as Zambia, the DRC, South Africa, Zimbabwe, Namibia and Angola have experienced mismanagement in their critical mineral development.[5] The extractive industry has also left a legacy of environmental degradation, adverse impacts on public health, marginalised communities and workers experiencing the worst inhumane living conditions, all in the quest of fuelling the transition towards a globalised low-carbon economy.[6]

[5] OP Maponga and C Musa, 'Domestication of the Role of the Mining Sector in Southern Africa through Local Content Requirements' (2020) 8(1) *The Extractive Industries and Society* 195.

[6] WT Selmier II and A Newenham-Kahindi, 'Communities of Place, Mining Multinationals and Sustainable Development in Africa' [2020] *Journal of Cleaner Production* 125709.

Table 4 Supply reserves (in metric tons) and major mining projects for key critical minerals in selected sub-Saharan countries

Lithium (Li)	Graphite (C)	Cobalt (Co)	Nickel (NiSO4)	Manganese (Mn)	PGMs
DRC (1 million reserves) AVZ Minerals: minerals exploration company Namibia (9000) Desert Lion Energy Zimbabwe (70,000) Prospect Resources; Bikita Minerals; Kamativi	Mozambique (2000) Battery Minerals Limited; Syrah Resources: Balama Graphite Mine Operation Tanzania (17,000) Magnis Resources: Nachu Graphite Project	Madagascar (150,000) Sumitomo; Ambatovy Namibia (112,400) Celsius Resources: Opuwo Cobalt Project DRC (3.5 million) GECAMINES SA; Glencore; China Molybdenum: Tenke Fungurume copper–cobalt mine Zambia (270,000) Arc Minerals: Zamsort Copper-Cobalt Project; ERG Africa: Chambishi Metals: Cobalt Refinery	Madagascar (1.6 million) Sumitomo; Ambatovy South Africa (3.7 million) Sulphide Project; Mintek – Nickel Beneficiation Project Zimbabwe (4.5 million) Bindura Nickel Corporation	South Africa (230,000) South32 Manganese Metal Company Botswana (unknown) Giyani Metals Corp: K Hill Manganese Project Exploration	South Africa (63,000) Anglo American Platinum – Bushveld Complex, including the world's most enormous open-pit PGM mines – Mogalakwena, Mototolo and Amendelbult; Impala Platinum Holdings (Implants) – Bushveld Complex Zimbabwe (1200) Anglo American Platinum – Unki mine; Impala Platinum Holdings (Implants) – Great Dyke area

Source: Illustration by author. Figures adapted from 'Mineral Commodity Summaries 2020' (US Geological Survey, 2000) https://doi.org/10.3133/mcs2020.

4.2.2. The Democratic Republic of Congo

Mining represents a critical sector for the development of the DRC. According to the World Bank, mining has dominated the Congolese economy since the early 1910s.[7] This domination is unsurprising, given that the country is incredibly mineral-rich. The DRC is among the world's wealthiest countries in mineral resources, with abundant tantalum, tungsten, cobalt and tin.[8] It also possesses the largest known diamond and gold deposits in the world. Its copper reserves make this region the second richest copper region globally, with 70 million metric tons, surpassed only by Chile.

The political instability in Congo is primarily due to the armed conflict that lasted for over two decades from the mid-1990s, killing over 5.4 million people, dubbed the deadliest conflict since World War II.[9] Furthermore, the DRC is also the largest country in the Central Africa region with an impoverished population. Despite the DRC having vast mineral resources, the armed conflict and the closed nature of large-scale mining operations mean that the extractive industry's benefits are not equitably distributed across the population, leaving most Congolese citizens living below the poverty line. Regardless of the DRC experiencing conflict and political instability, the country holds more than 50 per cent of global cobalt reserves. The increased demand for cobalt is mainly attributed to its industrial application in electroplating and the alloying of other metals that are used in the aerospace industry.[10] The energy transition and technological advancements since the twentieth century have seen cobalt used in mobile phones and laptops, stationary applications (energy storage) and electric mobility (electric or hybrid vehicles and charging stations).

Cobalt sourcing in the DRC is estimated to be produced mainly by large-scale mining operations.[11] The state-owned Gecamines has major interests in Kambove, Kipushi, Kamfundwa and Kolwezi.[12] The company has forged relationships and

[7] World Bank, 'Democratic Republic of Congo: Growth with Governance in the Mining Sector' (2008) https://openknowledge.worldbank.org/handle/10986/8072.

[8] L Prause, 'Conflicts Related to Resources: The Case of Cobalt Mining in the Democratic Republic of Congo' in A Bleicher and A Pehlken (eds), *The Material Basis of Energy Transitions* (Academic Press, 2020) 153–67.

[9] JL Kormoh, 'The Conflicts in the DRC: Wider Ramifications for the African Great Lakes Region' in K Omeje (ed), *The Governance, Security and Development Nexus* (Palgrave Macmillan, 2020) 341–53.

[10] RT Nguyen, RG Eggert, MH Severson and CG Anderson, 'Global Electrification of Vehicles and Intertwined Material Supply Chains of Cobalt, Copper and Nickel' [2020] *Resources, Conservation and Recycling* 105198.

[11] GK Byemba, 'Formalisation of Artisanal and Small-Scale Mining in Eastern Democratic Republic of the Congo: An Opportunity for Women in the New Tin, Tantalum, Tungsten and Gold (3TG) Supply Chain?' [2020] *The Extractive Industries and Society* 420.

[12] JP Otamonga and JW Poté, 'Abandoned Mines and Artisanal and Small-Scale Mining in Democratic Republic of the Congo (DRC): Survey and Agenda for Future Research' (2020) 208 *Journal of Geochemical Exploration* 106394.

joint ventures with foreign companies. These include the Anglo-Swiss Glencore International, American giant Freeport-McMOran, London-based Eurasian Natural Resources Corporation and the Hong Kong-listed China Non-Ferrous Metal Mining.[13] China Molybdenum Co announced a $2.51 billion investment in August 2021 to nearly double copper and cobalt production at its massive Tenke Fungurume mine in the DRC.[14] The investment would go towards constructing three ore production lines, increasing the mine's average annual copper output by 200,000 tonnes and cobalt output by 17,000 tonnes. China Moly owns an 80 per cent stake in Tenke Fungurume, one of the largest copper–cobalt deposits in the world, and Gecamines owns the other 20 per cent. In 2020, the mine produced approximately 182,600 tonnes of copper and 15,400 tonnes of cobalt.[15]

4.2.3. Zambia

Zambia is one of the most mineral-rich countries globally, with massive deposits ranging from cobalt, uranium, silver, zinc, semiprecious gemstones, lead, emeralds, gold and copper ore. The country has one of the highest-grade copper reserves in the world, is the world's seventh largest copper producer and ranks second in Africa. Copper mining has dominated Zambia's economy since the first commercial mine opened in 1928 at Roan Antelope (now Luanshya), although copper was produced in 1908 and 1911 at Kansanshi and Bwana Mkubwa, respectively.[16] The mining industry boomed during this period, and copper's high demand and favourable prices compelled the private mine owners to maximise their profits.[17] Improved floatation technology for separating copper sulphide minerals from ores enabled the production of large quantities of copper. As a result, mine owners invested in concentrators, smelters and other metal extraction facilities, which remained in operation until 1969.[18] The 1960s and 1970s were decades marked by increased metals demand (as a raw material in industries) from the industrialised economies, high international mineral prices and increased production.[19]

[13] ibid.

[14] T Daly, 'China Moly to Spend $2.5 Billion to Double Copper, Cobalt Output at Congo Mine' (Reuters, 6 August 2021) www.reuters.com/article/us-cmoc-congo-investment-idUSKBN2F712Z.

[15] ibid.

[16] P Sinkala, Y Fujii, JI Kodama and D Fukuda, 'An Overview of Copper Mining in Zambia's Copperbelt Province' in *Proceedings of Spring Meeting of MMIJ Hokkaido Branch* (MMIJ-Hokkaido Branch, 2018) 35–36.

[17] J Sikamo, A Mwanza and C Mweemba, 'Copper Mining in Zambia – History and Future' (2016) 116(6) *Journal of the Southern African Institute of Mining and Metallurgy* 491, https://dx.doi.org/10.17159/2411-9717/2016/v116n6a1.

[18] ibid.

[19] AFRODAD, 'Impacts of Fluctuating Commodity Prices on Government Revenue in the SADC Region: The Case of Copper for Zambia' (African Forum and Network on Debt and Development, 2016) https://media.africaportal.org/documents/IMPACTS_OF_FLUCTUATING_COMMODITY_PRICES_ZAMBIA_1.pdf.

Due to the position of copper today as a critical mineral and its role in the race to achieve net-zero emissions, this upward trajectory is expected to continue as nations and multinational corporations race to transition away from fossil fuel energy. According to the Zambia Extractive Industries Transparency Initiative, mining accounts for 77 per cent of Zambia's total exports and nearly 28 per cent of government revenue.[20] Zambia produced 882,061 tonnes of copper in 2020, up 10.8 per cent from 796,430 tonnes produced in 2019.[21]

Copper mining in Zambia is mainly concentrated in the Copperbelt, with mines located in Kitwe, Mufulira, Kalulushi, Chililabombwe, Chingola, Ndola and Luanshya.[22] According to Zambia's Chamber of Mines, there are four major mines, namely: FQM Kansanshi, owned by Canadian FQM (First Quantum Minerals); Barrick Lumwana, wholly owned by the Canadian company Barrick; KCM (Konkola Copper Mines), majorly owned by Vedanta Resources, an Indian diversified metals and mining group; and Mopani Copper Mines, mainly owned by Swiss-based Glencore.[23] The Zambian government is the biggest stakeholder in Zambia's mining industry as it is a minority shareholder in the majority of mining companies through its investment-holding company ZCCM-IH. These mines account for approximately 80 per cent of Zambia's annual copper production.[24] Mining activities have also grown in other parts of the country – for example, the FQM's Kansanshi mine is in Solwezi, the capital of North-Western Province, and 150 km away its Trident project consists of the Sentinel copper mine and the Enterprise nickel mine.[25] The Lumwana mine is located about 100 km from Solwezi and is owned by Barrick.

The incumbent President of Zambia, His Excellency Hakainde Hichilema, gave a keynote address at the Investing in African Mining Indaba in February 2024 in South Africa. He emphasised that certain investments have been made and have yielded positive results, for example, the Enterprise nickel mine, the largest nickel producer in Africa. This mine became operational after receiving a $100 million investment from First Quantum Minerals (FQM). FQM is also investing over $1 billion to expand the Kanshanshi mine and smelter, enhancing the downstream beneficiation industry. Moxico Resources commenced production at its Mimbula mine project in March 2023, yielding an output of 6000 metric tons of copper during the initial nine months of operation. The President also pointed out that Kobold Metals, utilising cutting-edge artificial intelligence (AI)

[20] Zambia Extractive Industry Transparency Initiative, https://eiti.org/zambia.

[21] Xinhua, 'Roundup: Expectations Remain High among Zambians as Copper Prices Rise' (*Xinhuanet*, 2021) www.xinhuanet.com/english/africa/2021-06/07/c_139994423.htm.

[22] RA Unceta, 'The Economic and Social Impact of Mining-Resources Exploitation in Zambia' (2021) 74 *Resources Policy* 102242.

[23] Mining for Zambia, 'Zambia's Mines – A Concentrated Mining Sector: Four Big Mines and Several Important Smaller Operations Make Up Zambia's Copper-Mining Landscape' (2016) https://miningforzambia.com/a-concentrated-mining-sector/.

[24] ibid.

[25] ibid.

technology, has achieved substantial advancements in delineating the orebody at its Mingomba project subsequent to a $150 million investment in 2022. Barrick Gold Corporation has reaffirmed its dedication by allocating a $2 billion investment to enhance its Lumwana mine, transforming it into a 'super-pit' that will have the capacity to yield 240,000 tonnes of copper annually upon its launch in 2028. The China Non-Ferrous Mining Corporation has committed to investing $1.3 billion in its activities in Zambia over the next five years. This investment includes $600 million specifically for reopening shaft 28 at the Luanshya Copper Mines, located in the Copperbelt region of Zambia.[26]

Zambia also possesses some copper refining facilities. By 2018, the country had four copper smelting operations, with a combined smelting capacity of up to 1.2 million tonnes of refined copper per year, making it Africa's largest.[27] Domestic copper market participants include the diversified miner Vedanta Resources, the Canadian metals and mining company FQM and the diversified miner Glencore, all of which have increased their efforts in establishing downstream facilities.[28] The Kansanshi copper smelter, completed in the first half of 2015, enabled FQM to increase the value of the copper it produces in Zambia and created about 700 specialist jobs.[29] KCM's Nchanga smelter produces REC copper cathodes, which are then refined at the Nkana refinery.[30] These cathodes have a purity level of 99.99 per cent copper, are registered as REC (A-Grade) on the London Metal Exchange (LME) and meet the highest international quality requirements. KCM's Tailings Leach Plant in Nchanga also produces copper cathodes.

4.2.4. China

China is a significant consumer of critical minerals for its industrial and domestic needs, as well as its processing and refining companies. In recent years, its refining and processing capacity has increased its share of global demand for minerals such as copper, lithium, nickel, iron ore and zinc.[31] The country is a

[26] President of the Republic of Zambia HE Hakainde Huchilema, 'Investing in African Mining Indaba 2024'.

[27] Creamer Media, 'Zambia's Refined Copper Outlook Positive' (*Mining Weekly*, 2018). https://www.miningweekly.com/article/zambias-refined-copper-outlook-positive-2018-08-17#:~:text=Zambia%20will%20remain%20one%20of,member%20of%20the%20Fitch%20Group.

[28] ibid.

[29] First-quantum.com, 'First Quantum Minerals Ltd – Our Operations', www.first-quantum.com/English/our-operations/default.aspx#module-operation--kansanshi.

[30] Kcm.co.zm. *Copper | Konkola Copper Mines Plc.* (2021) [online] Available at: http://kcm.co.zm/our-products/copper/.

[31] S Kalantzakos, 'The Race for Critical Minerals in an Era of Geopolitical Realignments' (2020) 55(3) *The International Spectator* 1.

significant mineral producer, but domestic production of critical minerals such as nickel, cobalt, iron ore and copper are insufficient to meet domestic demand. As a result, China's consumption needs continue to be met by international markets.[32] Chinese enterprises have locked up supplies of critical minerals and metals through a combination of state-directed investment and state-backed financing, making long-term strategic bets in niche markets with minimal transparency and often in politically unstable nations in which they operate.[33] China is, therefore, locked in a battle to control the raw materials necessary to run the digital economy through its foreign policy. Studies have revealed how quickly and effectively the country has carried out its national goals, with far-reaching consequences for the world.[34]

The White Paper on 'China's Policy on Mineral Resources', published in 2003,[35] highlighted China's 'going out policy' in minerals. The Chinese government asserted that allowing foreign mining companies to enter China and Chinese mining enterprises to expand into other countries was critical 'for the common prosperity and healthy development of global mineral resources prospecting and exploitation'.[36] This was accompanied by a rise in China's presence and equity stake in international mineral holdings. The Belt and Road Initiative (BRI) was established in 2013 as the primary vision for the country's international interactions. The BRI is a transcontinental Chinese government-led global development initiative to jointly establish a 'Silk Road' economic belt and a 'Maritime Silk Road'. It involves infrastructure projects to speed up economic integration across Asia, Europe, Africa, the Middle East and the Americas. The phrase originated from ancient China's trading activities and relationships with peoples and countries in Europe, Asia and Africa along the Silk Road and maritime voyages. The Initiative was first announced by China's president, Xi Jinping, in 2013 and was known as OBOR – One Belt, One Road – until 2016. With the approval of the State Council, the National Development and Reform Commission, the Ministry of Foreign Affairs and the Ministry of Commerce of the People's Republic of China announced the official framework for the BRI on 28 March 2015. Seventy-one nations are participating in the Initiative, accounting for more than one-third of

[32] Z Chen, L Zhang and Z Xu, 'Analysis of Cobalt Flows in Mainland China: Exploring the Potential Opportunities for Improving Resource Efficiency and Supply Security' (2020) 275 *Journal of Cleaner Production* 122841.

[33] ibid.

[34] G Keraval, 'Mining the Future: How China Is Set to Dominate the Next Industrial Revolution' (*FP*, 1 May 2019) https://foreignpolicy.com/2019/05/01/mining-the-future-china-critical-minerals-metals/.

[35] 'White Paper on China's Policy on Mineral Resources of 2003', www.chinadaily.com.cn/en/doc/2003-12/23/content_292806.htm.

[36] ibid.

the global GDP and two-thirds of the global population,[37] with investments in 52 out of the 54 African countries.[38]

The Chinese state-owned China Road and Bridge Corporation (CRBC) has invested over $14 billion in Kenya's Mombasa Port. At the same time, the CRBC has completed an agreement with an Omani construction company to overhaul and extend the Bagamoyo Port in Tanzania.[39] Both Kenya and Tanzania are competing to be dominant gateways of critical minerals such as copper, cobalt and coltan from the DRC and Zambia to global markets such as Europe, India and China. The Chinese Railway Engineering Corporation has also spent over $2 billion modernising the Benguela railway line, which links the Katanga Province of the DRC to the Angolan port of Lobito on the Atlantic coast, for the transportation of cobalt, copper and manganese.[40] The 'yen-driven development' influence in critical mineral resource corridors has mainly challenged South Africa. South Africa has a transport corridor stretching from the ports of East London, Cape Town, Port Elizabeth and Durban northward through Zimbabwe, Botswana, Zambia, Malawi and Tanzania to the Katanga province of the DRC and eastward into Mozambique for critical minerals.[41] Bilateral trade between China and the DRC increased in the first half of 2020, reaching a total value of $3.11 billion. China's imports from the DRC amounted to $2.31 billion, up 20.81 per cent year-on-year, while its exports to the DRC totalled $798 million.[42]

China has created a robust commercial presence in most African countries through the BRI over the last two decades. With its enticing economic investment package, focused development projects and flexible political strategy, the BRI offers tremendous opportunities for African countries.[43] However, the Initiative's unilateral nature, lack of transparency and accountability to African countries and lack of initiatives that help locals directly have generated doubts and fuelled local discontent, with some countries cancelling or postponing key projects.[44]

[37] The Belt and Road Initiative portal, https://eng.yidaiyilu.gov.cn/info/iList.jsp?cat_id=10076&cur_page=1.

[38] P Risberg, 'The Give-and-Take of BRI in Africa' (2019) 17 *New Perspectives in Foreign Policy* 43.

[39] U Wissenbach and Y Wang, 'African Politics Meets Chinese Engineers: The Chinese-Built Standard Gauge Railway Project in Kenya and East Africa' (Johns Hopkins University-SAIS, 2017) Working Paper 13.

[40] A Cain, 'Alternatives to African Commodity-Backed Urbanisation: The Case of China in Angola' (2017) 33(3) *Oxford Review of Economic Policy* 478.

[41] T Marshall, *Prisoners of Geography: Ten Maps That Tell You Everything You Need to Know About Global Politics* (Elliot & Thompson Limited, 2015).

[42] X Gu, C Dinkelbach, C Heidbrink, Y Huang, X Ke, M Mayer and HW Ohnesorge, *China's Engagement in Africa: Activities, Effects and Trends* (Centre for Global Studies, 2022).

[43] V Lokanathan, 'China's Belt and Road Initiative: Implications in Africa' (Observer Research Foundation, 2020) ORF Issue Brief No 395, www.orfonline.org/research/chinas-belt-and-road-initiative-implications-in-africa/.

[44] ibid.

In terms of value, coal production in China accounts for the most significant proportion of the global mining industry.[45] Coal is produced by China Shenhua Energy Co Ltd, the world's second-largest mining company. Besides coal, China Molybdenum, Zijin Mining Group, Chinalco Mining Corp (CMC), Jiangxi Copper and Shandong Gold Mining are the major Chinese mining corporations.[46] Copper, cobalt, niobium and phosphates production are among China Molybdenum's activities. The business has operations in Brazil, the DRC and Australia, with a few projects in China. The Hong Kong-listed Zijin Mining Group has diverse copper, gold, lead, iron ore, tungsten and zinc projects spread over 24 Chinese provinces and nine foreign countries. CMC is a resource development business that serves as a platform for the parent company, the state-controlled Aluminium Corp of China Ltd (Chinalco), to acquire, invest in, develop and operate non-ferrous and non-aluminium natural resources and projects around the world. Jiangxi Copper is a copper company and one of China's leading copper cathode producers, combining mining and processing operations. Although it owns a stake in the Escondida copper project in Chile, most of its operations are in China. Apart for Chinalco, a state-owned entity holding 85 per cent of the shares, none of the companies has significant state ownership; instead, the stakes are predominantly held by institutions through private or corporate investment funds.[47]

China has much control over processing critical minerals such as lithium, copper, cobalt, nickel and rare earth minerals, used in the energy transition, as Figure 3 shows. China is the world's largest copper consumer, accounting for over half of all production. Imports of unwrought copper and other products increased by 9.8 per cent in January–April 2021 compared to the previous year.[48] Moreover, the country also dominates cobalt chemicals used in battery manufacturing, accounting for more than 80 per cent of total cobalt chemical production,[49] and it controls a huge share of the world's cobalt sulphate and nearly all of the world's cobalt chemical refining capacity. The cobalt ore is refined into metal, powder and chemicals. Over the last decade, China's use of iron ore, copper, nickel and zinc has accounted for a growing share of world demand. In recent years, China's mineral consumption has remained a key indicator for

[45] STRADE, 'China's Mineral Sector and the Belt & Road Initiative' (Strategic Dialogue on Sustainable Raw Materials for Europe, March 2018) European Policy Brief No 2/2018, www.stradeproject.eu/fileadmin/user_upload/pdf/STRADE_PB_02-2018_One_Belt_One_Road.pdf.

[46] ibid.

[47] ibid.

[48] R Imahashi and J Nagumo, 'China and Green Energy Drive Copper Prices to Record High: Shares in Asian Miners and Nonferrous Producers Surge Despite Supply Concerns' (NIKKEI Asia, 24 May 2021) https://asia.nikkei.com/Spotlight/Market-Spotlight/China-and-green-energy-drive-copper-prices-to-record-high.

[49] J Farchy and H Warren, 'China Has a Secret Weapon in the Race to Dominate Electric Cars' (Bloomberg, 2 December 2018) www.bloomberg.com/graphics/2018-china-cobalt/.

forecasting worldwide demand for various minerals, including gold, lithium, copper and iron ore.[50]

Figure 3 China's share of the global processing of selected critical materials

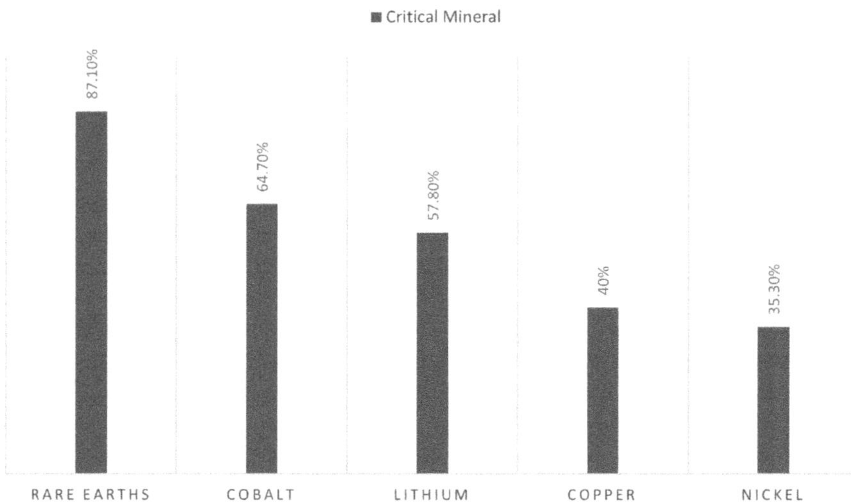

Source: Authors' own elaboration, based on information extracted from IEA, 'The Role of Critical Minerals in Clean Energy Transitions. World Energy Outlook Special Report' (International Energy Agency, 2021).

Figure 3 shows that China controls the processing of major energy transition minerals. For example, it accounts for over approximately 65 per cent of the global cobalt refining and 40 per cent of copper. This puts the country in a central position in the supply chains of much-needed minerals.

4.2.5. The European Union

The EU is the biggest consumer of critical minerals, although it has little mining or processing activity.[51] For example, it consumes 16 per cent of the total refined copper and has a high demand for cobalt for its electric vehicle batteries industry. Some EU Member States have a sizeable base of metal refining and manufacturing; for example, Finland refines approximately 10 per cent of the

[50] STRADE (n 45).

[51] M Leonard, J Pisani-Ferry, J Shapiro, S Tagliapietra and GB Wolff, *The Geopolitics of the European Green Deal* (Bruegel, 2021).

world's refined cobalt output.[52] The region is also home to major solar photovoltaic components, wind turbines and electric vehicles. The EU sources some of its critical minerals domestically. For example, Finland supplies 51 per cent of the germanium, Germany 35 per cent of the gallium, Spain 100 per cent of the strontium, France 34 per cent of the hafnium and Turkey 62 per cent of the antimony and 98 per cent of the borates.[53] However, as shown in Table 5, the region is almost entirely dependent on external mining supplies for several energy transition minerals, including lithium, cobalt and rare earth elements, exposing it to geopolitical issues in the supply chains.[54] The EU intends to pursue domestic sources of critical minerals, such as enhanced metal extraction in post-mining regions.[55] Further, the European Commission wants to establish strategic international partnerships to ensure the supply of critical raw materials that are not readily available in Europe, with pilot collaborations with interested African countries, Canada and the EU's neighbours starting in 2021.[56] The Commission undertakes to advocate for sustainable and responsible mining practices and transparency in these international undertakings.[57]

Table 5 Selected countries accounting for the largest share of the EU's supply of critical minerals

Country	Mineral	Percentage share
DRC	Cobalt	68
Chile	Lithium	78
Guinea	Bauxite	64
China	Rare earth elements	99
China	Magnesium	93
Brazil	Niobium	85
Kazakhstan	Phosphorous	71
Mexico	Fluorspar	25

Source: Author's own elaboration, based on information extracted from European Commission, *Study on the EU's List of Critical Raw Materials (2020) Final Report* (2020).

[52] IEA, 'The Role of Critical Minerals in Clean Energy Transitions. World Energy Outlook Special Report' (International Energy Agency, 2021).

[53] European Commission, 'Critical Raw Materials – Internal Market, Industry, Entrepreneurship and SMEs' (2021) https://ec.europa.eu/growth/sectors/raw-materials/specific-interest/critical_en.

[54] ibid; Kalantzakos (n 31).

[55] IEA (n 53).

[56] European Commission, 'Commission Announces Actions to Make Europe's Raw Materials Supply More Secure and Sustainable' (2020) https://ec.europa.eu/commission/presscorner/detail/en/ip_20_1542.

[57] ibid.

Critical raw materials (CRMs) are critical to the EU's economy, and the concept of criticality is frequently rewritten. Europe's economy relies on raw materials, which provide a robust industrial base and enable the manufacture of various goods and applications used in daily life and modern technologies.[58] Access to certain raw materials in a reliable and unhindered manner is a growing concern in the EU. To address this issue, the European Commission established a list of CRMs, which is reviewed and updated regularly.[59] In 2011, the European Commission published the first EU-wide list of CRMs. The 2020 CRMs list, which combined raw materials of critical importance to the EU economy and the associated supply risk, indicated that 30 elements or groups of elements were in the critical area, up from 14 in 2011, 20 in 2014 and 27 in 2017.[60] Along with bauxite, titanium and strontium, lithium was added to the list for the first time in 2020, demonstrating the region's commitment to growing the battery and electric vehicle manufacturing industries.[61] In 2023, a fifth list of 34 CRMs was published in Annex II of Regulation proposal COM(2023) based on the Study on the Critical Raw Materials for the EU 2023 – Final Report. The considerations used to determine the criticality of the minerals on the 2023 list were link to industry, use in modern technology and the mineral's importance in environmental protection, especially in terms of clean energy technologies.

The global climate change regime primarily drives the EU's critical mineral agenda. The EU is an exemplary region and is leading the fight against climate change through its functionaries to help raise global ambition.[62] It is a highly developed region, with an estimated nominal GDP of $18.8 trillion in 2018, accounting for 22 per cent of the nominal global GDP. The EU invested approximately $174 billion – 1.2 per cent of its GDP in climate change measures in 2019 alone. In 2020, the region committed to apportioning 21 per cent of the total $186.8 billion ($39.2 billion) set aside to finance projects into measures addressing climate change.[63] The EU is a signatory to the Paris Agreement, which aims to limit global warming below 2°C and pursue efforts to limit it to 1.5°C. In 2008, it set targets for 2020 that included reducing greenhouse gas emissions by 20 per cent (compared to 1990), increasing the share of renewable energy to 20 per cent and making a 20 per cent improvement in energy efficiency.[64] With undertakings like

[58] Kalantzakos (n 31).

[59] P Nurmi, 'Green Mining – a Holistic Concept for Sustainable and Acceptable Mineral Production' [2017] *Annals of Geophysics* 60.

[60] M Girtan, A Wittenberg, ML Grilli, DPS de Oliveira, C Giosuè and ML Ruello, 'The Critical Raw Materials Issue between Scarcity, Supply Risk, and Unique Properties' (2021) 14 *Materials* 1826; European Commission, *Study on the EU's List of Critical Raw Materials (2020) Final Report* (2020).

[61] IEA (n 53).

[62] C Dupont, 'The EU's Collective Securitisation of Climate Change' (2019) 42(2) *West European Politics* 369.

[63] C Farand, 'EU 2020 Budget Boosts Climate Action Spending' (*Climate Home News*, 19 November 2019) www.climatechangenews.com/2019/11/19/eu-2020-budget-boosts-climate-action-spending/.

[64] European Commission, 2020 Climate & Energy Package, https://eur-lex.europa.eu/EN/legal-content/summary/2020-climate-and-energy-package.html.

the European Green Deal, Renewable Energy Directive EU/2023/2413 and the EU Batteries Regulation (Regulation (EU) 2023/1542), the EU is a global driver of climate change and circular economy, thus offering the Global North perspective to this book.

The climate change agenda is primarily driven by the European Union, and it concerns the security of supply and economic importance of raw materials. The EU has implemented measures such as encouraging circular resource use, which includes establishing advanced recycling capacity, bolstering efforts to source sustainable products and promoting material substitution technology innovation. Some of the policies and measures are as follows.

4.2.5.1. *Circular Economy Action Plan*[65]

In March 2020, the European Commission adopted a new circular economy action plan (CEAP). It is a critical component of the European Green Deal, the EU's new agenda for sustainable growth. The EU's transition to a circular economy will alleviate pressure on natural resources and spur long-term growth and employment.[66] Additionally, it is a prerequisite for meeting the EU's 2050 climate neutrality goal and halting biodiversity loss. The new action plan details initiatives spanning the product's entire life cycle. It focuses on product design, encourages circular economy processes and promotes sustainable consumption to prevent waste and reuse resources in the EU economy for as long as possible.[67] It introduces legislative and non-legislative measures focusing on areas where EU action adds value. The first action plan was adopted in December 2015, followed by a series of other actions. There were proposals to amend the Waste Framework Directive of 2008 to incorporate measures to optimise the management of waste containing significant amounts of critical raw materials.[68] Further, the European Green Deal was adopted in December 2015; the CEAP in March 2020; a proposal for a new regulation on sustainable batteries in December 2020; and in February 2021, the EU launched the Global Alliance on Circular Economy and Resource Efficiency.

4.2.5.2. *The European Green Deal*[69]

The EU set the 2019 European Green Deal, whose overarching goal is to transform the EU into the world's first 'climate-neutral bloc' by 2050 by regulating

[65] European Commission, 'Circular Economy Action Plan: For a Cleaner and more Competitive Europe' COM(2020) 98 final, https://ec.europa.eu/environment/pdf/circular-economy/new_circular_economy_action_plan.pdf.

[66] ibid.

[67] ibid.

[68] European Commission, 'Report on Critical Raw Materials in the Circular Economy' (2018).

[69] European Green Deal, https://eur-lex.europa.eu/legal-content/EN/TXT/?qid=1576150542719&uri=COM%3A2019%3A640%3AFIN.

various sectors, including agriculture, oceans, industry, biodiversity, construction, transportation and energy. To achieve the Green Deal objectives, the European Commission adopted a set of proposals on 14 July 2021 to adapt the EU's economic sectors to achieve a net greenhouse gas emissions reduction of at least 55 per cent by 2030 relative to 1990 levels.[70] The strategy also includes a CEAP, a review and the possible revision of all relevant climate-related policy instruments.

4.2.5.3. The EU Raw Materials Initiative[71]

The Raw Materials Initiative aims to ensure the EU economy's access to raw materials. This strategy is founded on three pillars: (i) sustainable raw material sourcing from global markets; (ii) sustainable domestic raw material production; and (iii) resource efficiency and secondary raw material supply. In 2012, the European innovation partnership on raw materials was launched, reinforcing the policy. The European Commission also adopted a revised EU industrial policy strategy in September 2017 that emphasised the critical role of raw materials, more so critical minerals, in ensuring the competitiveness of all industrial value chains for the region's economy.[72] In September 2020, the European Commission published a set of policy documents to increase the security and sustainability of Europe's raw material supply and aligned the previous policy recommendations with new 2030 and 2050 climate targets.[73]

4.2.5.4. European Battery Alliance

The European Commission, EU Member States, industry and academia formed the European Battery Alliance (EBA) in 2017. The EBA's mission is to develop an innovative, competitive and sustainable European battery value chain; and one of the six priority areas is ensuring access to raw materials for batteries.

4.2.5.5. The EU Batteries Regulation

The EU Batteries Regulation[74] amended Directive 2008/98/EC and Regulation (EU) 2019/1020 and repealed Directive 2006/66/EC. The Batteries Regulation aims

[70] European Commission, 'Delivering the European Green Deal', https://ec.europa.eu/info/strategy/priorities-2019–2024/european-green-deal/delivering-european-green-deal_en.

[71] European Commission, 'The Raw Materials Initiative: Meeting Our Critical Needs for Growth and Jobs in Europe' COM(2008) 699.

[72] Commission to the European Parliament, the European Council, the Council, the European Economic and Social Committee and the Committee of the Regions and the European Investment Bank, 'Investing in a Smart, Innovative and Sustainable Industry: A Renewed EU Industrial Policy Strategy' COM(2017) 479 final.

[73] European Commission, 'Critical Raw Materials Resilience: Charting a Path Towards Greater Security and Sustainability' COM(2020) 474 final, https://ec.europa.eu/docsroom/documents/42849.

[74] Regulation (EU) 2023/1542 of the European Parliament and of the Council of 12 July 2023 concerning batteries and waste batteries.

to address social, economic and environmental concerns about all types of batteries, including those imported into the bloc. The sustainability standards relate to electric vehicle safety and rechargeable industrial batteries, including carbon footprint, QR code, recycled raw material content, battery passport, and electrochemical performance and durability. The regulation covers the entire battery life cycle, is directly applicable to the supply chains for cobalt, lithium, lead and nickel, and follows the circular economy principles of the EU and the EBA's objectives.

4.3. The Critical Minerals Value Chain

4.3.1. Overview

Critical minerals have always been valuable to human and international relations in the security, health and automotive industries. The demand for these minerals has spiked recently due to the need to address climate change and achieve the energy transition.[75] Both the DRC and Zambia are endowed with critical minerals, but most importantly, they have massive copper and cobalt deposits. However, the countries have been subject to the mining sector's human rights, fiscal and child labour concerns. Even though both countries are heavily reliant on natural resource-based development, they have suffered the resource curse due to the vast mineral presence in their territories. Also, the DRC and Zambia are members of the Southern African Development Community (SADC), depend on the same South African transport corridor and are the biggest recipients of the BRI from China. China plays a key role in the copper–cobalt value chain. Africa's biggest critical mineral investor, primarily through its BRI, has the most extensive mineral processing facilities.

DRC has a small share of global mined copper processing, at six per cent.[76] It remains the world's largest producer of mined cobalt, accounting for approximately 70 per cent of global cobalt mine production in 2020.[77] China was the world's largest cobalt refiner, with most of its output derived from cobalt imported from the DRC. China was also the world's largest consumer of cobalt, with the rechargeable battery industry accounting for more than 80 per cent of its consumption.[78] China also dominates the global cobalt chemical production and refining industry, refining and exporting cobalt concentrates derived from small-scale and large-scale mining. The DRC is the world's leading cobalt producer, and other producers include Australia, Russia, the Philippines and Cuba.[79]

[75] RJ Heffron, 'The Role of Justice in Developing Critical Minerals' (2020) 7(3) *The Extractive Industries and Society* 855.
[76] US Geological Survey, *Mineral Commodity Summaries 2021* (2021) https://doi.org/10.3133/mcs2021.
[77] ibid.
[78] ibid.
[79] ibid.

On the other hand, the copper supply chain is not geographically concentrated at the refining stage. China continues to be the world's largest copper smelter; it also has a 40 per cent share of the global copper refining capacity. Copper produced in the DRC is exported as ore and concentrates in blisters and cathodes, with the ore being refined primarily in China or Zambia.[80]

International commodities traders play a critical role in sourcing copper products exported from the DRC, which they deliver to smelters, refiners and fabricators for further processing and value addition.[81] Certain refiners have significant copper mining, concentration and refining operations in the DRC and other countries. China has approximately 41–48 per cent of global semi-fabricated copper production capacity and consumption of refined copper.[82] Japan, Russia, the USA and Chile also have copper refining capacity, while Germany, Japan and the USA deal in fabricated copper products, receiving concentrates and cathodes from the DRC and China. Jinchuan Group, for example, operates one copper and cobalt mine in the DRC and is the world's fourteenth largest and China's second largest copper refinery.[83] Other companies such as Glencore are engaged in copper mining, refining and international marketing. Other businesses keep cobalt fine refining facilities in China but manufacture copper cathodes in the DRC.[84]

Though China has the most processing facilities among the importers of critical minerals, the EU is the biggest end user. The EU and the UK aim to be carbon-neutral by 2050.[85] Countries like Norway and the UK have gone further to devise fiscal incentives (such as tax reductions) that would promote electric vehicles.[86] Countries like Germany, France, Italy and Spain have pledged to ban vehicles with internal combustion engines by 2030.[87] Such policies drive up the demand for critical minerals in the sub-Saharan African region. However, the region has no mechanism to retain value for its benefit. It leaves host communities largely relying on artisanal mining, bringing about violence and an influx of desperate workers for these minerals.

[80] ibid.

[81] OECD, 'Interconnected Supply Chains: A Comprehensive Look at Due Diligence Challenges and Opportunities Sourcing Cobalt and Copper from the Democratic Republic of the Congo' (2019) https://mneguidelines.oecd.org/Interconnected-supply-chains-acomprehensive-look-at-due-diligence-challenges-and-opportunitiessourcing-cobalt-and-copper-from-the-DRC.pdf.

[82] ICSG, *The World Copper Factbook 2018* (International Copper Study Group, 2018).

[83] Jinchuan Group International Resources, 'Business Overview' (*Jinchuan-intl.com*, 2021) www.jinchuan-intl.com/en/business_overview/.

[84] OECD, *Interconnected Supply Chains* (n 82).

[85] M Ram, A Aghahosseini and C Breyer, 'Job Creation During the Global Energy Transition Towards a 100% Renewable Power System by 2050' (2020) 151 *Technological Forecasting and Social Change* 119682.

[86] E Haites, 'A Dual-Track Transition to Global Carbon Pricing: Excellent Idea but Doomed to Fail' (2020) 20(10) *Climate Policy* 1344.

[87] ibid.

4.3.2. Gaps in the Value Chain

Different stages of the copper–cobalt value chain face distinct challenges.[88] At every stage of the value chain, several challenges arise – from the investment decisions and actual production in the DRC and Zambia; the refining and processing stage in China; consumption in the EU; and finally waste management and mine closure in the EU. Figure 4 summarises the major challenges and concerns in the copper–cobalt value chain, which are further elaborated on in the text.

Figure 4 The major challenges and concerns in the copper and cobalt value chain

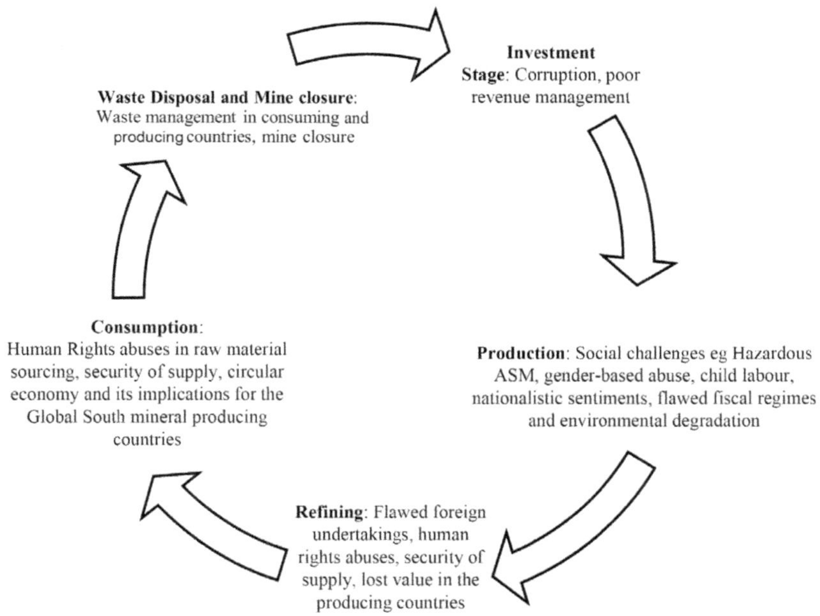

Source: S Nakanwagi, 'Critical Minerals and the Global Energy Transition: Recognising Global South Perspectives' (2023) 4(1–2) *Global Energy Law and Sustainability* 115.

4.3.2.1. *The Investment Stage and Production Stage*

The multinational corporations mainly initiate upstream investment decisions, but with ramifications in the mineral-producing states, in this case, the

[88] This is because the different segments of the value chain are in different states, which are subject to different sovereign powers and national circumstances. See the principle of permanent sovereignty over natural resources in AE Bastida, *The Law and Governance of Mining and Minerals: A Global Perspective* (Bloomsbury Publishing, 2020) ch 3.

DRC and Zambia. The state wholly owns underground minerals in both the DRC[89] and Zambia,[90] and the states reserve the right to issue mining rights for prospecting, exploration, production and disposal of minerals, among other things. Hence, the states reserve the right to determine how these mineral rights are given and under what conditions. The stage is crucial to the value chain because it determines how the mineral rights from prospecting to production are awarded as well as the terms and conditions of the mining rights, such as taxation, local content, environmental protection and disposal of the minerals.[91]

This stage of the value chain is of concern due to the concerns presented by the critical minerals' global valuation, governance, socio-legal and environmental issues, and the distribution of the benefits and ills occasioned by the copper and cobalt resources. Still, while mine closure occurs at the end of the mining activities, the ramifications of mining persist in the producing countries and sites of production.[92] The issues at the production stage range from social, environmental, corruption, ill management of revenues and the poor fiscal regimes which fail to capture value. For example, the DRC suffered conflict and political instability during the transition from President Kabila to President Tshisekedi in 2019. On the other hand, Zambia's failed fiscal regime has robbed the 18 million people from the Central African Copperbelt.[93]

(a) Critical Minerals Investments and Global Valuation

Climate change and the clean energy agenda are currently driving investment decisions in the critical mineral value chain.[94] For example, all 193 parties to the Paris Agreement have issued at least a first Nationally Determined Contribution (NDC) to the United Nations Framework Convention on Climate Change (UNFCCC). About 90 per cent of these pertain to renewable energy action in the power sector, while 71 per cent include quantifiable targets for renewable energy generation.[95] As the world shifts from the use of fossil fuels (the energy transition), the increase in clean energy investments is inevitably driving investments in the critical minerals that serve as the raw materials for the industry.[96]

[89] Act No 007/2002 of 11 July 2002 establishing the Mining Code, as amended by Act No 18-001 of 9 March 2018.

[90] Mines and Minerals Development Act No 11 of 2015.

[91] J Katz and C Pietrobelli, 'Natural Resource-Based Growth, Global Value Chains and Domestic Capabilities in the Mining Industry' (2018) 58 *Resources Policy* 11.

[92] S Nakanwagi, 'Mine Closure and Justice Implications' (*IJPIEL*, 13 August 2021) https://ijpiel.com/index.php/2021/08/13/mine-closure-and-justice-implications/.

[93] M Larmer, 'Nation-Making at the Border: Zambian Diplomacy in the Democratic Republic of Congo' (2019) 61(1) *Comparative Studies in Society and History* 145.

[94] IEA (n 53).

[95] IRENA, *Renewable Energy and Climate Pledges: Five Years After the Paris Agreement* (International Renewable Energy Agency, 2019); see also the UNFCCC, Nationally Determined Contributions under the Paris Agreement: Synthesis Report by the secretariat. United Nations Convention on Climate Change FCCC/PA/CMA/2021/8, Conference of the Parties serving as the meeting of the Parties to the Paris Agreement, Third Session, Glasgow, 31 November 2021.

[96] IEA (n 53).

Investments in critical minerals have always followed the demand patterns of the Global North. During the colonialism and nationalism era, industrial minerals like gold, aluminium, platinum and nickel were needed by industry. Since the rise of climate change awareness and consciousness in the 2000s, minerals like copper, cobalt, lithium, nickel and rare earth elements are in high demand to fuel the energy transition. Again, after the COVID-19 pandemic, there were calls for a green economic recovery,[97] which requires critical minerals. Similarly, the determinations of what amounts to critical minerals have followed the same patterns. For example, the US Federal Emergency Management Agency Report of 1982, the US National Research Council Reports of 2008 and the EU Commission Reports of 2010, 2014, 2017 and 2020 determine which minerals are critical by considering the prevailing national or regional circumstances. For example, 26 of the 27 CRMs in 2017 were confirmed on the 2020 list; bauxite, lithium and titanium are three CRMs on the 2020 list that were not considered vital on the 2017 list. On the other hand, helium was crucial in the 2017 CRM list but was not included in 2020.[98]

These critical mineral valuations and studies have a multiplier effect on the demand for the minerals and, consequently, the level of investment in the value chains. For example, the EU valuations show the importance of the critical minerals for the region to deliver on the climate ambition of the European Green Deal. According to a European Commission and Joint Research Centre study, projections show that for batteries for electric vehicles and energy storage, the EU would require up to 18 times more lithium and five times more cobalt in 2030.[99] By 2050, the region will need approximately 60 times more lithium and 15 times more cobalt than the current supply to the whole EU economy. Further, demand for rare earths used in permanent magnets, such as those used in electric vehicles, robots and wind turbines, is likely to increase tenfold.[100]

(b) Weak Governance

The major setback during the investment stage in SSA is rampant corruption, which is mainly prevalent in countries with weak political systems.[101] The DRC, for instance, faces significant levels of illicit financial flows, and as a result the country's development is jeopardised, with a sizeable portion of its population living in impoverished circumstances.[102] It has, for instance, attracted massive

[97] ibid; Heffron (n 76).
[98] European Commission, '2020 Study on the Review of the EU's list of Critical Raw Materials' (2020) https://rmis.jrc.ec.europa.eu/uploads/CRM_2020_Report_Final.pdf.
[99] European Commission, 'Critical Materials for Strategic Technologies and Sectors in the EU – A Foresight Study' (2020) https://rmis.jrc.ec.europa.eu/uploads/CRMs_for_Strategic_Technologies_and_Sectors_in_the_EU_2020.pdf.
[100] ibid.
[101] E Oshionebo, *Mineral Mining in Africa: Legal and Fiscal Regimes* (Routledge, 2020).
[102] SA Igbatayo, 'Combating Illicit Financial Flows from Africa's Extractive Industries and Implications for Good Governance' (2019) 44(3) *Africa Development/Afrique et Développement* 55.

foreign investments in the extractive sector, but it is still subjected to cruel corporate practices and does not follow global standards of due diligence. For example, Glencore, a substantial Swiss mining company, operates in the DRC through its subsidiary Katanga Mining Limited (KML).[103] KML owns two cobalt-producing sites, Kamoto and Mutanda, which are joint ventures with the state mining company.[104] Glencore obtained full ownership of the Mutanda assets through stake purchases from Gecamines and Dan Gertler (a US-sanctioned businessman).[105] The US Department of Treasury accused Gertler of using his 'close relationship' with the previous President of the DRC, Joseph Kabila, to act as a middleman for the cobalt and copper assets in the country.[106] Glencore is currently the subject of court action in the USA over its involvement with Gertler in the Congolese deals.[107] Under President Kabila, the country's public institutions were weak and constrained by powerful officials who routinely abused their public positions for private gain, which presented Gertler with an opportunity to take advantage of the loopholes and lax governance in the DRC's banks, corporate registries and mining sector to circumvent the sanction against him.[108]

(c) Social Challenges

The production stage faces several challenges, ranging from hazardous artisanal and small-scale mining (ASM) practices, child labour, gender-based violence and segregation, high crime rates, prostitution and environmental degradation. The DRC produces 70 per cent of the global cobalt, 15–30 per cent of which is by ASM.[109] Unregulated hazardous ASM has harmed the cobalt mining industry by orchestrating human rights violations such as women's exploitation, child labour and violence.[110] Some scholars liken it to modern-day slavery.[111]

[103] B Doherty, P Blum and O Zihlmann, 'The Inside Story of Glencore's Hidden Dealings in DRC' *The Guardian* (5 November 2017) www.theguardian.com/business/2017/nov/05/the-inside-story-of-glencore-hidden-dealings-in-drc.

[104] ibid.

[105] C Peyer, P Feeney and F Mercier, 'PR or Progress? Glencore's Corporate Responsibility in the Democratic Republic of the Congo' (Rights and Accountability in Development, 2014) 1, www.raiduk.org/sites/default/files/glencore-report-June2014.pdf.

[106] ibid.

[107] *Henry Church VI & Ors v Glencore Plc & Ors* Case No 2:18-cv-11477-SDW-CLW United States District Court District of New Jersey, www.stewartslaw.com/wp-content/uploads/2018/07/20200107-Amended-Class-Action-Complaint-Glencore.pdf.

[108] Global Witness, 'Undermining Sanctions: Evidence Suggests Scandal-Hit Billionaire Dan Gertler Is Trying to Dodge US Sanctions Using a Suspected Money Laundering Network' (2020) www.globalwitness.org/documents/19912/Undermining_Sanctions_-_July_2020.pdf.

[109] WEF, 'Making Mining Safe and Fair: Artisanal Cobalt Extraction in the Democratic Republic of the Congo', White Paper (World Economic Forum, 2020) www3.weforum.org/docs/WEF_Making_Mining_Safe_2020.pdf.

[110] ILO, 'Child Labour in Mining and Global Supply Chains' (International Labour Organisation, 2019) www.ilo.org/wcmsp5/groups/public/---asia/---ro-bangkok/---ilo-manila/documents/publication/wcms_720743.pdf.

[111] BK Sovacool, 'When Subterranean Slavery Supports Sustainability Transitions? Power, Patriarchy, and Child Labor in Artisanal Congolese Cobalt Mining' (2021) 8(1) *The Extractive Industries and Society* 271.

The DRC cobalt industry has caused social and environmental impacts that raise concern for the Congolese people's well-being. Further, abandoned mines in the DRC have led to a damaging legacy and environmental degradation. There is waterways pollution, use of toxic metals during dam construction, a build-up of silt, poor sanitation and effluent dumped in rivers, all of which were hangovers from past mining operations before the establishment of stringent mine closure regulations.[112] Moreover, ASM practices have a detrimental impact on the environment, which creates social and financial challenges that seriously hinder the nation's sustainable growth. In ASM areas, sanitation and essential health services are often lacking. Drug addiction, alcoholism and communicable diseases are continually growing.[113] Women and children are often involved in ASM operations and have their own health, physical and psychological problems. Host communities have little opportunity for legal remedy, considering that ASM is illegal and that monitoring and enforcement of regulations are hampered by informality, the remote location of mine operations and a lack of resources.[114]

(d) Environmental Challenges

Mining in mineral-producing countries continues to wreak havoc on the environment. Corruption, unaccountable extraction processes, the locations of the mines in environmentally vulnerable places and a lack of enforcement of mining laws contribute to the country's mining being an environmental disaster. Deforestation, dust/air pollution, eg in DRC's Katanga province,[115] landslides, tailing pollution[116] and fugitive emissions are just some of the challenges. Forty-three people were killed in 2019 in a landslide at Glencore's largest copper and cobalt mine in the DRC; the catastrophe happened at the KOV open pit, when terraces overlooking the main mine collapsed, forcing rocks to fall on miners working illegally at the site.[117] In Zambia, the mining activities have also led to significant environmental problems, namely sulphur dioxide (SO_2) and particulate matter emissions from smelters, heavy-metal effluents released into water streams and rivers, and siltation of local rivers like the Kafue river and other water bodies such as the underground aquifers used for drinking water near the mining town of Chingola.[118]

[112] Otamonga and Poté (n 12).

[113] ibid.

[114] SS Sharma and A Manthiram, 'Towards More Environmentally and Socially Responsible Batteries' (2020) 13(11) *Energy & Environmental Science* 4087.

[115] B Ngounou, 'Africa: The Impact of Mining on the Environment' (*Afrik21*, 10 June 2021) www.afrik21.africa/en/africa-the-impact-of-mining-on-the-environment/.

[116] AT Kaniki and K Tumba, 'Management of Mineral Processing Tailings and Metallurgical Slags of the Congolese Copperbelt: Environmental Stakes and Perspectives' (2019) 210 *Journal of Cleaner Production* 1406.

[117] N Hume, 'Death Toll at DRC Mine Rises to 43' *Financial Times* (2019) www.ft.com/content/ad0aafba-99a9-11e9-8cfb-30c211dcd229.

[118] AM Knoblauch, A Farnham, HR Zabré, M Owuor, C Archer, K Nduna, M Chisanga, L Zulu, G Musunka, J Utzinger and MJ Divall, 'Community Health Impacts of the Trident Copper Mine Project in Northwestern Zambia: Results from Repeated Cross-Sectional Surveys' (2020) 17(10) *International Journal of Environmental Research and Public Health* 3633.

Mineral mining consumes a large amount of water, resulting in the depletion of available water resources. Additionally, the areas are susceptible to water pollution; for example, mining waste rock frequently contains sulphide minerals, which form an acidic solution containing metals when combined with air and water. Acid mine drainage occurs when mining activity accelerates this process, and it has a detrimental effect on the environment, wreaking havoc on aquatic plant communities, fish species and humans. In the DRC, the Shinkolobwe, Lwisha and Kansonga rivers in the province of Katanga have been affected by mining activities.[119] In Zambia, soil and mango fruit grown near copper and cobalt mines were found to contain metals above the permissible limit.[120]

(e) Precarious Nationalisation and Privatisation Policies

Zambia experienced turmoil due to the failed nationalisation undertakings in the 1960s and 1970s, which saw the government obtaining 51 per cent and subsequently 60.3 per cent ownership of the existing mines.[121] This failure was attributed mainly to the global decline of copper prices at the time. Other reasons included the exorbitant price paid to the private sector for mining shares, the clientelist network surrounding the state mining system and the investment of Zambia Consolidated Copper Mines funds in inefficient parastatals outside the mining sector.[122] Following the failed nationalisation objectives and pressure from international forces such as the World Bank, Zambia's government began privatising copper mines in 1992. A new Mining Act – the Mines and Minerals Act, 1995 – was promulgated in 1995. It provided foreign investors with tax incentives in the form of reduced tax rates. For example, while the rest of the economy paid 35 per cent income tax, the mining sector paid only 25 per cent.[123] Loss carry-forward provisions were permitted for a period of 15–20 years.[124] Recurring and capital inputs were exempt, and interest costs and repatriated dividend income were tax-deductible. Also, the Act empowered the government to enter 'development agreements' (DAs) with specific businesses.[125]

[119] DM Kalonda, AK Tshikongo, FK Kule-koto, O Luboya, CKB Numbi, DK Kalonda, YK Bwalya, HM Cansa, AL Otshudi and ZL Kalala, 'Impact of Mining on Water of the Rivers Shinkolobwe, Lwisha and Kansonga in the Province of Katanga (DRC)' (2017) 3(2) *Journal of Medical Research* 71.

[120] P Kayika, SM Siachoono, C Kalinda and JM Kwenye, 'An Investigation of Concentrations of Copper, Cobalt and Cadmium Minerals in Soils and Mango Fruits Growing on Konkola Copper Mine Tailings Dam in Chingola, Zambia' (2017) 1(103) *Archival Science* 2.

[121] Unceta (n 22).

[122] P Collier, 'Zambia: A Time for Big Opportunities and Tough Decisions' in C Adam, P Collier, M Gondwe (eds), *Zambia: Building Prosperity from Resource Wealth* (Oxford University Press, 2014) 15–29.

[123] Sikamo et al (n 17).

[124] ibid.

[125] J Lungu, 'Copper Mining Agreements in Zambia: Renegotiation or Law Reform?' (2008) 35(117) *Review of African Political Economy* 403.

These agreements provided for additional tax incentives compared to those contained in the Act.

Due to the incentives extended to mining companies and investors, the privatisation of Zambia's copper mines increased foreign direct investment in the economy.[126] Regrettably, subsequent development agreements with mining companies were detrimental to the national public interest,[127] as they ignored the welfare of Copperbelt communities and the wider Zambian population.[128] Despite the increase in global copper prices, mining companies continued to provide reduced services to communities, compelling civil society to press the government to renegotiate the agreements.[129] Further, companies reaped substantial benefits from secret DAs during the windfall period of copper price increases between 2002 and 2008.[130] The government also entered fiscal stability agreements that committed it to not altering mineral fiscal policies for 15–20 years.[131]

Today, the government is making a U-turn on privatisation, going by its current actions. The previous President Edgar Lungu pushed for Zambians to acquire majority stakes in selected strategic mines to reap additional benefits from the country's mineral wealth.[132] Zambia Copper Consolidated Mines, the state-owned mining company, acquired 90 per cent of Mopani Copper Mines from Glencore in January 2021 for a nominal price of $1, which price does not accurately reflect the actual cost of the purchase.[133] Mopani Copper Mines owed up to $1.5 billion, which was included in the deal. The sale occurred after Glencore, which has been hard hit by the COVID pandemic and low copper prices, declared force majeure in April 2020, allowing it to disregard contractual obligations and close its Zambian mines.[134] Lungu's government responded by threatening to revoke the company's mining licence. Also, minimal information about the $1.5 billion (€1.2 billion) transaction has been made public.

(f) Flawed Fiscal Regimes

In 2008, the Zambian government promulgated another new Mining Act (Mines and Minerals Development Act, No 7 of 2008 – now repealed) which cancelled

[126] A Caramento, 'Cultivating Backward Linkages to Zambia's Copper Mines: Debating the Design of, and Obstacles to, Local Content' (2020) 7(2) *The Extractive Industries and Society* 310.

[127] M Gondwe and EM Pamu, 'Growth Strategies for Zambia: Harnessing Natural Resource Wealth for Sustainable Growth' in Adam et al (n 123) 3–14.

[128] J Lungu, 'Socio-economic Change and Natural Resource Exploitation: A Case Study of the Zambian Copper Mining Industry' (2008) 25(5) *Development Southern Africa* 543.

[129] ibid.

[130] ibid.

[131] ibid; Lungu, 'Copper Mining' (n 126); SP Ng'ambi, 'Stabilisation Clauses and the Zambian Windfall Tax' (2010) 1(1) *Zambia Social Science Journal*.

[132] K Mapila, 'Copper Can Save Zambia – Capitalizing on Rising Demand Will Have Long-Term Benefits if Handled Properly' (*The World Today*, 2021) www.chathamhouse.org/publications/the-world-today/2021-08/copper-can-save-zambia.

[133] ibid.

[134] ibid.

the DAs entered into during the privatisation undertakings.[135] It unilaterally imposed and ratified windfall taxes on large-scale mining companies to achieve a larger share of profits. The country went from having one of the lowest average effective tax rates globally to having an above-average effective tax rate and government take.[136] The government increased income tax and mineral royalty rates, reduced capital allowances and reinstated withholding tax. The mineral fiscal regime had the following tax structures:[137] a mineral royalty of three per cent of gross revenue; a 30 per cent corporate income tax; and a 15 per cent withholding tax on interest, management fees, royalties and other income. A windfall tax was also implemented, which was to be triggered at various cobalt and copper price thresholds.[138]

Furthermore, a variable profit tax of 15 per cent was imposed where the taxable income-to-sales ratio exceeded eight per cent, while capital allowances were reduced from 100 per cent to 25 per cent.[139] These fiscal measures resulted in a significant increase in mining revenues, which increased from a pitiful $20 million in 2007 to an estimated $400 million in 2008.[140] However, as international copper prices fell in the second half of 2008 and a new leadership was elected, the government repealed the windfall tax in 2009. The Zambian government recognised the country's institutions as being too weak and incapable of controlling pricing.[141] Soon after the windfall tax on copper prices was eliminated, copper production increased dramatically, but with little benefit to the Zambian people.[142]

4.3.2.2. The Processing/Refining Stage

China dominates the copper and cobalt processing stage.[143] For example, refining for the technology and electric vehicle industries involves companies engaged in processing cobalt ore to create chemicals such as cobalt sulphate. They also combine the chemicals with other metals, such as nickel and manganese, to create the cathode element of a lithium-ion battery, assembling the cathodes with other

[135] M Mukwasa, 'When Is Compensation Payable for Breach of a Stabilisation Clause? The Case for the Cancelled Mining Development Agreements in Zambia' (Doctoral Dissertation, University of Pretoria, 2010).

[136] O Lundstøl and J Isaksen, 'Zambia's Mining Windfall Tax' (UNU-WIDER, 2018) WIDER Working Paper 2018/51; L Rakner, 'Tax Bargains in Unlikely Places: The Politics of Zambian Mining Taxes' (2017) 4(3) *The Extractive Industries and Society* 525.

[137] Sikamo et al (n 17).

[138] ibid.

[139] ibid.

[140] Oshionebo (n 102).

[141] A Kabandula and J Seekings, 'Donor Influence, the Minister of Finance and Welfare Policy Reform in Zambia, 2003–11' (2016) CSSR Working Paper 395.

[142] C Adam and AM Simpasa, 'Copper Mining in Zambia: Plundered Nations?' [2011] *Successes and Failures in Natural Resource Extraction* 304.

[143] P Andersson, 'Chinese Assessments of "Critical" and "Strategic" Raw Materials: Concepts, Categories, Policies, and Implications' (2020) 7(1) *The Extractive Industries and Society* 127.

components to create battery cells and batteries.[144] The refining industry in China relies heavily on sub-Saharan Africa with most of the raw materials sourced from the DRC and Zambia, where China has a strong presence.[145] Securing the supply of minerals thus drives most of China's activities in the resource-rich countries.

However, there has been some debate around these engagements, with China being implicated in human rights breaches in the areas of operation, including the DRC and Zambia. Between 2013 and 2020, the Business and Human Rights Centre documented 679 allegations of human rights violations in connection with Chinese business conduct abroad and 102 company responses to these allegations.[146] Conflicts between Zambian miners and their Chinese bosses are not unusual in Chinese-owned mines.[147] In 2005, an explosion at a factory at the Chinese-owned Chambishi Copper Mine killed at least 50 Zambians, while in 2010, Chinese investors were accused of shooting Zambian miners at the Collum Coal Mine.[148] Further, Chinese companies, including Gecamines, have been named in incidences of forced evictions, for example, at Luisha.[149] According to Amnesty International, approximately 300 households were evicted forcibly in 2011 after a Chinese company, Congo International Mining Corporation, was granted the rights to a site in the heart of Luisha, where they had lived since 2007, in order to make way for the construction of a processing plant. Huayou Cobalt Co, Ltd is a significant cobalt refining company in China.[150] However, in its 2016 report, 'This Is What We Die For,' Amnesty International accused Huayou's subsidiary Congo Dongfang Mining International of human rights violations and child labour abuse in their cobalt sourcing practices.[151] This report traced how child labour-tainted cobalt enters the global supply chains.

China has benefited greatly from its processing industry.[152] The refining companies are a source of revenue for the country. They employ a huge portion of the population and are responsible for infrastructural development and technological advancements, among other things. Huayou Cobalt Co, Ltd, for example, has

[144] Farchy and Warren (n 49).

[145] ibid.

[146] Business and Human Rights Centre, '"Going Out" Responsibly: The Human Rights Impact of China's Global Investments (2021) https://media.business-humanrights.org/media/documents/2021_BHRRC_China_Briefing.pdf.

[147] Y Hairong and B Sautman, 'The Beginning of a World Empire'? Contesting the Discourse of Chinese Copper Mining in Zambia' (2013) 39(2) *Modern China* 131.

[148] A Okeowo, 'China, Zambia, and a Clash in a Coal Mine' (*The New Yorker*, 9 October 2013) www.newyorker.com/business/currency/china-zambia-and-a-clash-in-a-coal-mine.

[149] Amnesty International, 'Profits and Loss: Mining and Human Rights in Katanga, Democratic Republic of Congo' (2013) www.amnesty.org/en/wp-content/uploads/2021/06/afr620012013en.pdf.

[150] Amnesty International, 'Chinese Mining Industry Contributes to Abuses in Democratic Republic of the Congo' (2021) www.amnesty.org/en/latest/news/2013/06/chinese-mining-industry-contributes-abuses-democratic-republic-congo/.

[151] Amnesty International, 'Democratic Republic of Congo: "This Is What We Die For": Human Rights Abuses in the Democratic Republic of the Congo Power the Global Trade in Cobalt' (2016) www.amnesty.org/en/wp-content/uploads/2021/05/AFR6231832016ENGLISH.pdf.

[152] S Kalantzakos, *China and the Geopolitics of Rare Earths.* (Oxford University Press, 2017).

developed its processing technology and is a leading supplier of cobalt compounds such as cobalt oxide, cobalt tetroxide, cobalt hydroxide, cobalt carbonate, cobalt monoxide, cobalt hydroxide, cobalt sulphate and cobalt oxalate.[153] Umicore is present on all continents, including China, where, as Umicore (Guangzhou), it also engages in cobalt refining and serves a global customer base. The company's total revenue was expected to reach €3.2 billion in 2020, and it currently employs over 10,859 people globally.[154]

4.3.2.3. The Consumption Stage

The biggest challenge at the consumption stage is for the consumer countries to secure the supply of critical materials for their economies, especially for the energy transition.[155] This explains the huge critical raw materials agenda of the EU. Notwithstanding the EU's increased interest in recycling, domestic production and changing consumption patterns, meeting the region's mineral requirements remains challenging.[156] In 2020, Europe accounted for approximately 15.4 per cent of the global market on a purchasing power parity basis, but mined only five per cent.[157] The EU continues to rely on mineral imports from China and elsewhere to fuel its transitions. There are now concerns about China's increasing influence on the supply chains in the EU and elsewhere in the Global North.[158] In 2008, when China introduced a quota system for rare earth production, it gained control over the global rare earth market and made the rest of the world dependent on it.[159] The quest for the EU region to secure its CRM supply led some of its firms to intensify their sourcing from companies like Umicore, which deals directly with companies in the producing countries.

However, some of these EU companies have been implicated in cases of human rights abuse. For example, Umicore NV (Umicore), a Brussels-based metal and mining trader and a major consumer of cobalt, was cited in the DRC child labour case filed in the US courts. The court documents showed that children worked illegally in DRC mines controlled by Glencore, a UK mining corporation. Cobalt from Glencore-owned mines is allegedly supplied to Umicore. It subsequently sells battery-grade cobalt to Apple, Google, Alphabet, Samsung, Microsoft

[153] Huayou.com, Huayou Cobalt Co Ltd 浙江华友钴业股份有限公司_化工制品, www.huayou.com/.

[154] Umicore.cn. n.d. 主页, www.umicore.cn/.

[155] Y He, 'The Trade–Security Nexus and US Policy Making in Critical Minerals' (2018) 59 *Resources Policy* 238.

[156] ibid.

[157] Y Liu, R Ma, C Guan, B Chen and B Zhang, 'Global Trade Network and CH_4 Emission Outsourcing' (2021) *Science of The Total Environment* 150008.

[158] S Ladislaw and N Tsafos, 'Energy Spheres of Influence' (Center for Strategic and International Studies, 2019).

[159] I Alon, J Chang, C Lattemann, JR McIntyre, W Zhang and Y He, 'Reregulation of China's Rare Earth Production and Export' (2014) 9(2) *International Journal of Emerging Markets* 236.

and LG Chem (which supplies Dell and Tesla).[160] Umicore historically participated in King Leopold II of Belgium's ruthless exploitation of the DRC. The company was founded in 1906 as Union Minière du Haut Katanga to benefit from natural resource exploitation in King Leopold's private colony, the Congo Free State.[161] Glencore and Umicore announced in May 2019 that they had entered into a long-term revolving agreement to safeguard the cobalt supply lines for Umicore's battery material value chains. Sustainability was to be ensured based on Umicore's sustainable procurement framework for cobalt with the aim of eliminating artisanally mined and child labour tainted cobalt. However, Umicore allegedly intentionally mixes cobalt mined by children working in hazardous conditions with other cobalt in the refining process and takes other steps to impair the traceability of the DRC cobalt.[162]

4.3.2.4. Waste Management and Mine Closure

Mineral development generates massive amounts of waste and residues, both during extraction and after consumption, some of which are hazardous to human health and the environment.[163] The consuming countries must deal with the disposal of mineral-containing appliances such as batteries at the end of their usefulness.[164] On the other hand, the producing countries have to deal with the waste generated during mineral extraction, such as tailings management.[165] Further, they must face the ramifications of the end of the mine closure at the end of the production life cycle of the mines. This includes revegetation and returning the sites to a near pre-mining era state to support human activities.[166] It requires the governments to plan to cover the closure costs, such as financial assurances by the mining companies during the investment stage.[167] An exploration permit holder in DRC must submit a plan for the site's restoration upon closure to be considered for exploitation permission.[168] The Mining Code also requires mining

[160] A Kelly, 'Apple and Google Named in US Lawsuit Over Congolese Child Cobalt Mining Deaths' *The Guardian* (16 December 2019) www.theguardian.com/global-development/2019/dec/16/apple-and-google-named-in-us-lawsuit-over-congolese-child-cobalt-mining-deaths.

[161] Case 1:19-cv-03737 Document 1 Filed 15 December 2019, http://iradvocates.org/sites/iradvocates.org/files/stamped%20-Complaint.pdf.

[162] ibid.

[163] F Khelifi, A Melki, Y Hamed, P Adamo and AG Caporale, 'Environmental and Human Health Risk Assessment of Potentially Toxic Elements in Soil, Sediments, and Ore-Processing Wastes from a Mining Area of Southwestern Tunisia' (2020) 42(12) *Environmental Geochemistry and Health* 4125.

[164] C Church, 'Sustainability and Second Life: The Case for Cobalt and Lithium Recycling' (International Institute for Sustainable Development, 2019) www.iisd.org/system/files/publications/sustainability-second-life-cobalt-lithium-recycling.pdf.

[165] IEA (n 53); O Agboola, DE Babatunde, OSI Fayomi, ER Sadiku, P Popoola, L Moropeng, A Yahaya and OA Mamudu, 'A Review on the Impact of Mining Operation: Monitoring, Assessment and Management' [2020] *Results in Engineering* 100181.

[166] Nakanwagi (n 93).

[167] ibid.

[168] Law No 18/001 of 9 March 2018, amending and supplementing law No 007/2002 of 11 July 2002 providing for the Mining Code.

rights holders to obtain a sufficient financial guarantee to cover environmental rehabilitation costs.[169] However, law enforcement is still poor due to the weak governance structures.

4.4. Key Mitigation Measures in the Copper and Cobalt Value Chain

Several initiatives have been undertaken by the government, industry, civil society and international organisations to address the justice concerns in the copper and cobalt value chains. These are summarised in Figure 5, with some initiatives cutting across the various segments of the critical mineral value chain, such as the due diligence frameworks that the EU, for instance, adheres to, while others are specifically tailored to address the ills in the producing countries. The measures taken, as discussed below, reflect the perceptions towards the role of critical minerals in particular countries in the copper–cobalt value chain, with the producing countries focusing on addressing social, economic and environmental governance issues. In contrast, the refining and consuming countries concentrate on the security of supply and the economic importance of the resources.

Figure 5 Summary of key mitigation measures in the copper and cobalt value chain

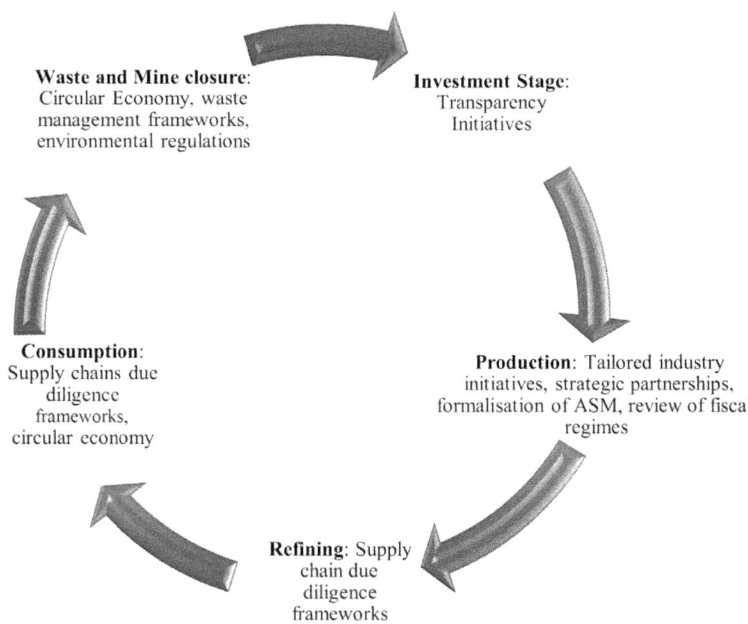

Source: Author's own elaboration.

[169] ibid.

4.4.1. Tailored Industry Initiatives and Strategic Partnerships

Industry initiatives to end child labour, especially in the DRC, have provided some measure of redress. For instance, the Fair Cobalt Alliance (FCA) is a collaborative action plan developed by The Impact Facility, Fairphone, Signify and Huayou Cobalt to assist organisations throughout the supply chain in engaging with and contributing to the transition to a 'fairer' production system.[170] Other members include the Responsible Cobalt Initiative; Glencore; Sono Motors; Lifesaver; the Miller Center for Social Entrepreneurship; and the Centre Arrupe pour la Recherche et la Formation.[171] The FCA seeks to address the intolerable socio-economic and working conditions that employees in the cobalt supply chain face. It strives to accomplish three objectives through collaboration with the DRC's national and provincial governments, civil society and technical partners.[172] These are: (i) expanding the supply of more ethically sourced cobalt by promoting the professionalisation of artisanal mine management and establishing safer and more environmentally responsible sites; (ii) contributing to eliminating child labour in the Kolwezi mining zone by assisting ASM operators in establishing credible control and monitoring mechanisms to keep children out of the mines and promoting child enrolment in school and youth access to education vocational training; and (iii) increasing household incomes through investments in community programmes for sustainable livelihoods besides mining, such as agriculture, entrepreneurship and business literacy.

Additionally, there are emerging industry efforts to eliminate child labour from the value chain, especially in DRC's cobalt mining industry. The London Metal Exchange (LME) adopted mineral sourcing standards requiring companies to address concerns over child labour.[173] The LME's standards adhere to the responsible sourcing guidelines of the Organisation for Economic Co-operation and Development (OECD), requiring companies trading on the LME to address child labour risks in their supply chains.[174] Companies that mine minerals and manufacture metals are required to demonstrate their commitment to responsible mineral sourcing.[175] In addition to addressing child labour, the LME has a policy

[170] See The Impact Facility, Fair Cobalt Alliance (FCA), www.theimpactfacility.com/commodities/cobalt/fair-cobalt-alliance/.

[171] ibid.

[172] The Impact Facility, 'Digging for Change Report – Towards a Responsible Cobalt Supply Chain' (2020) www.theimpactfacility.com/resources/downloads#cobalt.

[173] LME, 'LME Partners with Charities Pact and The Impact Facility to Fund Two Responsible Sourcing Projects' (London Metal Exchange, 2021) www.lme.com/News/Press-releases/2021/LME-partners-with-charities-Pact-and-The-Impact-Facility-to-fund-two-responsible-sourcing-projects.

[174] LME, 'LME Responsible Sourcing – Setting the Global Standard' (London Metal Exchange, 2019) www.lme.com/-/media/Files/About/Responsibility/Responsible-Sourcing/issued/LME-responsible-sourcing-October-2019.pdf?la=en-GB.

[175] ibid.

that prohibits discrimination between large-scale mining (LSM) and ASM to encourage sourcing from ASM mines.[176] Accordingly, the LME disputed a causal link between a brand's sourcing and its price being solely related to the type of mining employed, whether ASM or LSM, suggesting instead that a price discount associated with responsible sourcing could be due to any number of supply chain risks.[177]

The DRC is also benefiting from strategic partnerships with leading global entities to address the most pressing mining industry issues. For instance, the United Nations Children's Fund (UNICEF) and the Global Battery Alliance established the Fund for the Prevention of Child Labour in Mining Communities in November 2020, with a focus on the DRC's copperbelt in the Lualaba and Haut-Katanga provinces. This campaign aimed to raise $21 million over three years from public and private partners to fund a series of initiatives addressing the root causes of child labour in mining communities.[178] The funds would be administrated and programmed exclusively by UNICEF and implemented in collaboration with the DRC's government and civil society organisations.[179]

Even with all the advancements made by the government, industry and other stakeholders, children in the Republic of the Congo are still subjected to the most heinous forms of child labour.[180] In 2019, the Republic of the Congo made modest progress toward eliminating the most heinous forms of child labour; the government approved comprehensive anti-trafficking legislation. Existing programmes fail to address the full extent of child labour in all relevant sectors. Information on children's work is minimal, as the Republic of the Congo has never conducted a national child labour survey or similar research.[181]

4.4.2. Formalisation of the Artisanal and Small-Scale Mining Measures

The DRC has embarked on a drive to formalise the ASM sector to mitigate its associated negative impacts – both social and environmental. According to the OECD, two types of formalisation projects are currently underway. The first is where a mining company, the permit holder or operator, enters into a supply agreement with a cooperative on the formalised site.[182] The supply agreements

[176] ibid.
[177] ibid.
[178] UNICEF, 'Ground-breaking Multi-stakeholder Initiative to Address Child Labour in DRC Mining Communities' (Press Release, 16 November 2020) www.unicef.org/drcongo/en/press-releases/multi-stakeholder-initiative-address-child-labour-mining-communities#.
[179] ibid.
[180] US Department of Labor, '2019 Findings on the Worst Forms of Child Labor' www.dol.gov/sites/dolgov/files/ILAB/child_labor_reports/tda2019/Congo-Republic-of-the.pdf.
[181] ibid.
[182] OECD, *Interconnected Supply Chains* (n 82).

grant the permit holder exclusive purchasing rights to recoup its investment in the site's controls. The permittee or operator enforces the agreement by controlling site access and owning, controlling or managing the on-site purchasing stations. Additionally, they sometimes pay cooperative management fees, finance cooperative buying agents, own and operate on-site buying stations and provide trucks to transport ore from the artisanal mining area to the plant.[183]

The second type is when the government establishes a 'Zone d'Exploration Artisanal' (ZEA) on an artisanal site. For example, formalisation projects are being undertaken on the concessions of private, multinational, large-scale mining companies, such as Chemaf (Mutoshi) and Congo Dongfang International Mining (Kasulo). There are approximately 40 ZEAs in Lualaba province, each with its own registered cooperative.[184] According to the World Economic Forum, the presence of local cooperatives is critical to the success of formalisation projects since they have strong ties to the local community and serve as a central point of contact for mining companies, facilitating the implementation of agreed standards.[185]

In addition, the DRC issued two new legal directives – Decree 19/15 of 5 November 2019 and Decree 19/16 of 5 November 2019, which require that:[186] (i) cobalt from artisanal production be kept separate from industrial production; (ii) cobalt mined at ASM sites should be exclusively sold to the government; and (iii) a government oversight body should be created to ensure decent working conditions at ASM sites. As such, all ASM products sold to the government will require certification by this oversight body. However, DRC has been criticised for adopting a formalisation process that merely reinforces state control and does not address the actual hazards of ASM, leaving the affected population in a precarious state.[187]

4.4.3. Amendment of Fiscal Regimes

The mineral-producing states have often amended their laws. Several attempts have been made to obtain more value from the industry to cater to the producing countries' flawed fiscal regimes. For instance, in April 2012, the Zambian government implemented two significant changes to the mining industry's fiscal regime. Copper and cobalt mineral royalty rates were increased to six per cent,

[183] ibid.
[184] WEF (n 110).
[185] ibid.
[186] ibid. See Decree 19/15 of 5 November 2019 on the safeguarding of activities relating to strategic mineral substances of artisanal exploitation; Decree 19/16 of 5 November 2019 on the creation, organisation and operation of the Authority for the Regulation and Control of Strategic Mineral Substances Markets.
[187] BK Sovacool, 'The Precarious Political Economy of Cobalt: Balancing Prosperity, Poverty, and Brutality in Artisanal and Industrial Mining in the Democratic Republic of the Congo' (2019) 6(3) *The Extractive Industries and Society* 915.

and hedging and operating income were taxed separately. Further, in July 2015, the government set corporate income and profit tax rates at 30 per cent and mineral royalty rates at nine per cent for all mine output.[188] Nonetheless, the current fiscal regime is missing key tax instruments such as windfall and capital gains.[189]

Additionally, the country faces administrative capacity challenges, as evidenced by recent radical shifts away from profit-based to revenue-based tax instruments.[190] Zambia's Mines and Minerals Development Act No 11 of 2015 (MMDA) (as amended by the Mines and Minerals Development (Amendment) Act, No 14 of 2016 and the Mines and Minerals Development (Amendment) Act, No 29 of 2022) governs and regulates the country's mining industry. It deals with issues including the types of mining rights, their acquisition, the rights/obligations conferred on holders of mining rights, safety, health and environmental protection requirements, the export of minerals, mineral royalties, fees and charges, and environmental protection. In March 2018, the DRC also amended its Mining Code to increase its free-carry equity stake in mining companies to 10 per cent, with an additional five per cent taken on licence renewals. It also increased the amount of taxes and royalties payable. A 50 per cent super profit tax was also enacted in the MMDA. The super profit tax becomes due when commodity prices rise by 25 per cent compared to the feasibility studies. The profits subject to the super profit tax are then exempt from profit tax (ie the corporate income tax at 30 per cent).

4.4.4. Resource Transparency Initiatives

As a policy reaction to inadequate governance and its negative effects on development, both the DRC and Zambia joined the Extractive Industries Transparency Initiative (EITI), in 2014 and 2012 respectively. The EITI promotes transparency and accountability throughout the extractives value chain in resource-rich countries. Transparency and accountability, for example, require transparency in mineral-related decision-making, such as through transparent and competitive licensing procedures, allocating mineral exploration and production rights, and designing the legal, contractual and policy framework.[191] Other spheres include transparency in revenue management and strong monitoring and implementation institutions.

However, Zambia's copper mining sector scored 50/100 points on the 2017 Resource Governance Index, placing it fortieth out of 89 index assessments

[188] D Manley, 'Ninth Time Lucky: Is Zambia's Mining Tax the Best Approach to an Uncertain Future?' (NRGI Briefing, October 2017).

[189] W Banda, 'Zambia's Domestication of the Africa Mining Vision: A Gap Analysis' (Centre for Trade Policy and Development Lusaka, 2019).

[190] ibid.

[191] PD Cameron and MC Stanley, *Oil, Gas, and Mining: A Sourcebook for Understanding the Extractive Industries* (World Bank Publications, 2017).

and eleventh in sub-Saharan Africa.[192] This overall low score was exacerbated by poor revenue management – it received a low revenue management score of 35/100. Additionally, Zambia is one of the EITI's most resource-dependent members, with the mining sector accounting for more than one-fifth of government revenue.[193] Further, the Zambian government withholds information about its mining contracts, the beneficial owners of mining companies and any mining-sector assets held by government officials.[194] Likewise, the mining sector in the DRC scores a dismal 33/100 for overall resource governance, placing it seventy-fifth out of the 89 countries assessed in 2017.[195] Despite the mining sector's importance to the DRC, governance challenges persist, most notably in revenue management and creating an enabling environment.[196]

4.4.5. Supply Chains' Due Diligence Frameworks

Responsible sourcing has gained widespread attention from companies, consumers, businesses and policymakers to address the sustainability risks inherent in global mineral supply chains. The OECD established a practical framework for conducting due diligence on mineral resources supply chain with its *OECD Due Diligence Guidance for Responsible Supply Chains of Minerals from Conflict-Affected and High-Risk Areas* (*OECD Guidance*) in 2010.[197] It provides detailed recommendations to help companies respect human rights and avoid conflict through mineral purchasing decisions and practices. It defines due diligence as 'an on-going, proactive and reactive process through which companies can ensure that they respect human rights and do not contribute to conflict'. The *OECD Guidance* strives to guarantee that: (i) corporations do not profit from or contribute to serious human rights abuses in the mines from which they get materials or anywhere else in their supply chains; and (ii) companies must be upfront about their efforts to detect and address human rights issues and demonstrate that they acquire their minerals ethically.

The *OECD Guidance* outlines a five-step process for ensuring supply chain due diligence, which includes the following:[198] (1) establish strong company management systems; (2) identify and assess supply chain risks; (3) design and implement a response to identified risks; (4) conduct independent third-party

[192] Natural Resource Governance Institute, '2017 Resource Governance Index Democratic Republic of Congo (Mining)' https://api.resourcegovernanceindex.org/system/documents/documents/000/000/385/original/Resource_Governance_Index_Zambia_mining_profile.pdf?1623786473.
[193] ibid.
[194] ibid.
[195] Natural Resource Governance Institute (n 193).
[196] ibid.
[197] OECD, *OECD Due Diligence Guidance for Responsible Supply Chains of Minerals from Conflict-Affected and High-Risk Areas*, 3rd edn (OECD Publishing, 2016) http://dx.doi.org/10.1787/9789264252479-en.
[198] ibid, 17–19.

audits of supply chain due diligence at identified points in the supply chain; and (5) report annually on supply chain due diligence. The *OECD Guidance* applies to all minerals and companies throughout the mineral supply chain. This includes conflict-affected and high-risk areas (eg the DRC and Zambia), defined as areas that 'may include areas of political instability or repression, institutional weakness, insecurity, collapse of civil infrastructure and widespread violence. Such areas are often characterised by widespread human rights abuses and violations of national or international law.'[199]

Several due diligence frameworks are in operation, most of which incorporate the *OECD Guidance*. The 2019 Cobalt Industry Responsible Assessment Framework of the Cobalt Institute is a management framework that strengthens the ability of cobalt producers and buyers to assess, mitigate and report on responsible production and sourcing risks in their operations and supply chain. The Global Battery Alliance initiative includes developing a battery passport to ensure transparency on raw materials' origin, transformation, use and end of life. The passport will trace the origins of battery materials and monitor them throughout their entire life cycle on a global digital platform to help eradicate unacceptable social or environmental practices and push unsustainable materials out of the market. The Copper Mark provides an assurance framework for the responsible production of copper.[200]

Companies have also incorporated due diligence and sustainable sourcing into their policy statements. Umicore, for example, claims to be the first company to establish a Sustainable Procurement Framework for Cobalt and obtain external validation for its ethical procurement practices.[201] The company states that it seeks to minimise the risk of any link between cobalt in its supply chain and, thus, in its customers' supply chains and human rights violations or unethical business practices.[202] Umicore also supports the development of traceability projects across the industry, for example, reporting on its supply chains through the International Reference Centre for the Life Cycle of Products, Processes and Services (CIRAIG).[203] It is also a member of the Global Battery Alliance, which supports the battery passport. Studies conducted, however, show that the existence of a company's human rights policy does not necessarily translate into positive action in preventing allegations of abuse.[204] This implies that current company policies are either insufficient or not enforced adequately in their supply chains.[205] Also, human rights indicators utilised in existing sustainability reporting requirements

[199] ibid 13.
[200] The Copper Mark, https://coppermark.org.
[201] Umicore's Sustainable Procurement Framework for Cobalt, www.umicore.com/storage/group/sustainablecobaltsupplybrochurefinal.pdfm.
[202] ibid.
[203] ibid.
[204] R McCorquodale, L Smit, S Neely and R Brooks, 'Human Rights Due Diligence in Law and Practice: Good Practices and Challenges for Business Enterprises' (2017) 2(2) *Business and Human Rights Journal* 195.
[205] ibid.

are frequently invalid or based on the most easily gathered data rather than the most significant facts – they do not reflect what is on the ground.[206]

4.4.6. Circular Economy Undertakings

The processing and consuming states have embarked on a campaign for a circular economy to secure supply and prolong the life of mineral resources in their economies. In the EU, these are backed by policies and regulations such as the European Green Deal, the EU Raw Materials Initiative, the EBA and the EU Sustainable Batteries Regulation. The circular economy concept is gaining traction among consumers, governments and industry, with the EU taking the lead.[207] The linear use of resources in the economies – raw materials, production, usage and waste – is replaced with circular use, which entails reusing, repurposing or recycling materials at every economic stage. Recovery and recycling of end-of-life materials are vital sustainable management strategies for ensuring the long-term supply of critical raw material resources for the Global North. The EU, for instance, has rules concerning treating waste from electrical and electronic equipment like mobile phones, computers and fridges to contribute to sustainable production and consumption.[208] A 2018 EU report identified the major sources of critical mineral waste. These include electrical and electronic equipment, batteries, the automotive sector and the renewable energy sector.[209] Some companies have gained ground in recycling. For example, Umicore (Umicore Cobalt & Specialty Materials – CSM), based in Belgium, is top in the recycling, refining, transformation and marketing of cobalt and nickel speciality chemicals;[210] Nord-Schrott, based in Germany, focuses on metal recycling;[211] while Regulator-Cetrisa, based in Sweden, specialises in manufacturing and providing equipment and installations for recycling and sorting metals.[212]

Some of the most outstanding persuasive circular economy models, such as the Ellen MacArthur Foundation's, include mining and beneficiation operations that

[206] D Hess, 'The Transparency Trap: Non-financial Disclosure and the Responsibility of Business to Respect Human Rights' (2019) 56(1) *American Business Law Journal* 5.

[207] K Mantalovas, G Di Mino, A Jimenez Del Barco Carrion, E Keijzer, B Kalman, T Parry and D Lo Presti, 'European National Road Authorities and Circular Economy: An Insight into Their Approaches' (2020) 12(17) *Sustainability* 7160.

[208] Directive 2012/19/EU of the European Parliament and of the Council of 4 July 2012 on Waste Electrical and Electronic Equipment (WEEE).

[209] European Commission, 'Report on Critical Raw Materials in the Circular Economy' (2018) https://weee4future.eitrawmaterials.eu/wp-content/uploads/2020/09/09_report-of-CRM-and-CE.pdf.

[210] Environmental-expert.com, 'Umicore S.A. Profile' (2021) www.environmental-expert.com/companies/umicore-sa-19383.

[211] Environmental-expert.com, 'Nord-Schrott Profile' (2021) www.environmental-expert.com/companies/nord-schrott-41688.

[212] Environmental-expert.com, 'Regulator-Cetrisa Profile' (2021) www.environmental-expert.com/companies/regulator-cetrisa-33197.

are not part of the earlier circular depiction.[213] Unlike in the initial take, which saw mining as against the concept of circularity,[214] now mining is prepositioned as a prospect rather than a threat, for example, by institutions such as the International Council on Mining and Metals.[215] The OECD identified four significant themes of analysis that encompass the concept of circular economy in mining. These are:[216] (i) metal is infinitely recyclable, and recycling can often be significantly less expensive than mining new metal; (ii) metals may be present in tailings from older mining facilities because of inefficient or uneconomic extraction techniques used during their initial processing. Technological advancement and increased mineral prices or policy incentives may currently make the metals in tailings more economically viable; (iii) because of the improved capacity to monitor metal and mineral commodities from their place of origin, new business models, such as mining corporations retaining responsibility for processing and recycling the metals they sell, are possible; and (iv) mining businesses in integrated business models function more like commodities corporations, selling metals from their own recycling plants and mines.

4.5. Summary

Chapter four shows that the sub-Saharan Africa region is a prominent supplier and producer of critical minerals, but is not a prominent consumer. The minerals are refined and consumed miles away in China and the EU. The lack of domestic consumption of critical minerals is attributed to several factors, such as the lack of infrastructure to facilitate the downstream sector for critical minerals in the sub-Saharan Africa region. Mining critical metals in the region has alienated host communities from the benefits of their resources, leading to child and forced labour, gender-based exploitation, environmental degradation and infrastructural destruction of impoverished communities. Even the mitigation measures currently being employed have not yielded the much-needed results. For instance, the circular economy pushed by the Global North is focused on securing supply and extending the life of critical minerals for the developed economies, which raises questions for the Global South economies that rely on resources for their growth and development.

[213] A Vasiljevic-Shikaleska, B Gjozinska and M Stojanovikj, 'The Circular Economy – a Pathway to Sustainable Future' (2017) 7(17) *Journal of Sustainable Development* 13. E Lèbre, G Corder and A Golev, 'The Role of the Mining Industry in a Circular Economy: A Framework for Resource Management at the Mine Site Level' (2017) 21(3) *Journal of Industrial Ecology* 662.

[214] S Thimmiah, 'Where Are Miners and Metals in the Circular Economy?' *The Guardian* (20 February 2024) www.theguardian.com/sustainable-business/mining-metals-circular-economy.

[215] M Tayebi-Khorami, M Edraki, G Corder and A Golev, 'Re-thinking Mining Waste Through an Integrative Approach Led by Circular Economy Aspirations' (2019) 9(5) *Minerals* 286.

[216] OECD, *Mining and Green Growth in the EECCA Region*, OECD Green Growth Studies (OECD Publishing, 2019) https://doi.org/10.1787/1926a45a-en.

5

Critical Minerals in the Just Holistic Framework

5.1. Introduction

Critical minerals have long been crucial for society, but now they are 'super critical'.[1] That is why the valuation and assessment of critical minerals remain essential as, at its simplest, it concerns the management of resources in the most efficient way.[2] Today, however, society is faced with a multipolar perspective towards the development of critical minerals. First are the accepted consequences of climate change, and through international legal agreements (for example, the Paris Agreement (COP21) of December 2015), society has agreed to develop a low-carbon economy.[3] Secondly, the critical mineral host countries need to utilise these minerals for domestic purposes, such as elevating poverty, creating channels for affordable access to energy and developing a domestic critical mineral industry.[4] Indeed, most developing countries, the biggest consumers and importers of critical minerals, have evaluated and assessed these minerals according to their peculiar needs, such as transportation, creating low-carbon technologies, military and security purposes, fashion and industry.[5] However, assessing and evaluating critical minerals leaves room for irregularities that cause injustice across the critical mineral value chain.

The number and definition of critical minerals have changed over time due to the development of multiple assessment studies, particularly in developing countries (Global North). This will probably remain the case as technological development increases for the demands of a low-carbon society.[6] However, there

[1] SM Hayes and EA McCullough, 'Critical Minerals: A Review of Elemental Trends in Comprehensive Criticality Studies' (2018) 59 *Resources Policy* 192.

[2] J Wang, L Yang, J Lin and Y Bentley, 'The Availability of Critical Minerals for China's Renewable Energy Development: An Analysis of Physical Supply' (2020) *Natural Resources Research* 1.

[3] BC McLellan, E Yamasue, T Tezuka, G Corder, A Golev and D Giurco, 'Critical Minerals and Energy – Impacts and Limitations of Moving to Unconventional Resources' (2016) 5(2) *Resources* 19.

[4] S Kalantzakos, 'The Race for Critical Minerals in an Era of Geopolitical Realignments' (2020) 55(3) *The International Spectator* 1.

[5] P Viebahn, O Soukup, S Samadi, J Teubler, K Wiesen and M Ritthoff, 'Assessing the Need for Critical Minerals to Shift the German Energy System Towards a High Proportion of Renewables' (2015) 49 *Renewable and Sustainable Energy Reviews* 655.

[6] RJ Heffron, 'The Role of Justice in Developing Critical Minerals' (2020) 7(3) *The Extractive Industries and Society* 855.

is little literature concerning critical minerals and their role in developing countries such as Zambia and the Democratic Republic of Congo (DRC), which are among the largest exporters of critical minerals. This chapter establishes the premise of the role of critical minerals in developing countries, building analysis in the perspective of justice as more and more of these critical minerals are extracted and used in society. This follows some recent research in the extractives industry that has begun to highlight justice issues (in particular, distributive justice) from a taxation perspective on critical mineral extraction in sub-Saharan Africa.[7]

5.2. Critical Minerals Evaluation

Raw material criticality methodologies and evaluation mechanisms assess the economic and technical reliance on a particular material and the likelihood of supply disruptions for a defined stakeholder group over a specified period.[8] Criticality assessments are critical for industry and policymakers alike, for example, in material selection, product and process design, investment decisions, trade agreements, collaboration strategies, prioritising research projects, policy agendas and initiatives to increase value chain transparency.[9]

Criticality assessments have been undertaken at different levels and for a specified reason, such as technology,[10] or by a company,[11] country, region[12] or event at the global level.[13] The criticality assessments of raw materials can be considered in both the short and long term due to the specifications needed.[14] The criticality studies employ a broad selection of pre-determined indicators by companies, raw material-consuming countries and the key players of the critical mineral value chain. Their considerations can be geological, technological, geopolitical, social

[7] M Hazrati and RJ Heffron, 'Conceptualising Restorative Justice in the Energy Transition: Changing the Perspectives of Fossil Fuels' (2021) 78 *Energy Research & Social Science* 102115.

[8] D Schrijvers, A Hool, GA Blengini, WQ Chen, J Dewulf, R Eggert, L van Ellen, R Gauss, J Goddin, K Habib and C Hagelüken, 'A Review of Methods and Data to Determine Raw Material Criticality' (2020) 155 *Resources, Conservation and Recycling* 104617.

[9] R Arendt, M Muhl, V Bach and M Finkbeiner, 'Criticality Assessment of Abiotic Resource Use for Europe – Application of the SCARCE Method' (2020) 67 *Resources Policy* 101650; Schrijvers et al (n 8); S Kosai, K Matsui, K Matsubae, E Yamasue and T Nagasaka, 'Natural Resource Use of Gasoline, Hybrid, Electric and Fuel Cell Vehicles Considering Land Disturbances' (2021) 166 *Resources, Conservation and Recycling* 105256.

[10] C Helbig, AM Bradshaw, A Thorenz and A Tuma, 'Supply Risk Considerations for the Elements in Nickel-Based Superalloys' (2020) 9(9) *Resources* 106; Schrijvers et al (n 8).

[11] SJ Duclos, JP Otto and DG Konitzer, 'Design in an Era of Constrained Resources' (2010) 132(9) *Mechanical Engineering* 36.

[12] European Commission, 'Methodology for Establishing the EU List of Critical Raw Materials' (2017) 30 EC 10.2873/769526.

[13] TE Graedel, EM Harper, NT Nassar, P Nuss and BK Reck, 'Criticality of Metals and Metalloids' (2015) 112(14) *Proceedings of the National Academy of Sciences* 4257.

[14] ME Riddle, E Tatara, C Olson, BJ Smith, AB Irion, B Harker, D Pineault, E Alonso and DJ Graziano, 'Agent-Based Modeling of Supply Disruptions in the Global Rare Earths Market' (2021) 164 *Resources, Conservation and Recycling* 105193.

or environmental. The shortfall of these considerations does not span to the local level of the critical mineral-producing countries where the atrocities associated with the industry occur.[15] Hence, factors such as child labour, human rights violations and the proliferation of militia are 'said' to be considered in the social aspect of criticality. Nevertheless, they are not tailored to the day's contextual realities since the architects of these considerations are not the victims of the critical mineral value chain.

The absence of 'all' stakeholders in the criticality methodologies and studies brings about diverse perspectives and motivations in carrying out such criticality studies and their associated variations.[16] As Eggert puts it, 'criticality is in the eye of the beholder'.[17] The lack of a defined and well-established generic determination and a standardised approach in conducting criticality assessments undermines the legitimacy of the criticality studies. This is because the localities where these resources are found are not considered beyond geological aspects of criticality. The Just Framework bridges this gap by simultaneously addressing the contextual realities of sourcing critical metals with the global concerns of addressing climate change and its ramifications and sustainable development.

The National Research Council developed considerations used in criticality studies. The main factors considered were global and national risks affecting the supply of critical metals.[18] The frequency of criticality assessments is drawn from several considerations, ranging from economic to supply risk, leaving out the pertinent issues facing the critical mineral-producing countries such as the DRC and Zambia. Different authors and critical mineral scholars have highlighted the need to identify criticality assessment factors and indicators that better quantify the degree of criticality.[19]

The International Round Table on Materials Criticality brings together international experts to address the challenges in critical metal methodologies and the development of future raw material criticality assessments. This is a raw materials project under the European Institute of Innovation and Technology. It was created to address the uniformity and harmonisation of criticality studies. Though commendable, such initiatives do not include marginalised stakeholders, making their findings superficial and leading to a resource curse in critical metal-rich countries. Because the resource does not address the contextual inequalities, Table 6 shows the considerations, goals and priorities driving criticality assessments and methodologies. Countries such as the USA, Germany, Japan, China

[15] C Helbig, D Schrijvers and A Hool, 'Selecting and Prioritizing Material Resources by Criticality Assessments' (2021) 4(3) *One Earth* 339.

[16] L Erdmann, TE Graedel, 'Criticality of Non-Fuel Minerals: A Review of Major Approaches and Analyses' (2011) 45 *Environmental Science Technology* 7620.

[17] RG Eggert, 'Minerals Go Critical' (2011) 3(9) *Nature Chemistry* 688.

[18] NSTC, 'Critical and Strategic Mineral Supply Chains Assessment of Critical Minerals' (National Science and Technology Council, 2016) Report 2016-03-16 FINAL.

[19] TE Graedel and BK Reck, 'Six Years of Criticality Assessments: What Have We Learned So Far?' (2016) 20(4) *Journal of Industrial Ecology* 692.

and Korea have all limited their determination to national security and defence, particularly in the twentieth century.[20]

Table 6 Country/regional priority on the use of critical metals/raw materials

	Countries				
Concerns	**UK**	**China**	**EU**	**DRC**	**Zambia**
Economic growth and stability	Priority	Priority	Priority	Priority	Priority
Poverty alleviation				Priority	Priority
Clean technology	Priority	Priority	Priority		
Increased income/accumulation of rents				Priority	Priority
Security and defence	Priority	Priority	Priority		
Supply risk	Priority	Priority	Priority		
Infrastructural development				Priority	Priority
Fashion and industry	Priority	Priority	Priority		
Clean sources of energy	Priority	Priority	Priority	Priority	Priority
Development of indigenous communities				Priority	Priority
Nationalisation of resources				Priority	Priority
Corruption				Priority	Priority

Source: Author's Own Elaboration.

The security and defence considerations led to countries building their military material stockpiles in response to anticipated high demand and potential supply constraints, particularly during World Wars I and II and the Cold War.[21] Furthermore, defence and security are not the only drivers of raw material criticality assessments. There was massive industrialisation between the mid-twentieth and early twenty-first century, specifically in developed countries (Global North).[22] Industrialisation saw a rapid acceleration of economic growth that fuelled technological advancements associated with a growing population. Europe had a scarcity of locally sourced materials for industrial purposes, while China's export restrictions on rare earth elements (REEs) dominated the critical metal industry and supply chain.[23]

[20] MF Ashby, *Materials and Sustainable Development* (Butterworth-Heinemann, 2015).

[21] JS Thomason, RJ Atwell, Y Bajraktari, JP Bell, DS Barnett, NS Karvonides, MF Niles and EL Schwartz, 'From National Defense Stockpile (NDS) to Strategic Materials Security Program (SMSP): Evidence and Analytic Support' (Institute for Defense Analyses, 2010) IDA Paper P-4593.

[22] E Kastanaki and A Giannis, 'Dynamic Estimation of Future Obsolete Laptop Flows and Embedded Critical Raw Materials: The Case Study of Greece' (2021) 132 *Waste Management* 74.

[23] M Frenzel, J Kullik, MA Reuter and J Gutzmer, 'Raw Material "Criticality" – Sense or Nonsense?' (2017) 50(12) *Journal of Physics D: Applied Physics* 123002.

Industrial developments, technology and security advancements increased reliance on raw material imports. As such, Japan, Korea, the USA and the EU have begun systematically assessing the security of their raw material supply chains.[24] The USA and the EU developed criticality assessments with economic and geopolitical factors playing a significant role. Methods for assessing the criticality of raw materials for specific industrial sectors, such as low-carbon energy technologies and other emerging technologies, have continued to be developed according to the needs of developed countries.[25] These techniques are intended to identify potential supply risks for materials necessary for modern lifestyles and the development and growth of national or regional economies.[26]

Additionally, criticality assessments also attracted increased interest when businesses advanced the criticality aspect in their perspective.[27] As a subset of these approaches, methods have been developed to determine whether potential supply risks will affect the supply of raw or intermediate materials for a particular product. Furthermore, some criticality assessments are made to analyse the possibility of future generations facing a raw material supply shortage.[28]

As much as global development seems 'generic', the problems and challenges facing countries and regions are peculiar, as shown in Table 6. For example, despite the DRC supplying over 60 per cent of the world's cobalt, the country is not inclined to use the metal for industrialisation or for the creation and generation of clean energy, but for poverty alleviation and human development. Countries such as China intend to capitalise on their REE domination of the supply chain for market manipulation and control, such as the ban on REE exports to Japan. The ramifications of climate change affect the whole world. Still, countries in the Global South, like the DRC and Zambia, are concerned with growing militia, human rights violations and disastrous artisanal mining brought by the new Gold Rush of critical minerals in the Global South.

The mechanisms adopted by Zambia and the DRC to control their destiny by instituting national mining companies gave the government greater control. Consequently, private investors' roles were reduced to contract management or marketing, and investment fell precipitously.[29] This motivated criticality

[24] ibid.

[25] GS Seck, E Hache, C Bonnet, M Simoën and S Carcanague, 'Copper at the Crossroads: Assessment of the Interactions between Low-Carbon Energy Transition and Supply Limitations' (2020) 163 *Resources, Conservation and Recycling* 105072.

[26] *Strategic Metal Report* (2011) https://strategic-metal.typepad.com/strategic-metal-report/2011/09/the-british-geological-survey-risk-list-2011.

[27] E Hache, GS Seck, M Simoen, C Bonnet and S Carcanague, 'Critical Raw Materials and Transportation Sector Electrification: A Detailed Bottom-Up Analysis in World Transport' (2019) 240 *Applied Energy* 6.

[28] G Calvo, A Valero and A Valero, 'Thermodynamic Approach to Evaluate the Criticality of Raw Materials and Its Application through a Material Flow Analysis in Europe' (2018) 22(4) *Journal of Industrial Ecology* 839.

[29] A Fent and E Kojola, 'Political Ecologies of Time and Temporality in Resource Extraction' (2020) 27(1) *Journal of Political Ecology* 819.

assessment studies based on the security of supply, the threat to the Global North's economic stability and a threat to further technological advancement due to strict rules and regulations brought about by the nationalisation of critical metal mines. The change in mining industry dynamics in the 1980s led to low levels of investment, declining operational efficiency and low prices, bringing both Zambia and the DRC's national mining companies to the verge of bankruptcy. These factors are not considered in the 1980s criticality assessments.[30]

The DRC's mining industry faced decades of financial plunder, with deteriorating mining infrastructure exacerbated by widespread asset pillage.[31] The DRC was then engulfed in a bloody civil war, which effectively halted all formal mining activities.[32] The civil war led to an unpopular privatisation move by President Laurent Kabila; Gécamines lost its monopoly over the country's minerals in the province of Katanga, though it retains rights to valuable mineral assets.[33] The mining sector continues to generate relatively little tax revenue for the government, owing to low royalty rates and a moderate corporate income tax.[34] While Gécamines receives dividends from its mining interests as well as royalties and signing bonuses, very little or no revenue ever makes its way into the national budget.[35] Gécamines retains de facto control over the selection of private partners for its portfolio projects, and contracts are awarded without due process, resulting in suboptimal partner selection and intermediary companies profiting handsomely from the sale of their assets to major international players.[36]

The concerns about fiscal reforms, militia presence, local community development and financing poverty alleviation cannot be addressed under the current criticality assessments. Criticality studies can consider various risks, depending on the assessment's objective and scope, including disrupted trade flows, material scarcity, price fluctuations and reputational risks.[37] In practice, many assessments consider a combination of these risks, but ignore the vast issues facing the critical mineral host communities of Zambia and the DRC. Furthermore, compiling a list of critical minerals and ranking them introduces the challenge of aggregating various criticality indicators.[38] Aggregation can obscure the underlying indicator

[30] RA Unceta, 'The Economic and Social Impact of Mining-Resources Exploitation in Zambia' (2021) 74 *Resources Policy* 102242.

[31] DB Bakamana, 'Impacts of Political Dynamics and Implications to Development in the Democratic Republic of Congo (DRC)' (2021) 5(1) *Journal of African Interdisciplinary Studies* 32.

[32] ibid.

[33] F Calvão, CEA Mcdonald and M Bolay, 'Cobalt Mining and the Corporate Outsourcing of Responsibility in the Democratic Republic of Congo' (2021) 8(4) *The Extractive Industries and Society* 100884.

[34] M Mangu and SD Kamga, 'Corporate Social Responsibility and the Right to Development in Local Communities: The Case of the Democratic Republic of Congo' in CC Ngang and SAD Kamga (eds), *Natural Resource Sovereignty and the Right to Development in Africa* (Routledge, 2021) 229–45.

[35] L Gnassou, 'Tax Base Erosion: A Cautionary Tale of the DRC' [2020] *Africa Policy Journal* 27.

[36] ibid.

[37] S Glöser, LT Espinoza, C Gandenberger and M Faulstich, 'Raw Material Criticality in the Context of Classical Risk Assessment' (2015) 44 *Resources Policy* 35.

[38] ibid.

values and is thus not recommended for identifying risk sources and appropriate mitigation options. Another difficulty in developing critical raw material lists is defining criticality indicator threshold values (eg what constitutes a 'high' probability of supply disruption or 'high' vulnerability to disruption?).[39] Furthermore, criticality assessments rely on geological and trade data that approximate the flows under consideration. Considering any given criticality study's objective and scope, data quality limitations can present substantial uncertainty in criticality assessments.

5.3. The Just Framework and the Critical Mineral Supply Chain

The Just Framework builds significant theoretical assumptions that can be used as building blocks for attaining justice in the critical mineral value chain. Each of the Just Framework components is examined across the critical mineral value chain, giving a microscopic analysis of society's key issues to ensure social welfare and overall economic benefit to the stakeholders and potential beneficiaries.

5.3.1. Distributive Justice

Distributive justice acknowledges the physically unequal distribution of environmental benefits and harms and the unequal distribution of the associated responsibilities.[40] It assesses where 'general questions about the desirability of technologies become entangled with issues specific to specific localities' and serves as a call for an equitable distribution of benefits and costs across society, regardless of income, race or any other specification.[41] Resources like critical minerals are inescapably unequally distributed (for example, the vast cobalt deposits in the DRC compared to cobalt deposits in the EU). As such, claims for justice necessitate that the prevailing explicit inequality should occur alongside an argument for fair treatment.[42] Thus, one avenue for empirical research is to examine how the sourcing and extraction of critical minerals result in distributional injustices.

[39] T Sonderegger, M Berger, R Alvarenga, V Bach, A Cimprich, J Dewulf, R Frischknecht, J Guinée, C Helbig, T Huppertz and O Jolliet, 'Mineral Resources in Life Cycle Impact Assessment – Part I: A Critical Review of Existing Methods' (2020) 25(4) *International Journal of Life Cycle Assessment* 784.

[40] G Walker, 'Beyond Distribution and Proximity: Exploring the Multiple Spatialities of Environmental Justice' (2009) 41(4) *Antipode* 614.

[41] S Owens and L Driffill, 'How to Change Attitudes and Behaviours in the Context of Energy' (2008) 36(12) *Energy Policy* 4412.

[42] K Jenkins, D McCauley, RJ Heffron, H Stephan and R Rehner, 'Energy Justice: A Conceptual Review' (2016) 11 *Energy Research & Social Science* 174.

Distributive justice encompasses the ramifications of the mining industry and the distribution of rents/income acquired from the critical mineral value chain. The technology needed to drive the energy transition has exposed the unequal distribution of burdens associated with developing climate change technology, mitigation and adaptation.[43] In this regard, the Just Framework concerns physical aspects of the critical mineral value chain and questions to what extent the climate change mitigation and adaptation mechanisms damage the social welfare of marginalised communities.

Furthermore, taxation is the core element of distributive justice; hence, there is a need to understand where and how revenue from critical minerals is distributed.[44] Some authors and researchers hold that distributive justice should be regarded as the cornerstone of tax law, as the 'primary or sovereign virtue of a society's tax system'.[45] There is a need to make distributive justice the cornerstone of fiscal regimes using legal tools and mechanisms for the development of future generations. For example, the copper mining industry accounts for nearly three-quarters of Zambia's export earnings. Nevertheless, the sector has already seen as many as 10 changes to its tax and royalty regime.[46] The Zambian copper industry has lost billions in tax revenue due to tax avoidance, mispricing and illicit trade of copper. Zambia's copper giants, such as Glencore and Vedanta, have used complex corporate structures and mispricing to avoid paying billions in tax revenues over the years.[47] Further, Glencore's Mopani Copper Mines was found guilty of avoiding over $13 million in taxes.[48] Such acts call for distributive justice in the critical mineral industry because the industry robs the current generation of their welfare and the prosperity of future generations.

Furthermore, the critical mineral value chain may inherently be unable to establish the equitable distribution of the ills and benefits of the industry. This is mainly attributed to the vast differences in investment structures, the infrastructural context, the breadth and width of economic linkage development, and capabilities within a given economy. Hitherto, explicit mechanisms could be established to redistribute benefits in countries like the DRC and Zambia. For example, Zambia and the DRC could adopt Botswana's Pula Fund approach.[49] Here, the

[43] AM Levenda, I Behrsin and F Disano, 'Renewable Energy for Whom? A Global Systematic Review of the Environmental Justice Implications of Renewable Energy Technologies' (2021) 71 *Energy Research & Social Science* 101837.

[44] Heffron, 'The Role of Justice' (n 6).

[45] ibid.

[46] P Carmody and P Kragelund, 'Who Is in Charge – State Power and Agency in Sino-African Relations?' (2016) 49 *Cornell International Law Journal* 1.

[47] G Dobler and R Kesselring, 'Swiss Extractivism: Switzerland's Role in Zambia's Copper Sector' (2019) 57(2) *Journal of Modern African Studies* 223.

[48] Business and Human Resource Centre, Zambia, 'Court Fines Glencore's Mopani Copper $13 Million for Tax Avoidance (27 May 2021) www.business-humanrights.org/en/latest-news/zambia-court-fines-glencores-mopani-copper-13-million-for-tax-avoidance/.

[49] KA Alsweilem, A Cummine, M Rietveld and K Tweedie, 'A Comparative Study of Sovereign Investor Models: Sovereign Fund Profiles' (Harvard Kennedy School, Belfer Center for Science and International Affairs and Center for International Development at Harvard University, 2015).

government of Botswana ring-fenced part of the proceeds from the diamond mining industry for the development of current and future generations, given that the diamond resources are finite and may be depleted by 2030.[50] Secondly, the issue of shared use or open access to resource infrastructure in the DRC and Zambia is concerned with identifying ways to leverage extractive industry-related infrastructure investments in developing countries for the greater good of the national and regional communities.[51]

Non-renewable resource extraction must be used to fund long-term assets, such as infrastructure, that promote sustainable and inclusive growth.[52] This can be accomplished in various ways, including capitalising on the potential for resource taxation and reinvesting tax revenues in all-weather roads. However, it can also be achieved by requiring shared use of resource infrastructure. The shared use of resources can be a means of distributing justice, such that the shared infrastructure can benefit a country's development.

5.3.2. Recognition Justice

Recognition justice is more than mere tolerance; it requires fairly represented individuals, protected from physical harm and with absolute and equal political rights.[53] Lack of recognition can manifest in various ways, including cultural and political hegemony, insults, degradation and devaluation.[54] Jenkins et al state that 'it may manifest as a failure to recognise, but also as misrecognition – a distortion of people's perspectives that may appear demeaning or contemptible'.[55] As such, recognition justice calls for recognising the different perspectives based on social, cultural, ethnic, racial and gender differences.[56] Furthermore, Fraser classifies misrecognition into three broad categories – cultural domination, non-recognition and disrespect – in the categorisation of recognition justice.[57]

[50] W Ma and P Downs, *The Hunt for Unicorns: How Sovereign Funds Are Reshaping Investment in the Digital Economy* (John Wiley & Sons, 2020).

[51] K Hund, JM Schure and A van der Goes, 'Extractive Industries in Forest Landscapes: Options for Synergy with REDD+ and Development of Standards in the Democratic Republic of Congo' (2017) 54 *Resources Policy* 97.

[52] C Atlin and R Gibson, 'Lasting Regional Gains from Non-Renewable Resource Extraction: The Role of Sustainability-Based Cumulative Effects Assessment and Regional Planning for Mining Development in Canada' (2017) 4(1) *The Extractive Industries and Society* 36.

[53] D Schlosberg, 'The Justice of Environmental Justice: Reconciling Equity, Recognition, and Participation in a Political Movement' (2003) 77 *Moral and Political Reasoning in Environmental Practice* 106.

[54] BK Sovacool and MH Dworkin, 'Energy Justice: Conceptual Insights and Practical Applications' (2015) 142 *Applied Energy* 435.

[55] Jenkins et al (n 42).

[56] N Fraser, 'Social Justice in the Age of Identity Politics. Geographic Thought: A Praxis Perspective' in GL Henderson and M Waterstone (eds), *Geographic Thought: A Praxis Perspective* (Routledge, 2009) 72–91.

[57] ibid.

Divergent perspectives have been recognised in various legal instruments ranging from international to local legal and regulatory frameworks. For example, under international law, indigenous communities are recognised in the United Nations Declaration of the Rights of Indigenous Peoples (UNDRIP).[58] A crucial part of that treaty is Article 10, which states:

> Indigenous peoples shall not be forcibly removed from their lands or territory. No relocation shall take place without the free, prior and informed consent of the indigenous people, and after agreement on just and fair compensation and, where possible, with the option of return.[59]

Recognising indigenous communities' rights requires that new legal and regulatory structures amplify their presence and voice. The amplification of these legal and regulatory recognition structures has led to the device of particular mechanisms, such as the social licence to operate, local content policies and corporate social responsibility (CSR).[60] These mechanisms establish the platform for the recognition of indigenous and marginalised communities.

5.3.2.1. Injustice as a Non-recognition

In the DRC, tensions between industrial and artisanal miners are high. State security forces intervened in 2019 in the mineral-rich provinces of Haut-Katanga and Lualaba to evict over 10,000 artisanal miners encroaching on two of the country's largest industrial mining sites.[61] Economic opportunities are scarce for artisanal miners, and they are frequently denied access to industrial sites, even when the deposits are commercially unviable and the region lacks artisanal mining zones.[62] Most Congolese miners are artisanal, making up over 63 per cent of the 75 million Congolese citizens living in extreme poverty, surviving on less than one dollar a day.[63] The failure to recognise specific groups, such as artisanal miners, leads to violence, insecurity and the spread of impoverishment to a significant part of the population. Justice as recognition brings the artisanal miners closer to global value chains, providing nascent avenues of growth.

[58] United Nations Declaration on the Rights of Indigenous Peoples (A/RES/61/295) of 2007.

[59] UN Department of Economic and Social Affairs, 'United Nations Declaration on the Rights of Indigenous Peoples' (2021) www.un.org/development/desa/indigenouspeoples/declaration-on-the-rights-of-indigenous-peoples.html.

[60] RJ Heffron, L Downes, OMR Rodriguez and D McCauley, 'The Emergence of the "Social Licence to Operate" in the Extractive Industries?' [2018] *Resources Policy* 101272.

[61] B Rubbers, 'Mining Boom, Labour Market Segmentation and Social Inequality in the Congolese Copperbelt' (2020) 51(6) *Development and Change* 1555.

[62] G Hilson, T Sauerwein and J Owen, 'Large and Artisanal Scale Mine Development: The Case for Autonomous Co-Existence' (2020) 130 *World Development* 104919.

[63] ibid.

5.3.2.2. *Injustice as Misrecognition and Disrespect*

The mining industry in the DRC and Zambia has brought about decades of conflict accompanied by the mismanagement of the mining industry. Consequently, traditional sectors of the economy, such as agriculture, have been eroded since the pivotal stage of their economies.[64] Marginalised communities and groups such as divorced/single women had no other option but to engage in the mining industry. Moreover, between 500,000 and two million people are estimated to be working informally in Zambia and the DRC's mining industries.[65] The majority of this group is formed by women, who are thereby reduced to second-class citizens in their countries. Women experience human rights violations and systematic and institutional blockage from participating in the mining industry.[66] Women are generally considered a bad omen in mining communities, leading to the misrecognition and disrespect of women in the mining industry, particularly in artisanal mining in Zambia and the DRC. Hence, the characterisation and categorisation of women as a marginalised sub-sect of the mining ecological construct creates gendering within the mining industry.[67] Gendering refers to the process of socialisation according to the dominant gender norms. It may also refer to adopting an alternative gender identity and the transcendence of all the recognised modes of how to live and subvert gender.[68] Recognition justice provides a comprehensive and diverse overview of gender, particularly in the artisanal and small-scale mining (ASM) segment of the industry. It balances the gender norms and the methodological tools that form the gendered social inequalities created. The overall input of the Just Framework affords an intervention into gender relations, gendered labour, gendered authority and power dynamics within mining zones, households, property regimes and broader communities.

5.3.3. Procedural Justice

Bell and Rowe define procedural justice as fairness in the process of decision-making and policy-making.[69] What, then, constitutes a 'fair decision' in critical mineral assessment, development and value chain, and what aspects are likely to be significant in shaping stakeholder perceptions of

[64] G Ayittey (ed), *Africa Unchained: The Blueprint for Africa's Future* (Springer, 2016).

[65] G Hilson, A Hilson and J McQuilken, 'Ethical Minerals: Fairer Trade for Whom?' (2016) 49 *Resources Policy* 232.

[66] CP Willis, 'Sexual Violence by the State: The Role of Political Institutions in Sexual Violence Perpetration' (2021) 65(3) *International Studies Quarterly* 768.

[67] B Rutherford and D Buss, 'Gendered Governance and Socio-Economic Differentiation Among Women Artisanal and Small-Scale Miners in Central and East Africa' (2019) 4(1) *Third World Thematics: A TWQ Journal* 63.

[68] ibid.

[69] D Bell and F Rowe, *Are Climate Policies Fairly Made?* (Joseph Rowntree Foundation, 2012).

procedural (in)justice? Stakeholder perspectives affect access to decision-making processes that govern any industry,[70] especially the critical mineral industry. Procedural justice demands equitable procedures that engage all stakeholders in a non-discriminatory manner.[71] It has since been applied to race, gender and religion, and in this book, the concept of procedural justice is extended to critical mineral development.[72]

The Just Framework recognises that procedural justice has multiple dimensions, which entail the fundamental criteria used to determine the fairness of a decision-making process.[73] Procedural justice advocates and integrates three particularly significant dimensions in the critical mineral value chain: inclusion, influence and information. Jenkins et al classified procedural justice based on three mechanisms of inclusion to achieve just outcomes: mobilising indigenous knowledge, increasing information disclosure and improving institutional representation.[74] In this case, procedural justice advocates for the legal process of providing a legitimate opportunity to participate in any value chain.[75] The assessment and evaluation of a decision-making process must meet the fairness criteria. Furthermore, it is influenced by softer, non-regulatory factors such as practices, norms, values and behaviours.[76]

Influence refers to the extent to which various participants' opinions, suggestions and concerns shape decision outcomes.[77] Hence, an individual or a group of people can exercise varying degrees of influence during a decision-making process, classified as 'listening as a spectator', 'consultative influence' and 'direct authority'.[78] The term 'listening as a spectator' refers to a situation in which a stakeholder learns about a decision but has no influence over it.[79] If a stakeholder has 'consultative influence', they can express their viewpoint and perspective on an issue, but others make the ultimate decision.[80] Finally, the term 'direct authority' refers to a situation in which a stakeholder has the formal ability to influence the outcome of a decision – either by making the decision alone or through a power-sharing agreement such as a democratic process (like voting).[81]

[70] D Schlosberg, *Defining Environmental Justice: Theories, Movements, and Nature* (Oxford University Press, 2019).
[71] R Nagtegaal, 'The Impact of Using Algorithms for Managerial Decisions on Public Employees' Procedural Justice' (2021) 38(1) *Government Information Quarterly* 101536.
[72] ibid.
[73] Heffron, 'The Role of Justice' (n 6).
[74] Jenkins et al (n 42).
[75] ibid.
[76] MZ Bell, 'Spatialising Procedural Justice: Fairness and Local Knowledge Mobilisation in Nuclear Waste Siting' (2021) 26(1) *Local Environment* 165.
[77] G Smith, *Democratic Innovations: Designing Institutions for Citizen Participation* (Cambridge University Press, 2019).
[78] ibid.
[79] C Hunold and IM Young, 'Justice, Democracy, and Hazardous Siting' (1998) 46(1) *Political Studies* 82.
[80] ibid.
[81] ibid.

In the critical mineral value chain, sourcing and exporting countries such as Zambia and the DRC are relegated to 'listening spectators' since they do not influence the valuation and assessment of critical minerals. Looking back at the main drivers of demand for critical minerals, such as war, the Cold War led to the stockpiling of critical minerals to build war machinery.[82] The need to develop climate change mitigation technology, critical minerals for transportation or critical minerals in fashion and industry all relegate Zambia and the DRC (as well as the whole Global South) to 'listening spectators'.[83] It can be argued that if critical mineral exporting countries were provided with adequate, sufficient and accurate information pertaining to the critical mineral resources, the outcome of the valuation of these metals would not be limited to economic and supply risk considerations. Procedural justice calls for mobilising local knowledge, disclosing information and adequate institutional representation;[84] these aspects are discussed in turn below.

5.3.3.1. Mobilising Local Knowledge

Local knowledge is notably a significant motivator for including and engaging the affected public. The concept is intertwined with the welfare of indigenous peoples. In the critical mineral value chain, there is a pattern of ignoring indigenous knowledge about the ramifications of the industry on host communities, to the detriment of communities and decision-making sustainability. In 2003, the World Bank funded the Copperbelt Environment Project to eliminate lead contamination in impacted townships in Zambia and to treat its health consequences. These were mainly a result of the Zambia Consolidated Copper Mines Ltd (ZCCM) operations before it was privatised. However, the Zambian government failed to develop an appropriate approach to fulfilling the project's objectives. It could not mobilise the indigenous communities' knowledge of the closed copper mines' negative health impacts. High lead levels remain in the soil and dust around the mine, particularly in the Kabwe townships of Kasanda and Makandanyama. Procedural justice would be critical if there were early consultative intervention and community engagement.

5.3.3.2. Disclosing Information

Procedural justice necessitates meaningful participation, government, industry impartiality and full disclosure of information,[85] as well as appropriate and

[82] D Humpheys, 'Whatever Happened to Security of Supply? Mineral's Policy in the Post-Cold War World' (1995) 21(2) *Resources Policy* 91.
[83] Viebahn et al (n 5).
[84] Bell (n 76).
[85] AR Davies, 'Environmental Justice as Subtext or Omission: Examining Discourses of Anti-Incineration Campaigning in Ireland' (2006) 37(5) *Geoforum* 708.

sympathetic engagement mechanisms.[86] In this context, many governments and key international players in the critical mineral value chain prioritise public consultation for the industry's sustainability. This can be state-induced or voluntary disclosure, both of which have varying degrees of effectiveness.[87] Information disclosure can catalyse more ethical[88] and sustainable[89] consumption practices and society's energy choices on a global scale.[90] Furthermore, disclosing information could serve as a means of redress when a community is confronted with an injustice.[91]

Disclosure of the negative socio-economic impacts of the critical mineral value chain and the probable economic gains of the industry is gaining traction as a mechanism for resolving distributive injustices.[92] The disclosure of information in the critical mineral value chain is increasingly geared towards low-income countries' marginalised host communities. The dissemination of information aims, first and foremost, to provide hints and tips for reducing detrimental environmental impacts. These strategies can help promote more socio-economic sustainable practices and facilitate the inclusion of marginalised communities in resolving distributive injustices.

5.3.3.3. *Representation Institutions*

Inequality in representation across a range of institutions, including business, national and international governmental entities, and non-state players affects decision-making.[93] Inequalities driven by gender and ethnic minorities have been documented in governing organisations for a lengthy period of time.[94] It is challenging for a community with no technology, skills, capital or infrastructure to integrate the critical global value chains.[95] Hence, the created enclave in the critical mineral industry creates a flight of capital and critical metals from the interior of

[86] H Todd and C Zografos, 'Justice for the Environment: Developing a Set of Indicators of Environmental Justice for Scotland' (2005) 14(4) *Environmental Values* 483.

[87] DC Matisoff, 'Different Rays of Sunlight: Understanding Information Disclosure and Carbon Transparency' (2013) 55 *Energy Policy* 579.

[88] SM Hall, 'Energy Justice and Ethical Consumption: Comparison, Synbook and Lesson Drawing' (2013) 18(4) *Local Environment* 422.

[89] K Hobson, 'Environmental Psychology and the Geographies of Ethical and Sustainable Consumption: Aligning, Triangulating, Challenging?' (2006) 38(3) *Area* 292.

[90] VJ Schwanitz, F Piontek, C Bertram and G Luderer, 'Long-term Climate Policy Implications of Phasing Out Fossil Fuel Subsidies' (2014) 67 *Energy Policy* 882.

[91] G Walker and R Day, 'Fuel Poverty as Injustice: Integrating Distribution, Recognition and Procedure in the Struggle for Affordable Warmth' (2012) 49 *Energy Policy* 69.

[92] Kalantzakos (n 4).

[93] N Palladino, 'The Role of Epistemic Communities in the "Constitutionalization" of Internet Governance: The Example of the European Commission High-Level Expert Group on Artificial Intelligence' (2021) 45(6) *Telecommunications Policy* 102149.

[94] ibid.

[95] NA Phelps, M Atienza and M Arias, 'Encore for the Enclave: The Changing Nature of the Industry Enclave with Illustrations from the Mining Industry in Chile' (2015) 91(2) *Economic Geography* 119.

critical mineral sourcing countries like the DRC and Zambia without touching the banks or government coffers of the given countries. For example, the collapse in commodity prices after the 2008 economic crisis, particularly those of minerals, was a global act causing local catastrophe.[96] The DRC and Zambia were adversely affected by the decline in the price of copper and cobalt.[97] This is because Glencore, the largest investor in the region, shut down several mines.[98] The mining industry in the DRC and Zambia employs thousands of people and their families, and the mine closures resulted in significant loss of jobs and livelihoods.[99] The nature of the critical mineral industry creates an enclave for the marginalised mining communities since crucial decisions are made on an international scale but with local impact.

5.3.4. Restorative Justice

The critical mineral industry is a huge part of the traditional mining industry. The mining industry has been associated with several injustices over the years,[100] and legislation and policy have been called for to rectify these wrongs/injustices. Nevertheless, restorative justice goes beyond addressing the injustice of the mining industry to restoring the community to its original position before the mining operations for the welfare of the host community.[101] Restorative justice has facilitated and enforced laws, regulations and policies towards waste management and community social welfare.[102] Additionally, by implementing restorative practices and avoiding a mine's linear structure, one can mitigate the negative consequences of mining while also providing economic incentives through secondary activities and more complex enterprises.[103]

5.3.5. Cosmopolitan Justice

Cosmopolitan justice entails that we are all global citizens; thus, the acts and deeds of one person in one part of the world affect other people in different

[96] R Baxter, 'The Global Economic Crisis and Its Impact on South Africa and the Country's Mining Industry' [2009] *Challenges for Monetary Policy-Makers in Emerging Markets* 105.

[97] J Smart, E Nel and T Binns, 'Economic Crisis and Food Security in Africa: Exploring the Significance of Urban Agriculture in Zambia's Copperbelt Province' (2015) 65 *Geoforum* 37.

[98] R Kesselring, 'What Zambia and Switzerland Have in Common: Copper and Resistance to Extractivism' (2018) 43(172) *Afrika Bulletin* 3.

[99] M Nakazwe, 'Life Beyond the Glitz and Glamour of Mining: Strengthening the Mine Closure Regime in Zambia' (2017) 35(3) *Journal of Energy & Natural Resources Law* 325.

[100] S Nakanwagi, 'Mine Closure and Justice Implications' (*IJPIEL*, 13 August 2021) https://ijpiel.com/index.php/2021/08/13/mine-closure-and-justice-implications/.

[101] Hazrati and Heffron (n 7).

[102] ibid.

[103] N Tripathi, RS Singh and CD Hills, *Reclamation of Mine-impacted Land for Ecosystem Recovery* (John Wiley & Sons 2016).

regions.[104] The critical mineral value chain is a perfect example of cosmopolitan justice. The demand and supply of critical minerals exist in global value chains,[105] with demand in the Global North and the supply of critical minerals coming from the Global South, in countries like Zambia and the DRC. Cosmopolitan justice brings to light the issue of cross-border consequences and interests in the critical mineral value chain.[106] For example, as of 2024, the total number of mobile phones in the world is 8.31 billion, and of these 7.21 billion are smartphones.[107] Coltan is a significant raw material for the manufacture of mobile phones. The pay in the coltan mines attracted and still attracts the majority of the population in DRC, including children. A case study undertaken by Polinares found that more than 30 per cent of children drop out of school to mine coltan.[108]

Economic gains in the DRC and Zambia's mining sectors have also attracted armed groups and militia. For example, the RCD rebels, at a point in time, made over $1 million monthly exporting coltan, compared to $200,000 monthly from exporting diamonds.[109] This has led to competition over the control of mines and minerals between armed groups, leading to devastating violence and abuse of human rights.

Other than the explosive demand for mobile phones, the other cosmopolitan factor affecting critical minerals is the emerging awareness of climate change. The need to mitigate and adapt to the new reality has transformed energy from fossil fuels to cleaner energy sources.[110] International agreements and policies such as the Paris Agreement (COP21) have become the main driver of trade flows, and environmental policies have created a new scramble for critical minerals to create a low-carbon economy.[111] The constant recognition of the DRC and Zambia's resources on the global stage should be matched by the ramifications of the critical mineral industry to the marginalised mineral host communities.

[104] CR Maboloc, 'Liberal Environmentalism and Global Climate Justice' (2020) 30(2) *Eubios Journal of Asian and International Bioethics*.

[105] Z Atakhanova and P Howie, 'Metal Intensity of Use in the Era of Global Value Chains' (2020) 33(1) *Mineral Economics* 101.

[106] RJ Heffron, MF Körner, M Schöpf, J Wagner and M Weibelzahl, 'The Role of Flexibility in the Light of the COVID-19 Pandemic and Beyond: Contributing to a Sustainable and Resilient Energy Future in Europe' (2021) 140 *Renewable and Sustainable Energy Reviews* 110743.

[107] A Turner, 'Number of Smartphone Users Worldwide (Billions)' (BankMyCell.com, 2024) www.bankmycell.com/blog/how-many-phones-are-in-the-world.

[108] POLINARES, 'Framework for Understanding the Sources of Conflict and Tension'. Work Package 1, Internal Project document, April 2010. L Galvez, 'Your Smartphone Could Have Contributed to Devastation in the DRC' (*Impakter*, 10 July 2021) https://impakter.com/your-smartphone-could-have-contributed-to-devastation-in-the-drc/.

[109] EF Kisangani, 'Conflict in the Democratic Republic of Congo: A Mosaic of Insurgent Groups' (2003) *International Journal on World Peace* 51.

[110] C Church and A Crawford, 'Minerals and the Metals for the Energy Transition: Exploring the Conflict Implications for Mineral-Rich, Fragile States' in M Hafner and S Tagliapietra (eds), *The Geopolitics of the Global Energy Transition* (Springer International Publishing, 2020) 279–304.

[111] ibid.

5.3.6. Space

The space aspect is an essential factor in critical mineral development since critical minerals are developed in different geographical spaces, each with its own peculiar jurisdictions and necessity.[112] The following aspects are key in illustrating the space aspect in critical mineral development.

1. Location – critical mineral value chains occur in a disintegrated linear supply chain,[113] which usually originates from the Global South and terminates in the Global North (with a few exceptions, like Australia).
2. At the local, national and international levels, critical minerals are vital raw materials and components for several global outputs and industries. Mostly, demand is driven by international agreements that shape individual habits, such as climate change mitigation and adaptation, which increase the demand for critical minerals.[114] Furthermore, the national level devises policies, rules and regulations that govern the issuance of licences and enhance the local level's critical mineral investment climate, whereby the marginalised host communities experience the negative impact of the critical mineral value chain.[115] Geopolitics is also involved due to the global nature of the critical mineral supply chain.[116] The stakeholders vary from multinational corporations investing in critical minerals to local businesses within the vicinity of the mining operations and artisanal miners involved in critical mineral sourcing.[117]
3. The peculiar needs of the place where critical minerals are sourced or extracted is not usually the same space in which the minerals are evaluated, assessed, and valued. This makes 'space' an important, if not critical, component of the critical mineral value chain. The spatial dimension of the critical mineral industry calls for a generic perspective when valuing critical minerals.[118] Additionally, Heffron et al note that evaluating mining earnings and where profits from the critical minerals sector will end up is vital.[119] Thus, there must be a major concern about how the industry evolves, demonstrating why ensuring justice in the critical minerals sector's development is important.

[112] TM Mose and M Hazrati, 'Is Energy Justice in the Fossil Fuel Industry a Paradox?' in G Wood and K Baker (eds), *The Palgrave Handbook of Managing Fossil Fuels and Energy Transitions* (Palgrave Macmillan, 2020) 529–49.

[113] Kalantzakos (n 4).

[114] Church and Crawford (n 110); RJ Heffron and K Talus, 'The Evolution of Energy Law and Energy Jurisprudence: Insights for Energy Analysts and Researchers' (2016) 19 *Energy Research & Social Science* 1.

[115] Church and Crawford (n 110).

[116] Kalantzakos (n 4).

[117] RT Shackleton, 'Loss of Land and Livelihoods from Mining Operations: A Case in the Limpopo Province, South Africa' (2020) 99 *Land Use Policy* 104825; AE Bastida, *The Law and Governance of Mining and Minerals: A Global Perspective* (Bloomsbury Publishing, 2020) chs 3 and 6.

[118] ID Qurbani, RJ Heffron and ATS Rifano, 'Justice and Critical Mineral Development in Indonesia and Across ASEAN' (2020) 8(1) *The Extractive Industries and Society* 355.

[119] Heffron et al, 'The Role of Flexibility' (n 106).

5.3.7. Time

Time is an important factor in critical mineral development. International climate change agreements increase the demand for these minerals based on the time set to achieve the climate commitments.[120] For instance, according to Africa's Agenda 2063, along with other key international agreements such as the Paris Agreement, the region must obtain carbon neutrality by 2050.[121] Also, 52 African countries filed their first nationally determined contributions (NDCs) since the ratification of Paris Agreement, while 45 had submitted updated NDCs in May 2022. However, the region lacks capital, infrastructure and skills to fulfil its carbon neutrality ambitions within the given time.[122] The aspect of time in critical mineral development is also important because the main driver of critical minerals is the energy transition, which has incorporated transition targets such as 2030, 2040, 2050 and 2080, which increases the demand for the minerals.[123]

5.4. A Just Framework for the Critical Mineral Industry

This book has established the importance of critical minerals in the energy transition, showing the role these minerals play in developing technology pertinent to climate change adaptation and mitigation. However, the polarised interests of states and regions regarding critical minerals, as shown from the consideration of criticality studies, have been evaluated against the principles and tenets of justice. The book thus establishes a holistic framework (Figure 6) beyond the current economic importance and threat of supply considerations that are largely the interests of the Global North. The book holds that the considerations for criticality must go beyond the supply risk and economic importance matrix to considerations of the following: (i) the process; (ii) the decision-making; (iii) the access; (iv) the benefits; (v) the restoration; and (vi) cosmopolitanism.

[120] Heffron and Talus (n 114).

[121] I Todd and D McCauley, 'Assessing Policy Barriers to the Energy Transition in South Africa' (2021) 158 *Energy Policy* 112529.

[122] M Weigel and A Demissie, 'Achieving the SDGs in Africa Through South-South Cooperation on Climate Change with China' in S Chaturvedi, H Janus, S Klingebiel, X Li, A Mello e Souza, E Sidiropoulos and D Wehrmann (eds), *The Palgrave Handbook of Development Cooperation for Achieving the 2030 Agenda: Contested Collaboration* (Palgrave Macmillan, 2021) 605–23.

[123] M Ojala, A Cunsolo, CA Ogunbode and J Middleton, 'Anxiety, Worry, and Grief in a Time of Environmental and Climate Crisis: A Narrative Review' (2021) 46 *Annual Review of Environment and Resources* 35.

Figure 6 The Just Holistic Framework for critical minerals value chains

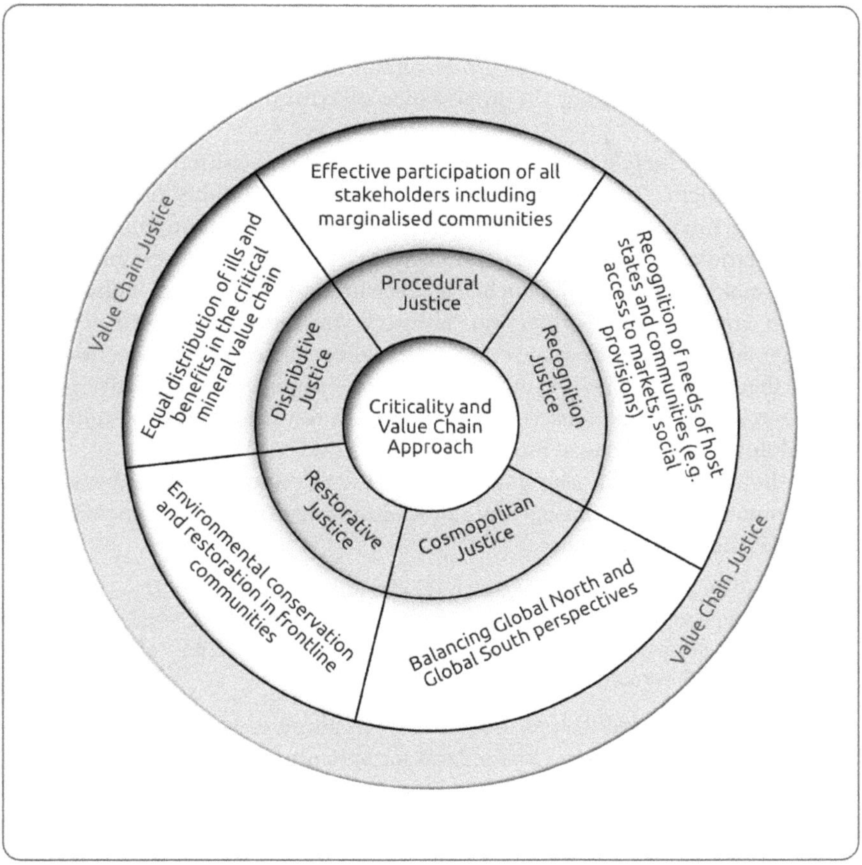

Source: Author's own elaboration.

The UN Guiding Principle No 11 states: 'Business enterprises should respect human rights. This means that they should avoid infringing on the human rights of others and should address adverse human rights impacts with which they are involved.'[124] The principle coincides with the procedural principle of

[124] See United Nations, 'Guiding Principles on Business and Human Rights, Implementing the United Nations "Protect, Respect and Remedy" Framework' (2011). See also J Ruggie, 'Report of the Special Representative of the Secretary-General on the Issue of Human Rights and Transnational Corporations and Other Business Enterprises: Guiding Principles on Business and Human Rights: Implementing the United Nations "Protect, Respect and Remedy" Framework' (2011) 29(2) *Netherlands Quarterly of Human Rights* 224; J Bonnitcha and R McCorquodale, 'The Concept of "Due Diligence" in the UN Guiding Principles on Business and Human Rights' (2017) 28(3) *European Journal of International Law* 899.

the new criticality framework. The criticality considerations must be systemic throughout the business relationships, ensuring that the criticality assessments and investment process addresses the challenges in given regions/countries/sectors. Hence, the process paradigm facilitates the creation of commonly identified formulae for defining the importance of critical minerals and criticality considerations.

The second principle in the holistic framework is recognition in the decision-making paradigm. The mining industry creates expectations for consumers, civil society, foreign investors, host governments and host communities. Thus, criticality studies, methodologies and value chain integration need an inclusive decision-making model. The inclusive decision-making model highlights all voices in environmental protection, industry standards, social and economic market trajectories, transparency and governance of the critical mineral industry. Furthermore, the decision-making paradigm impacts the legislative process and enforcement of the desired holistic approach towards criticality studies and methodologies of the critical mineral industry.

The holistic approach also guarantees access to remedies and redress of the critical mineral industry through both procedural and distributive justice. The UN Guiding Principle No 25 states:

> As part of their duty to protect against business-related human rights abuse, States must take appropriate steps to ensure, through judicial, administrative, legislative or other appropriate means, that when such abuses occur within their territory and jurisdiction, those affected have access to an effective remedy.[125]

The critical mineral industry is associated with abuse of human rights, such as child labour, slave-like wages, loss of land for agricultural and spiritual practices, and the loss of livelihoods for the host communities. Even though measures have been advanced that ensure favourable value chain practices using block-chain technologies, the host communities should be awarded legal remedies due to the negative impacts associated with the critical mineral industry.

Several court cases have recently emerged on justice in critical mineral development in different parts of the world. Just provisions such as environmental impact assessments (EIAs) are crucial to resource extraction within any society,[126] although they have been criticised when used as a single tool.[127] Such studies evaluate the most likely environmental impacts of a proposed project or mineral

[125] S Carrera and M Stefan, 'Introduction: Justicing Europe's Frontiers: Effective Access to Remedies and Justice in Bordering and Expulsion Policies' in S Carrera, M Stefan (eds), *Fundamental Rights Challenges in Border Controls and Expulsion of Irregular Immigrants in the European Union* (Routledge, 2020) 1–21.

[126] FP Retief, TB Fischer, RC Alberts, C Roos and DP Cilliers, 'An Administrative Justice Perspective on Improving EIA Effectiveness' (2020) 38(2) *Impact Assessment and Project Appraisal* 151.

[127] T Yang, 'The Emergence of the Environmental Impact Assessment Duty as a Global Legal Norm and General Principle of Law' (2018) 70 *Hastings Law Journal* 525.

development, taking into account the interrelated socio-economic, cultural and human health impacts, especially within a given host community.[128] The EIA studies must be made public, with full access to the information, to notify society of a proposed project's adverse and beneficial aspects.[129]

In South Africa, a critical case on climate change and EIA made its findings and conclusion based on justice in EIA studies. On 8 March 2017, the North Gauteng High Court in South Africa handed down judgment in the matter of *Earthlife Africa, Johannesburg v The Minister of Environmental Affairs and others*.[130] The case follows the government's plan to get an independent power producer to build a 1200 MW coal-fired power station near the town of Lephalale in the Limpopo Province. The construction of the coal-fired plant was intended to address the severe energy challenges that hamper South Africa's socio-economic development;[131] South Africa is one of the heaviest emitters of global greenhouse gas emissions in sub-Saharan Africa.[132] The Chief Director of the Department of Environmental Affairs granted an environmental authorisation for the project without the benefit of a separate, independently researched climate change impact report.[133] The judgment was against the construction of the coal plant. It was found that climate change poses a substantial risk to sustainable development in South Africa. Therefore, future generations must assess and consider climate change's impact, linking sustainable development with the principle of intergenerational justice. Further, in 2019, a judge in Australia held that a coal mine should not receive permission to open due to the effects of the carbon dioxide that would be produced in other places in the world once that coal was transported and burnt outside of Australia.[134]

Restorative justice also aims to address the massive pollution, environmental degradation and social challenges associated with the critical mineral industry. Furthermore, the industry creates rent-seeking tendencies. Hence, restoration must go beyond environmental conservation to socio-economic structures. Restoration must be intertwined with criticality aspects, looking at environmental considerations the same way the threat to supply of minerals is looked at. The paradigms of the holistic approach before 'restoration' will not create any

[128] RM Deus, FD Mele, BS Bezerra and RAG Battistelle, 'A Municipal Solid Waste Indicator for Environmental Impact: Assessment and Identification of Best Management Practices' (2020) 242 *Journal of Cleaner Production* 118433.

[129] D McCauley and R Heffron, 'Just Transition: Integrating Climate, Energy and Environmental Justice' (2018) 119 *Energy Policy* 1.

[130] TL Humby, 'The Thabametsi Case: Case No 65662/16 Earthlife Africa Johannesburg v Minister of Environmental Affairs' (2018) 30(1) *Journal of Environmental Law* 145.

[131] ibid.

[132] G Vural, 'How Do Output, Trade, Renewable Energy and Non-Renewable Energy Impact Carbon Emissions in Selected Sub-Saharan African Countries?' (2020) 69 *Resources Policy* 101840.

[133] Humby (n 130).

[134] *Gloucester Resources Limited v Minister for Planning* [2019] NSWLEC 7; R White, J Hallinan and B Rayment, 'Environmental Law: Climate Change Takes Centre Stage in Land and Environment Court' (2019) 54 *Law Society Journal: Law Society of New South Wales Journal* 80.

sustainable results if host communities and, in a larger context, the host countries do not restore their communities to the situation they were in before discovering these critical minerals. This is also in line with the Mining Principles of the International Council on Mining and Metals (ICMM), which define good practice environmental, social and governance requirements for the mining and metals industry.[135]

The cosmopolitan paradigm of the holistic approach entails treating all people as citizens of earth. Thus, the paradigm acknowledges that the industrial development of one region led to ramifications being experienced in another region. The developments in mitigating and adapting to climate change in the Global North have implications for the Global South. For example, moving away from fossil fuels to cleaner energy sources threatens stranded assets in developing critical mineral-producing countries. Hence, the cosmopolitan paradigm emphasises the equal treatment of people across the critical mineral value chain while considering their context.

The holistic approach enhances the considerations of criticality studies and methodologies, moving beyond jurisdictional and regional bias due to the origin of the study. Furthermore, the holistic approach considers 'dark or lost voices' that are yet to be considered in global decision-making corridors on climate change and the energy transition. The holistic approach also moves beyond the supply and economic importance considerations of criticality studies by integrating justice as a pertinent consideration. Below is the integration of the 'Just Holistic Framework' and the critical mineral value chain.

5.5. The Integration and Resolve of the Just Framework into the Critical Mineral Industry

Justice is a significant component of critical mineral development across borders. However, the legal and regulatory frameworks in countries such as the DRC and Zambia have left loopholes through legal insufficiency for stakeholders to integrate justice in the given industry. This part proposes interdisciplinary pathways to integrate the Just Framework into the critical mineral value chain. Figure 7 shows the possible pathways at each value chain stage.

[135] The ICMM Guiding Principles are a set of 10 guidelines and principles on conducting ethical business, incorporating sustainable development in decision-making processes, respect for human rights, effective risk-management strategies, health and safety performance, environmental performance, conservation of biodiversity, responsible production, social performance and stakeholder engagement. See www.icmm.com/en-gb/about-us/member-commitments/icmm-10-principles.

Figure 7 Just Framework pathways into the critical mineral value chain

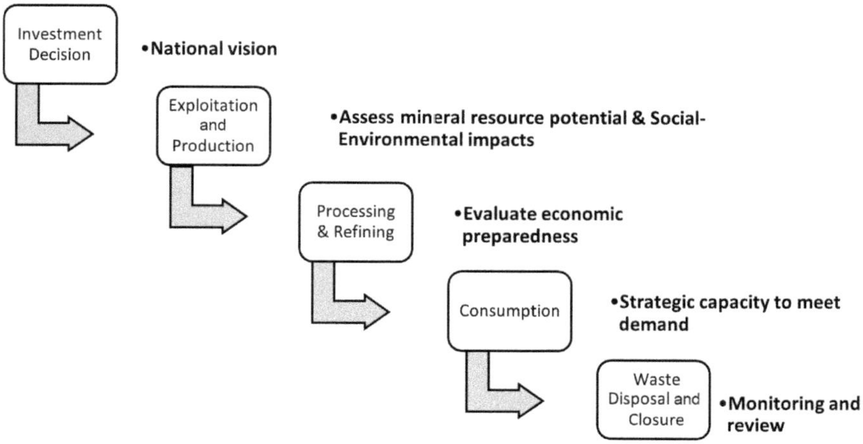

Source: S Nakanwagi, 'Critical Minerals and the Global Energy Transition: Recognising Global South Perspectives' (2023) 4(1–2) *Global Energy Law and Sustainability* 115.

5.5.1. The Investment Decision Stage

The first step is the investment stage – this stage must be intertwined with the nation's objectives to integrate the Just Framework into the critical mineral value chain. This stage requires clear strategies for using the critical minerals for the country's development, such as powering renewable energy and local consumption, thus boosting the industrialisation of a given country such as the DRC and Zambia. Additionally, the stakeholders could anticipate clear and stable rules and policies regarding critical mineral extraction and development while making their investment decisions.[136] Thus, the nation's objective should be to manage its natural resources to maximise the welfare of its people; this is critical because it becomes a state responsibility due to being incorporated into the constitution, as is the case for countries like Indonesia.[137] According to Article 33(3) of the Indonesian Constitutional Law 1945, land, water and natural resources contained within the territory shall be controlled by the state and used for the greatest prosperity of the people. The Indonesian Constitution accords with the current societal

[136] H Hamzah, 'Legal Policy of Legislation in the Field of Natural Resources in Indonesia' (2016) 1(1) *Hasanuddin Law Review* 108.

[137] RJ Heffron and J Sheehan, 'Rethinking International Taxation and Energy Policy Post COVID-19 and the Financial Crisis for Developing Countries' (2020) 73 *Journal of Energy & Natural Resources Law* 465.

push for greater justice in critical mineral development. It addresses the fundamental goal of justice, which is to create a more inclusive society in which no one is left behind.

Consequently, the industry meets the demands of procedural, recognition and distributive justice by first recognising local businesses and individuals. Secondly, it provides a procedural assurance that they can compete on an equal footing with foreign firms, considering any disadvantages associated with operating in a developing country. Thirdly, it helps the government to balance the imperative of monetising the resource through exports and creating opportunities for the local population and the welfare of the state.[138]

5.5.2. The Exploitation and Production Stage

The second stage of the critical mineral value chain, the exploitation and production phase, entails incorporating the Just Framework based on a resource potential assessment, as shown in Figure 8. In this stage, coupled with the nation's objectives, the scope and duration of the mining activities are critical factors in the design and implementation of policies to promote justice integration. The stage of development of the resource base is also vital. The activities of the critical mining industry during exploration, development and production present distinct opportunities for value capture and the welfare of the nation, especially the marginalised host communities.[139] Based on the geological make-up of the minerals, governments should ask themselves in each circumstance and at each stage of the process, from initial exploration to production, 'what opportunities exist to develop the types of skills, goods and services that are required, and when are they required?'

Governments should request early data on their needs throughout the project development life cycle from foreign critical mineral companies and share it with educational institutions and local suppliers. Through procedural justice, the Just Framework needs to mobilise local knowledge on the geological structure of the minerals as this would deter unsafe, unhealthy and unethical industrial practices, such as ASM. Furthermore, the government should also meet procedural justice by disclosing information on the commodity cycles and broader economic cycles so that the local population can understand the value of their minerals according to international prices and not their own circumstances.[140] Lastly, adequate institutional representation would ensure that a just optimisation of lowering

[138] MZ Ngoasong, 'How International Oil and Gas Companies Respond to Local Content Policies in Petroleum-Producing Developing Countries: A Narrative Enquiry' (2014) 73 *Energy Policy* 471.

[139] Qurbani et al (n 118).

[140] BK Sovacool and M Martiskainen, A Hook and L Baker, 'Decarbonization and Its Discontents: A Critical Energy Justice Perspective on Four Low-Carbon Transitions' (2019) 155(4) *Climatic Change* 581.

operating costs by the critical mineral investors is not at the detriment of the host communities.

Figure 8 Just Framework integration based on the geological make-up of the resources

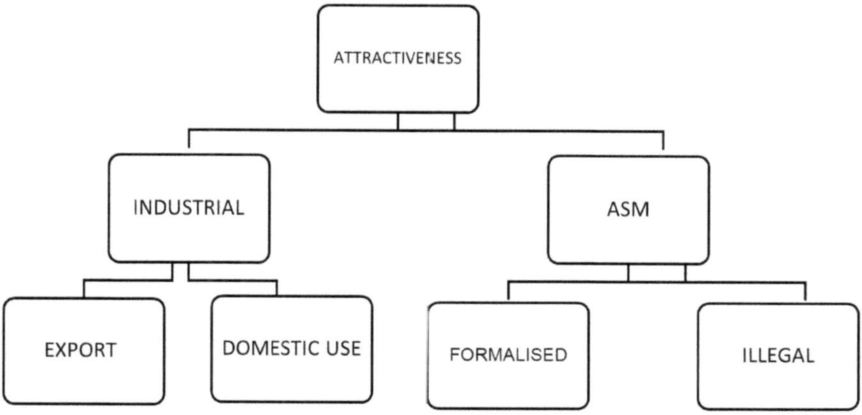

Source: Author's own elaboration.

Governments should determine resource geology to ensure distributive justice and integrate the Just Framework into the critical mineral value chain. The data on the geology of the resources creates a valuation based on the government and not any foreign entity.[141] This would solve the undervaluation of critical minerals in developing countries, particularly in the DRC and Zambia. According to the above illustration, if the resources found are attractive for large industrial practices, there will be limited opportunities for the host community, as most host communities engage in ASM. The variations between large and small deposits facilitate the efficient speculation of a risk-averse government.[142]

By commissioning valuation and assessment studies, governments can gain early knowledge of and control the resource base. For example, the platinum-group metals (PGMs) industry is South Africa's largest employer.[143] However, the labour-intensive nature of older operations in South Africa has been argued to pose a real risk to the industry's long-term viability.[144] The increased and intensive costs have been exacerbated by recycling, a significant factor in recent years. Nevertheless, PGMs faced lower global prices in 2020, which led to the recycling

[141] AE Hilson and JS Ovadia, 'Local Content in Developing and Middle-Income Countries: Towards a More Holistic Strategy' (2020) 7(2) *The Extractive Industries and Society* 253.

[142] PL Têtu and F Lasserre, 'Chinese Investment in Greenland's Mining Industry: Toward a New Framework for Foreign Direct Investment' (2017) 4(3) *The Extractive Industries and Society* 661.

[143] B Genc, T Mlangena and M Onifade, 'Safety Towards Zero Harm in the South African Platinum Sector' in *Proceedings of the 27th International Symposium on Mine Planning and Equipment Selection – MPES* (Springer, 2018) 535–44.

[144] ibid.

supply competing with the primary production supply.[145] The wages and rents flowing to local communities remained low despite the recent profit spikes.

5.5.3. The Processing and Refining Stage

The processing and refining stage is the value chain segment that most developing countries lose out on. The justice rhetoric cannot be achieved without an economy bearing the absorptive capacity that creates or provides the economic preparedness to absorb and take advantage of the critical mineral supply chain. Hence, to achieve justice in the processing and refining stage of the critical mineral industry, several factors must be considered, such as the expected level of activity and the demand for national skills, goods and services. Additionally, there must be an examination of the proximity of the critical mineral operations to the country's economic hubs. Such factors assess the economic readiness to absorb and create just outcomes in the critical mineral industry, as shown in Figure 9.

Figure 9 Economic preparedness to ensure justice in the critical mineral industry

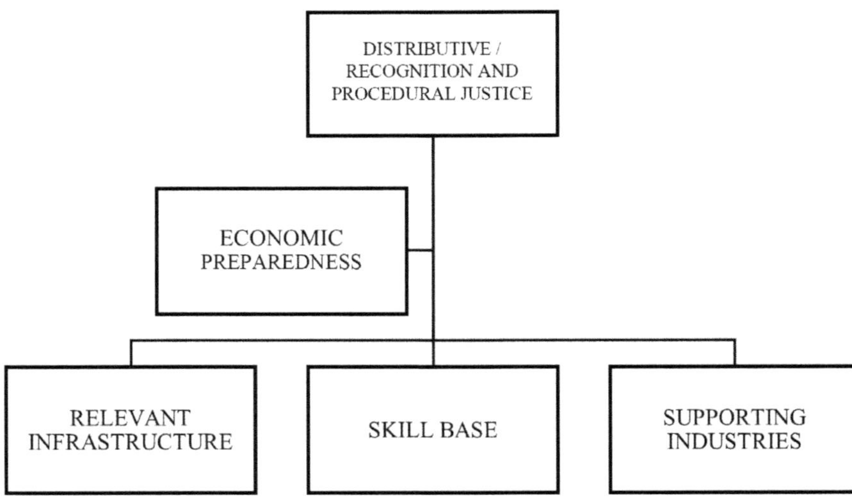

Source: S Nakanwagi, 'Critical Minerals and the Global Energy Transition: Recognising Global South Perspectives' (2023) 4(1–2) *Global Energy Law and Sustainability* 115.

Suppose an economy has well-developed supporting industries capable of meeting the demands of the critical mineral industry. In that case, efforts should be

[145] D Xun, H Hao, X Sun, Z Liu and F Zhao, 'End-of-life Recycling Rates of Platinum Group Metals in the Automotive Industry: Insight into Regional Disparities' (2020) 266 *Journal of Cleaner Production* 121942.

made to leverage that capacity and source locally to adhere to distributive and recognition justice.[146] However, compared to developed economies, critical mineral-rich nations in the Global South have limited resources for developing the downstream industry. Governments must collaborate with the critical mineral investors and other associated stakeholders to determine, for instance, the capability of the available infrastructure, the demand for goods and services, the available local capacity and services, the training and the supplier development strategy to close the gaps that could cause injustice to the locals and marginalised host communities.

Furthermore, the skill base is a significant factor in achieving justice in the critical mineral value chain. Multinational companies must provide adequate information on the requirements of the opportunities offered to the local people.[147] The industry and government must forge partnerships and finance the cost of bridging gaps and loopholes that can create injustice for the local population. The local economy may also assess the existing supporting industries.[148] Suppose the economy cannot supply goods and services through its supporting industries. In that case, the government should assess whether the national supporting environment is conducive to developing these industries.[149] The ease of doing business can be established. Changes in government policy create strategies needed to develop justice in the critical mineral industry. The benefits of supporting industries can only be materialised through vibrant cost-of-doing-business-associated legislation that emphasises justice.[150] Significant developments in environmental concerns, proposals for more equitable distribution of financial revenue generated and overall simplification of legislation can meet the demands of the Just Framework. The Just Framework advocating or promoting policies can entail the following:

1. Implementing fiscal incentives to promote the formation of small and medium-sized businesses. The fiscal incentive for critical mineral supply chains should be weighed against the fiscal incentives for other industrial sectors that may be more successful or have a greater chance of success.[151]
2. Developing infrastructure (roads, airports and telecommunications) to enable the private sector to provide goods and services. Infrastructure development

[146] Sovacool et al (n 140).

[147] S Patnaik, Y Temouri, J Tuffour, S Tarba and SK Singh, 'Corporate Social Responsibility and Multinational Enterprise Identity: Insights from a Mining Company's Attempt to Localise in Ghana' (2018) 24(5) *Social Identities* 604.

[148] ibid.

[149] S Geenen, 'Gold and Godfathers: Local Content, Politics, and Capitalism in Extractive Industries' (2019) 123 *World Development* 104605.

[150] RJ Heffron, 'Justice Should Govern the New Momentum for COP26' (2021) 2(1) *Global Energy Law and Sustainability* 5.

[151] F Chien, QT Ngo, CC Hsu, KY Chau and R Iram, 'Assessing the Mechanism of Barriers Towards Green Finance and Public Spending in Small and Medium Enterprises from Developed Countries' (2021) *Environmental Science and Pollution Research* 1.

should prioritise establishing synergies between the mining project and other economic activities (for example, facilitating access to new agricultural land or tourist attractions).[152]

3. Educating the private sector about the standards and accreditations required for the delivery of goods and services by the critical mining sector.[153]
4. Encouraging collaboration among critical mineral companies in order to reduce costs and develop markets for standardised products and services.
5. Providing reliable information promptly to enable local businesses to make sound investment decisions. Defining the categories of goods and services to which local residents may be granted preferential access.

5.5.4. The Consumption Stage

Consumption of critical minerals is mainly concentrated in the Global North, especially for their climate change agenda. As a result, the consuming countries have undertaken a massive drive to achieve a circular economy and the recycling of critical materials to increase their lifespan – hence securing the availability of the minerals. The EU is leading in this sphere, with legislative actions like the Green Battery Deal. In its 'perfect' form, transforming sectors, especially energy, into a more circular economy represents a significant paradigm shift with the potential to significantly reduce waste and carbon emissions while increasing the supply of parts and materials.[154] It also mitigates the environmental degradation caused by mining, which generates large amounts of contaminated waste, ecological degradation and biodiversity loss.[155] However, the circular economy has been criticised by some researchers for having a weak conceptual foundation and a lack of coherence in terms of how it can contribute to long-term sustainable development. By 2017, only 12 per cent of the circular economy definitions integrated sustainable development.[156] Furthermore, as one might want or expect, sustainability is not as well incorporated into the implementation of circular economy techniques, nor as prevalent in circular economy research.[157] For example, the Ellen MacArthur Foundation has positioned the circular economy squarely within the narrative

[152] JY Lin, 'New Structural Economics: A Framework for Rethinking Development' (2011) 26(2) *The World Bank Research Observer* 193.
[153] MJ Mayer and M Altman, 'South Africa's Economic Development Trajectory: Implications for Skills Development' (2005) 18(1) *Journal of Education and Work* 33.
[154] AP Velenturf, SA Archer, HI Gomes, B Christgen, AJ Lag-Brotons and P Purnell, 'Circular Economy and the Matter of Integrated Resources' (2019) 689 *Science of the Total Environment* 963.
[155] G Gaustad, M Krystofik, M Bustamante and K Badami, 'Circular Economy Strategies for Mitigating Critical Material Supply Issues' (2018) 135 *Resources, Conservation and Recycling* 24.
[156] M Geissdoerfer, P Savaget, NM Bocken and EJ Hultink, 'The Circular Economy – A New Sustainability Paradigm?' (2017) 143 *Journal of Cleaner Production* 757.
[157] AP Velenturf and P Purnell, 'Principles for a Sustainable Circular Economy' (2021) 27 *Sustainable Production and Consumption* 1437.

of 'green growth', implying that primary resource consumption and associated emissions can be divorced from GDP to justify continued economic expansion.[158]

Globally, the structural transition to a circular economy poses significant implications. Primary raw material flows, value chains and international trade relations will be reshaped.[159] Some economies often experience declines in import and export demand for primary materials, secondary materials and waste.[160] As a result, a strategy with immense promise for sustainable development risks losing momentum, necessitating the integration of sustainability into the design, implementation and appraisal of circular economies.[161] It is thus critical to investigate the extent to which the circular economy can contribute to sustainable development, more so in the developing resource-rich countries that rely on the extraction of their mineral wealth for their development needs.

Further, a circular economy can safeguard resource supply by reducing primary raw material dependency, mitigating geopolitical supply risks and balancing global markets.[162] In the medium to long term, low- and middle-income countries relying heavily on extractive industries stand to suffer, with more dire consequences for those relying heavily on resource exports for economic growth and tax revenue.[163] Consequently, this may also harm those countries' ability to achieve sustainable development.[164] While it is natural to be fearful when considering the magnitude of mineral requirements for the energy transition, evidence suggests that the world is unlikely to run out of any mineral, due to the improved extraction and recycling technologies.[165] Analysts have consistently underestimated the size of reserves for as long as commodities have been traded, noting that the commodity business is cyclical.[166] With mines opening and closing and ramping up or slowing down production in response to market conditions, demand and supply never perfectly match; but this does

[158] T Parrique, J Barth, F Briens, C Kerschner, A Kraus-Polk, A Kuokkanen and JH Spangenberg, 'Decoupling Debunked. Evidence and Arguments Against Green Growth as a Sole Strategy for Sustainability' (European Environment Bureau, 2019).

[159] OECD, *International Trade and the Transition to a Circular Economy* (OECD Publishing, 2018) www.oecd.org/environment/waste/policy-highlights-international-trade-and-the-transition-to-a-circular-economy.pdf.

[160] ibid.

[161] Velenturf and Purnell (n 157).

[162] A McCarthy, R Dellink and R Bibas, 'The Macroeconomics of the Circular Economy Transition: A Critical Review of Modelling Approaches' (OECD, 2018) Environment Working Paper No 130, www.oecd.org/officialdocuments/publicdisplaydocumentpdf/?cote=ENV/WKP(2018)4&docLanguage=En.

[163] P Schröder, 'Promoting a Just Transition to an Inclusive Circular Economy' (Royal Institute of International Affairs, 2020) www.chathamhouse.org/sites/default/files/2020-04-01-inclusive-circular-economy-schroder.pdf.

[164] ibid.

[165] S Kirsch, 'Running Out? Rethinking Resource Depletion' (2020) 7(3) *The Extractive Industries and Society* 838. N Ferris, 'Why Critical Mineral Supplies Won't Scupper the Energy Transition (*Energy Monitor*, 2021) https://energymonitor.ai/finance/risk-management/why-we-need-a-level-headed-approach-to-energy-transition-minerals.

[166] Ferris (n 165).

not mean we are running out of supplies.[167] However, scholars like Kirsch have opined that the focus should instead be on the consequences of environmental deterioration induced by the extraction of resources rather than on running out of minerals.[168] Circularity should, therefore, be based on the environmental benefits it provides.

5.5.5. The Waste Disposal and Closure Stage

Regarding waste disposal and mine closures, governments should have clearly defined terms for what is expected and what is meant by restorative justice.[169] This stage must emphasise returning the environment and surroundings to their original form or even better. Hence, quantifiable targets must facilitate the local community's monitoring, reporting and enhancement after the mining operations have been completed and the minerals depleted.[170] Heffron and McCauley state that at its most fundamental level, energy justice entails restoring an energy site (in this case, a mining site) to its original purpose.[171] It is a critical step in developing a project, and there is growing recognition that insufficient action is taken on this issue far too frequently.

5.6. Summary

The critical minerals industry is growing rapidly and there is potential for more growth in the sub-Saharan Africa region, particularly in the DRC and Zambia. This chapter aims to shed light on the underappreciated role of justice in the development of this critical industry in these two countries as the global community and society seek to meet the demands of sustainable development. It is critical to address the societal issue of inequality and ensure justice in the mining industry, especially the critical mining industry. Furthermore, the utilisation of the Just Framework illustrates that the nation's natural resources, such as critical minerals, must be used to maximise the people's prosperity. Secondly, developing countries such as Zambia and the DRC must transplant mechanisms from traditional mining industries to crack through the critical mineral industry's enclave and do so in a prosperous and sustainable manner.

[167] ibid.

[168] Kirsch (n 162).

[169] RS Muhongo, *Energy Justice: A Local Content Analytical Framework for Sub-Saharan Africa* (Springer Nature, 2020).

[170] P Amoah and G Eweje, 'Impact Mitigation or Ecological Restoration? Examining the Environmental Sustainability Practices of Multinational Mining Companies' (2021) 30(1) *Business Strategy and the Environment* 551.

[171] RJ Heffron and D McCauley, 'The Concept of Energy Justice Across the Disciplines' (2017) 105 *Energy Policy* 658.

6

Conclusion

6.1. Introduction

This book has evaluated and analysed critical metals' evaluation and assessment criteria. It has already been established that these metals are critical for economic and social development and, most importantly, for achieving Sustainable Development Goals. The consumption of these critical metals exploded in the twenty-first century, posing a greater demand and supply risk for the world's metal resources.[1] Most Global North (including China) countries have taken adequate measures to address the future supply risk of critical metals.[2] For example, to reduce the dependence on imports, the USA advanced supply security by effectively promoting the extraction and recycling of critical domestic resources.[3] The EU bolstered their regional mineral resource development and facilitated safe access to raw materials to ensure a stable supply of critical minerals.[4]

Additionally, countries such as Canada and Australia have enhanced the efficiency and quality of mining operations for these critical minerals.[5] The Chinese National Plan for Mineral Resources (2016–2020) unequivocally asserts that for national security strategy, management improvements are required to ensure the safe supply of resources.[6] These illustrations show how the criticality and evaluation of these metals have been predominantly managed and led by developed countries, notably the Global North. Thus, the considerations have been limited to economic and scientific reasons, with defence and health gaining traction in recent years.

[1] E Barteková and R Kemp, Critical Raw Material Strategies in Different World Regions (2016) *The United Nations University-Maastricht Economic and Social Research Institute on Innovation and Technology (UNU-MERIT) Working Papers*, 5.

[2] P Andersson, 'Chinese Assessments of "Critical" and "Strategic" Raw Materials: Concepts, Categories, Policies, and Implications' (2020) 7(1) *The Extractive Industries and Society* 127.

[3] SM Fortier, NT Nassar, GW Lederer, J Brainard, J Gambogi and EA McCullough, 'Draft Critical Mineral List – Summary of Methodology and Background Information' (US Geological Survey, 2018) US Geological Survey technical input document in response to Secretarial Order No 3359 (No 2018-1021).

[4] V Bach, N Finogenova, M Berger, L Winter and M Finkbeiner, 'Enhancing the Assessment of Critical Resource Use at the Country Level with the SCARCE Method – Case Study of Germany' (2017) 53 *Resources Policy* 283.

[5] ibid.

[6] W Yan, Z Wang, H Cao, Y Zhang and Z Sun, 'Criticality Assessment of Metal Resources in China' (2021) 24(6) *iScience* 102524.

Most studies and evaluations conducted by researchers and critical metal scholars have offered a three-dimensional system that accounts for supply chain risk, economic volatility and environmental risk.[7] The assessment and critical metal evaluation studies are conducted under the parameters of a material's supply risk and economic importance.

This book asserts that broader considerations need to be taken into account, considering the stakeholders involved and the spatial dimension of the critical mineral value chain. Furthermore, it is evident from the above illustration that the criticality studies have predominantly emphasised the industrial needs and supply of these metals.[8] Machacek holds that the criticality construct highlights the role of experts in constructing mineral criticality.[9] For example, EU and US experts construct criticality by means of classification. These experts have estimated mineral criticality by allotting data to a set of parameters in a framework established for assessing criticality.[10] Hence, Machacek holds that 'in a bureaucratic practice of classification, key materials are turned into critical materials'.[11] This criticality criterion has been criticised for being a one-sided approach by 'experts' from critical mineral-consuming countries, particularly the Global North. Hence, they are the 'legitimitisers' of constructing the conceptual meaning of what should be critical.

The one-sided approach shows how other aspects of mineral criticality can be silenced in this process. Furthermore, the experts have politicised criticality studies – when defining some minerals as 'critical', experts influence policymakers who seek to mitigate criticality by emphasising certain issues. Consequently, this leads to the redistribution of public wealth toward a few beneficiaries. Following these arguments, the book adopted a Just Framework for the critical mineral value chain, to integrate distributive, procedural and recognition justice principles into the critical mineral value chain.

Such considerations emanate from the Global South, being the custodian of these minerals but not the beneficiary thereof, hindering sustainable development objectives. This book, therefore, presents justice as a vessel for operationalising and achieving sustainable development and sustainability, especially in the resource-rich Global South countries, through the justice elements – procedural justice (for the governance dimension of sustainable development); recognition justice (for the social dimension of sustainable development); distributive justice (for the social and economic dimension of sustainable development); and restorative justice (for the environmental dimension of sustainable development). Hence,

[7] TE Graedel, J Allwood, JP Birat, M Buchert, C Hagelüken, BK Reck, SF Sibley and G Sonnemann, 'What Do We Know About Metal Recycling Rates?' (2011) 15(3) *Journal of Industrial Ecology* 355.

[8] E Machacek, 'Constructing Criticality by Classification: Expert Assessments of Mineral Raw Materials' (2017) 84 *Geoforum* 368.

[9] ibid.

[10] PL Têtu and F Lasserre, 'Chinese Investment in Greenland's Mining Industry: Toward a New Framework for Foreign Direct Investment' (2017) 4(3) *The Extractive Industries and Society* 661.

[11] Machacek (n 8).

the book investigated the 'criticality' aspects of significant issues such as sustainable development aspirations and the critical minerals value chain.

6.2. The Just Holistic Framework Implications

The Just Holistic Framework has social implications for developing countries such as the Democratic Republic of Congo (DRC). Cobalt mining villages such as Kolwezi and Kivu can gain an 'equitable' stake in the energy transition. This can be done by attracting impact investments that have implications beyond the financial gains of the industry. The Just Holistic Framework creates avenues and channels for developing policies that bring about equitable distribution of benefits and recognition of marginalised host communities and people, such as the women and children of Zambia and the DRC. The income gap between women and men engaged in artisanal mining can be addressed through such channels and frameworks by shaping policy, laws and regulations in developing countries guided by regional and international policies.

The Just Holistic Framework has economic policy implications. Developing countries with extractive resources suffer from the resource curse, or the paradox of plenty.[12] Countries such as Nigeria, the DRC, Chad and Angola have failed to change their natural resources into agents of economic change. The resource curse has largely been caused by single-industry dependency when countries neglect investment in other major sectors such as manufacturing, agriculture and tourism.[13] The Just Holistic Framework provides avenues for decision-making and participatory engagements from the top down between the host communities, marginalised communities, investors and international policy stewards. Through the proposed framework, channels of access and benefits create linkage development between industries for the aggregate development of the economy.

The Just Holistic Framework has international geopolitical implications. The critical mineral industry has massive geopolitical implications. Countries such as China are dominant in rare earth element production. On the other hand, South Africa is the major transportation corridor in sub-Saharan Africa to the European and Asian markets.[14] The Just Framework's application balances the geopolitical aspects of countries such as the DRC and Zambia without getaway borders through the redistribution of supply channels and the development of

[12] MB Rapanyane, 'China's Involvement in the Democratic Republic of Congo's Resource Curse Mineral Driven Conflict: An Afrocentric Review' (2021) *Contemporary Social Science* 1.

[13] ibid.

[14] H Paulick and E Machacek, 'The Global Rare Earth Element Exploration Boom: An Analysis of Resources Outside of China and Discussion of Development Perspectives' (2017) 52 *Resources Policy* 134; ASM Quium, 'Transport Corridors for Wider Socio-economic Development' (2019) 11(19) *Sustainability* 5248.

new transport corridors based on cosmopolitanism and recognition in the critical mineral industry and supply chain. DRC has recently joined the East African Community, increasing the market to over 400 million people.[15] Through the Just Framework that facilitates increased in-country value, largely retained skills and technological transfer, developing countries such as the DRC and Zambia will have an opportunity to accelerate and diversify their economies.

The Just Holistic Framework has implications for criticality assessments. Criticality assessments have a lot of extraterritorial implications, such as the resource curse (they lead to increased demand for minerals from areas with weak governance), as discussed above. Criticality studies currently have two predominant considerations: economic considerations and supply risk.[16] As shown throughout the book, these two considerations show that myriad considerations and factors are not considered or added to the criticality equation. These include restorative justice for host communities, the synergy of business and human rights, and the development of decision-making platforms for remote host communities. These considerations are significant to criticality studies that can be applied if the Just Holistic Framework is efficiently implemented. Thus, there is a need for action from the international community regarding how the exploitation of the minerals should occur. Therefore, criticality assessments should be done differently to look beyond the economic importance and supply risk considerations.

The Just Holistic Framework influences developments in shaping law, policy and regulations in host countries such as the DRC and Zambia. The countries will look beyond concentrating on only the accumulation of rents from their fiscal regimes. Using the framework, they will develop appropriate regulations and policies from the grassroots. This will involve considering the real explicit needs of marginalised communities, such as the pricing of the metals, advocating for more rigorous corporate social responsibility practices, and developing local content regimes that are considerate of the energy transition to ensure jobs and skills within the transition.

The Just Holistic Framework expands the legal discipline into a socio-legal perspective, especially concerning environmental, climate, energy, natural resource and mining laws. The framework proposes a study that seeks to remedy the injustices of the extractive industry and economy across multiple disciplines, such as geology in criticality considerations, economics in metric formulations and policy in considering legal impacts and remedies.

The Just Holistic Framework impacts the DRC, Zambia and other resource-rich countries' supply chains, especially with more inclusive pricing of metals

[15] R Mugume and KA Nattabi, 'The Potential Trade Effects of Democratic Republic of Congo Joining the East African Community Bloc' (2021) 9(4) *African Journal of Economic Review* 291.

[16] L Erdmann, TE Graedel, 'Criticality of Non-Fuel Minerals: A Review of Major Approaches and Analyses' (2011) 45 *Environmental Science Technology* 7620.

and climate change policies. The readjusting of the pricing of these critical metals to include considerations of the Global South make critical mining projects economically and socially viable within the given framework. Furthermore, the adequate valuation of these metals using the Just Holistic Framework will drive more equitable benefits, such as community development and public health, as well as the delivery of social services and other benefits, to the marginalised host communities.

The Just Holistic Framework provides possible avenues for modifying and reconfiguring business ways. It manages the transition of exploitative extractive methodologies to sustainable business models that include involving marginalised host communities in decision-making, distributing benefits and ills and recognising the peculiar needs of these countries for the development of the supply chain. The framework sets targets within the value chain from the investment decision to the decommissioning phase of critical mining projects, ensuring justice adherence and just outcomes within the new business models.

Further, the Just Holistic Framework provides lenses of justice through which many international actions could be triggered. These include avenues for international cooperation, liaising with ministries of foreign affairs, business and human rights models, and prompting international regulation of the critical mineral industry. It also includes the coherency of foreign policy to consider the needs of developing countries.

6.3. Lessons for Critical Mineral-Rich Countries

Global South countries must conduct studies to identify the gaps in policy and the critical mineral value chain that are detrimental to the host communities and countries. Such customisation will enable safeguards in mineral resource governance and transparency, revenue maximisation and utilisation, and adoption of environmental, social and governance investment strategies rather than developing and depending on rent-oriented strategies when negotiating with multinational mining companies. In this regard, they limit the environmental and social impacts on the community due to the responsible and sustainable mining strategies implemented at the beginning of the value chain.

Mineral-rich countries must prioritise initiatives to foster economic diversification and maximise the value derived from mineral resources. They should consider policies that bolster local processing and add value to the minerals before exportation, thereby catalysing economic linkages through the growth of downstream sectors such as mineral processing, manufacturing and technological innovation. Such measures are essential for stimulating domestic economic expansion, fostering job creation and augmenting the intrinsic worth of mineral resources.

The Global South should also invest in the technological transfer that creates domestic value-added advantages due to the high demand for critical minerals. The domestic consumption of these minerals will increase energy access and employment opportunities, increase government revenue and integrate artisanal small-scale miners who engage in harmful practices to gain some minerals.

Concerted efforts to understand the ever-changing needs of humanity are essential. Sustainable development is being pushed and realigned with international policies and governance mechanisms to meet the latest needs of humanity. Criticality studies, especially in the Global South, are crucial as the needs and wants are not universal, though the need to curb climate change is. Therefore, the Global South needs to establish goals and developmental targets that synergise the global demands of critical minerals.

Regional bodies in the Global South should promote a collaborative approach towards aligning sustainability standards and negotiating and allocating resource rights. Regional regulatory frameworks should offer credibility criteria for multinational companies to adhere to while responsibly investing in the region.

6.4. Further Considerations

Analysis of geopolitical aspects: As established throughout the book, copper and cobalt minerals in sub-Saharan Africa are predominantly found in Zambia and the DRC. The geopolitical aspects of the region must therefore be analysed to determine how regional organisations and neighbouring governments will affect aspects of governance, markets, criticality studies and mineral processing and refining in the future, with these metals' increased demands. For example, in 2018, African countries established the African Continental Free Trade Area. The largest free trade area in the world will indeed have ramifications on critical mineral development. Since countries like South Africa are moving towards assembling and manufacturing electric cars, most critical minerals may remain in sub-Saharan Africa for domestic consumption. These issues raise a need for research in human geography to understand how the change in corporate and economic interactions affects the critical mineral industry.

There is a need to analyse the issues of sovereignty and legality of criticality assessments within different regions. Every country has the right to self-determination, and how criticality assessments and studies are determined falls under the sovereignty of the determining country or region. This brings about a collision of ideologies and beliefs since these exercised sovereign rights by developed countries impact critical mineral-rich countries, which are mainly developing countries. Therefore, further research could investigate the issues of cosmopolitan justice (highlighting that we are the citizens of one world) against the principles of sovereignty and self-determination.

Development of the Just Holistic Framework in other disciplines beyond socio-legal aspects such as geology in criticality formulae and economics: The methodologies, valuations and criticality studies have always followed economic and scientific concerns, overlooking other pressing considerations not significantly experienced by the evaluating countries. For example, companies have employed sustainability metrics and indices to quantify sustainability beyond the general rhetoric.[17] This book has identified gaps in the critical minerals value chain and established the unequivocal need to incorporate the Just Framework in the copper–cobalt value chain. Economists, physicists and developmental studies can create justice framework metrics and indices to show how far the Just Framework is being materialised in the copper–cobalt value chain.

Development of legal and regulatory regimes based on justice for the mining industry: For instance, research should be considered on a joint Zambia–DRC binational mineral policy to envision accelerated growth of critical mineral production and address the need for a downstream sector. This binational critical mineral agreement between Zambia and the DRC would facilitate the exploration and extraction of these minerals for domestic benefit. Furthermore, such recommendations would necessitate a conducive investment environment for investors and relevant stakeholders. Such initiatives show that legal and policy experts need to devise policies tailored to critical mineral evaluation, exploitation and exportation. Thus, countries such as the DRC and Zambia may enact a 'Critical Mineral Development Act' compatible with international legal and policy regimes and adhere to the principles and tenets of the Just Framework.

Development of a synergy between the Just Holistic Framework and other emerging trends such as blockchain technology and environmental, social and governance standards in the mining industry: Blockchain technologies, for instance, have been employed to ensure the ethical sourcing of gemstones such as diamonds.[18] Additionally, blockchain can be considered a distributed public ledger disseminated via a peer-to-peer network in which participants validate transactions and maintain a copy of the ledger.[19] Changes to the ledger can be made only with the consent of all blockchain participants.[20] This process is governed by a consensus protocol establishing who is authorised to validate transactions. All blockchain participants, a majority, a select few or a random selection could be the decision-makers. Blockchain technologies have been seen as an alternative to tracking

[17] R Slager, JP Gond and D Crilly, 'Reactivity to Sustainability Metrics: A Configurational Study of Motivation and Capacity' (2021) 31(2) *Business Ethics Quarterly* 275.

[18] C Chow, 'Blockchain for Good? Improving Supply Chain Transparency and Human Rights Management' (2018) 70(1) *Governance Directions* 39.

[19] SA Abeyratne and RP Monfared, 'Blockchain Ready Manufacturing Supply Chain Using Distributed Ledger' (2016) 5(9) *International Journal of Research in Engineering and Technology*, 1.

[20] ibid.

human rights abuse and irregularities in sourcing critical minerals.[21] However, blockchain technology was created to verify cryptocurrency transactions and provide transparency without an intermediary such as a bank. Therefore, further research is needed in critical mineral development to incorporate blockchain technology demonstrating the provenance of goods and indicating that a commodity is free of child labour and slave-like wages.

[21] U Thakker, R Patel, S Tanwar, N Kumar and H Song, 'Blockchain for Diamond Industry: Opportunities and Challenges' (2020) 8(11) *IEEE Internet of Things Journal* 8747.

BIBLIOGRAPHY

Books

Anghie, A, Chimni, B, Mickelson, K and Okafor, OC (eds), *The Third World and International Order: Law, Politics and Globalization* (Brill, 2021).

Ashby, MF, *Materials and Sustainable Development* (Butterworth-Heinemann, 2015).

Ayittey, G (ed), *Africa Unchained: The Blueprint for Africa's Future* (Springer, 2016).

Bastida, AE, *The Law and Governance of Mining and Minerals: A Global Perspective* (Bloomsbury Publishing, 2020).

Bell, D and Rowe, F, *Are Climate Policies Fairly Made?* (Joseph Rowntree Foundation, 2012).

Bell, S, *Fighting King Coal: The Challenges to Micro mobilization in Central Appalachia* (MIT Press, 2016).

Cameron, PD and Stanley, MC, *Oil, Gas, and Mining: A Sourcebook for Understanding the Extractive Industries* (World Bank Publications, 2017).

Field, TL, *State Governance of Mining, Development and Sustainability* (Edward Elgar Publishing, 2019).

Gates, B, *How to Avoid a Climate Disaster: The Solutions We Have and the Breakthroughs We Need* (Allen Lane, 2021).

Gelbard, ME and Xu, R, *Building Resilience in Sub-Saharan Africa's Fragile States* (International Monetary Fund, 2015)

Heffron, RJ, *Energy Law: An Introduction* (Springer, 2014).

Le Billon, P, *Wars of Plunder: Conflicts, Profits and The Politics of Resources* (Columbia University Press, 2012).

LeBlanc, SA and Register, KE, *Constant Battles: Why We Fight* (Macmillan, 2004).

Leonard, M, Pisani-Ferry, J, Shapiro, J, Tagliapietra, S and Wolff, GB, *The Geopolitics of the European Green Deal* (Bruegel, 2021).

Lerner, S, *Sacrifice Zones: The Front Lines of Toxic Chemical Exposure in the United States* (MIT Press, 2012).

Limbaugh, RH, *Tungsten in Peace and War, 1918–1946* (University of Nevada Press, 2010).

Ma, W and Downs, P, *The Hunt for Unicorns: How Sovereign Funds Are Reshaping Investment in the Digital Economy* (John Wiley & Sons, 2020).

Malthus, TR, Winch, D and James, P, *Malthus: 'An Essay on the Principle of Population'* (Cambridge University Press, 1992).

Marshall, T, *Prisoners of Geography: Ten Maps That Tell You Everything You Need to Know About Global Politics* (Elliot & Thompson Limited, 2015).

Martinez-Alier, J, *The Environmentalism of the Poor: A Study of Ecological Conflicts and Valuation* (Edward Elgar Publishing, 2003).

Muhongo, RS, *Energy Justice: A Local Content Analytical Framework for Sub-Saharan Africa* (Springer Nature, 2020).

Nightingale, AJ, Böhler, T, Campbell, B and Karlsson, L (eds), *Environment and Sustainability in a Globalizing World* (Routledge, 2019).

Olawuyi, DS, *Extractives Industry Law in Africa* (Springer International Publishing, 2018).

Oshionebo, E, *Mineral Mining in Africa: Legal and Fiscal Regimes* (Routledge 2020).

Piketty, T, *Capital and Ideology* (Harvard University Press, 2020).

Pinkse, J and Kolk, A, *International Business and Global Climate Change* (Routledge 2009).

Rawls, J, *A Theory of Justice* (Harvard University Press, 1971).

Robinson, CJ, *Black Marxism Revised and Updated Third Edition: The Making of the Black Radical Tradition* (University of North Carolina Press Books, 2020).
Roeser, S (ed), *Handbook of Risk Theory: Epistemology, Decision Theory, Ethics, and Social Implications of Risk* (Springer Science & Business Media, 2012).
Sbert, C, *The Lens of Ecological Law: A Look at Mining* (Edward Elgar Publishing, 2020).
Schlosberg, D, *Defining Environmental Justice: Theories, Movements, and Nature* (Oxford University Press, 2019).
Skirrow, RG, Huston, DL, Mernagh, TP, Thorne, JP, Duffer, H and Senior, A, *Critical Commodities for a High-Tech World: Australia's Potential to Supply Global Demand* (Geoscience Australia, 2013).
Smil, V, *Energy Myths and Realities* (AEI Press, 2010).
Smith, AK, *Creating a World Economy: Merchant Capital, Colonialism, and World Trade, 1400–1825* (Routledge, 2019).
Smith, G, *Democratic Innovations: Designing Institutions for Citizen Participation* (Cambridge University Press, 2019).
Tripathi, N, Singh, RS and Hills, CD, *Reclamation of Mine-impacted Land for Ecosystem Recovery* (John Wiley & Sons 2016).

Chapters in Books

Akpan, O and Umoh, UE, '"Resource Curse" and "Resource Wars" and the Proliferation of Small Arms in Africa' in UA Tar and CP Onwurah (eds), *The Palgrave Handbook of Small Arms and Conflicts in Africa* (Palgrave Macmillan, 2021) 245.
Carrera, S and Stefan, M, 'Introduction: Justicing Europe's Frontiers: Effective Access to Remedies and Justice in Bordering and Expulsion Policies' in S Carrera and M Stefan (eds), *Fundamental Rights Challenges in Border Controls and Expulsion of Irregular Immigrants in the European Union* (Routledge, 2020) 1–21.
Caruana, C and Pace, P, 'Local Agenda 21 Processes and their Implications for the SDGs' in W Leal Filho, M Mifsud and P Pace (eds), *Handbook of Lifelong Learning for Sustainable Development* (Springer, 2018) 293–305.
Church, C and Crawford, A, 'Minerals and the Metals for the Energy Transition: Exploring the Conflict Implications for Mineral-Rich, Fragile States' in M Hafner and S Tagliapietra (eds), *The Geopolitics of the Global Energy Transition* (Springer International Publishing, 2020) 279–304.
Collier, P, 'Zambia: A Time for Big Opportunities and Tough Decisions' in C Adam, P Collier and M Gondwe (eds), *Zambia: Building Prosperity from Resource Wealth* (Oxford University Press, 2014) 15–29.
Foth, M, Mann, M, Bedford, L, Fieuw, W and Walters, R, 'A Capitalocentric Review of Technology for Sustainable Development: The Case for More-Than-Human Design' in A Finlay (ed), *Global Information Society Watch 2020: Technology, the Environment and a Sustainable World: Responses from the Global South* (Association for Progressive Communications, 2021) 78–82.
Fraser, N, 'Social Justice in the Age of Identity Politics. Geographic Thought: A Praxis Perspective' in GL Henderson and M Waterstone (eds), *Geographic Thought: A Praxis Perspective* (Routledge, 2009) 72–91.
Gilbert, PR, 'Making Critical Materials Valuable: Decarbonization, Investment and 'Political Risk' in A Bleicher and A Pehlken (eds), *The Material Basis of Energy Transitions* (Academic Press, 2020) 91–108.
Gondwe, M and Pamu, EM, 'Growth Strategies for Zambia: Harnessing Natural Resource Wealth for Sustainable Growth' in C Adam, P Collier and M Gondwe (eds), *Zambia: Building Prosperity from Resource Wealth* (Oxford University Press, 2014) 3–14.
Hafner, M and Tagliapietra, S, 'The Global Energy Transition: A Review of the Existing Literature' in M Hafner and S Tagliapietra (eds), *The Geopolitics of the Global Energy Transition. Lecture Notes in Energy*, vol 73 (Springer, 2020).

Heffron, RJ, 'The Just Framework' in RJ Heffron (ed), *Achieving a Just Transition to a Low-Carbon Economy* (Palgrave Macmillan, 2021) 21–42.
Heffron, RJ, 'Energy Law Principles' in RJ Heffron (ed), *Energy Law: An Introduction* (Springer, 2021) 75–90.
Horner, R and Carmody, P, 'Global North/South' in A Kobayashi (ed), *International Encyclopedia of Human Geography* (Elsevier BV, 2019) 181–87.
Humphreys, D, 'The Mining Industry and the Supply of Critical Minerals' in G Gunn (ed), *Critical Metals Handbook* (John Wiley & Sons, 2014) 20–40.
Jennings SN, 'Towards a Sustainable Role for Artisanal and Small-Scale Mining in Mineral Production' in E Bastida, WT Waelde and J Warden-Fernández (eds), *International and Comparative Mineral Law and Policy: Trends and Prospects* (Kluwer Law International, 2005) 505–16.
Kormoh, JL, 'The Conflicts in the DRC: Wider Ramifications for the African Great Lakes Region' in K Omeje (ed), *The Governance, Security and Development Nexus* (Palgrave Macmillan, 2020) 341–53.
Leal Filho, W, de Sousa, LO and Pretorius, R, 'Future Prospects of Sustainable Development in Africa' in W Leal Filho, R Pretorius and LO de Sousa (eds), *Sustainable Development in Africa: Fostering Sustainability in One of the World's Most Promising Continents* (Springer International Publishing, 2021) 733–41.
Mangu, M and Kamga, SD, 'Corporate Social Responsibility and the Right to Development in Local Communities: The Case of the Democratic Republic of Congo' in CC Ngang and SAD Kamga (eds), *Natural Resource Sovereignty and the Right to Development in Africa* (Routledge, 2021) 229–45.
Martinez-Alier, J, 'The Environmentalism of the Poor: Its Origins and Spread' in JR McNeill and ES Mauldin (eds), *A Companion to Global Environmental History* (Wiley Blackwell, 2012) 513–29.
Martinez-Alier, J, 'Global Environmental Justice and the Environmentalism of the Poor' in T Gabrielson, C Hall, JM Meyer and D Schlosberg (eds), *The Oxford Handbook of Environmental Political Theory* (Oxford University Press, 2016) 563–79.
Maupin, A, 'Energy and Regional Integration: The Grand Inga Project in the DR Congo' in S Scholvin (ed), *A New Scramble for Africa? The Rush for Energy Resources in Sub-Saharan Africa* (Routledge, 2015) 53–69.
Menegaki, M and Kaliampakos, D, 'Dealing with NIMBYism in Mining Operations' in C Drebenstedt and R Singhal (eds), *Mine Planning and Equipment Selection: Proceedings of the 22nd MPES Conference, Dresden, Germany, 14th–19th October 2013* (Springer International Publishing, 2014) 1437–46.
Mengolini, A and Masera, M, 'EU Energy Policy: A Socio-Energy Perspective for an Inclusive Energy Transition' in MPC Weijnen, Z Lukszo and S Farahani (eds), *Shaping an Inclusive Energy Transition* (Springer, 2021).
Mose, TM and Hazrati, M, 'Is Energy Justice in the Fossil Fuel Industry a Paradox?' in G Wood and K Baker (eds), *The Palgrave Handbook of Managing Fossil Fuels and Energy Transitions* (Palgrave Macmillan, 2020) 529–49.
Moyo, T, 'Industrialisation in Southern Africa: Towards a Developmental and Strategic Perspective' in S Adejumobi and C Obi (eds), *Developmental Regionalism and Economic Transformation in Southern Africa* (Routledge, 2020) 70–105.
Ohno, H, Matsubae, K, Nakajima, K, Nakamura, S and Nagasaka, T, 'Development of Efficient Recycling System for Steel Alloying Elements in End-of-Life Vehicles' in A Kvithyld et al (eds), *REWAS 2013: Enabling Materials Resource Sustainability* (Springer, 2013) 414–22.
Prause, L, 'Conflicts Related to Resources: The Case of Cobalt Mining in the Democratic Republic of Congo' in A Bleicher and A Pehlken (eds), *The Material Basis of Energy Transitions* (Academic Press, 2020) 153–67.
Schmitz, H.B, 'The Rise of the East: What Does It Mean for Development Studies?' in O Kenichi and O Izumi (eds), *Eastern and Western Ideas for African Growth* (Routledge, 2013) 84–96.

Journal Articles

Abeyratne, SA and Monfared, RP, 'Blockchain Ready Manufacturing Supply Chain Using Distributed Ledger' (2016) 5(9) *International Journal of Research in Engineering and Technology* 1.

Achzet, B and Helbig, C, 'How to Evaluate Raw Material Supply Risks – An Overview' (2013) 38(4) *Resources Policy* 435.

Adam, C and Simpasa, AM, 'Copper Mining in Zambia: Plundered Nations?' [2011] *Successes and Failures in Natural Resource Extraction* 304.

Adekunle, AA, 'Critical Notes on Environmental Justice and Sustainable Development' (2018) 10(3) *International Journal of Sociology and Anthropology* 21.

Agboola, O, Babatunde, DE, Fayomi, OSI, Sadiku, ER, Popoola, P, Moropeng, L, Yahaya, A and Mamudu, OA, 'A Review on the Impact of Mining Operation: Monitoring, Assessment and Management' [2020] *Results in Engineering* 100181.

Ahn, TW, Lee, HS and Yi, JS, 'A Study on the Keyword Extraction for ESG Controversies Through Association Rule Mining' (2021) 30(1) *Journal of Information Systems* 123.

Ali, S, Akter, S and Fogarassy, C, 'The Role of the Key Components of Renewable Energy (Combustible Renewables and Waste) in the Context of CO_2 Emissions and Economic Growth of Selected Countries in Europe' (2021) 14(8) *Energies* 2034.

Ali, SH, Giurco, D, Arndt, N, Nickless, E, Brown, G, Demetriades, A, Durrheim, R, Enriquez, MA, Kinnaird, J, Littleboy, A and Meinert, LD, 'Mineral Supply for Sustainable Development Requires Resource Governance' (2017) 543(7645) *Nature* 367–372.

Almond, REA, Grooten, M and Petersen, T, 'Living Planet Report 2020 – Bending the Curve of Biodiversity Loss' (2021) 35(3) *Natural Resources & Environment* 62.

Alon, I, Chang, J, Lattemann, C, McIntyre, JR, Zhang, W and He, Y, 'Reregulation of China's Rare Earth Production and Export' (2014) 9(2) *International Journal of Emerging Markets* 236.

Amoah, P and Eweje, G, 'Impact Mitigation or Ecological Restoration? Examining the Environmental Sustainability Practices of Multinational Mining Companies' (2021) 30(1) *Business Strategy and the Environment* 551.

Amoah, P, Eweje, G and Bathurst, R, 'Understanding Grand Challenges in Sustainability Implementation Within Mining in Developing Countries' (2020) 10(2) *Social Business* 123.

Andersson, P, 'Chinese Assessments of "Critical" and "Strategic" Raw Materials: Concepts, Categories, Policies, and Implications' (2020) 7(1) *The Extractive Industries and Society* 127.

Angelopulo, G, 'A Comparative Measure of Inclusive Urbanisation in the Cities of Africa' (2021) 22 *World Development Perspectives* 100313.

Anghie, A, 'Inequality, Human Rights, and the New International Economic Order' (2019) 10(3) *Humanity: An International Journal of Human Rights, Humanitarianism, and Development* 429.

Anzolin, G and Pietrobelli, C, 'Local Content Policies: Why Mining Need Consistent Policy Packages to Support Capabilities Development' (2021) 8(1) *The Extractive Industries and Society* 395.

Ard, K, 'By All Measures: An Examination of the Relationship Between Segregation and Health Risk from Air Pollution' (2016) 38(1) *Population and Environment* 1.

Arendt, R, Muhl, M, Bach, V and Finkbeiner, M, 'Criticality Assessment of Abiotic Resource Use for Europe–Application of the SCARCE Method' (2020) 67 *Resources Policy* 101650.

Atakhanova, Z and Howie, P, 'Metal Intensity of Use in the Era of Global Value Chains' (2020) 33(1) *Mineral Economics* 101.

Atlin, C and Gibson, R, 'Lasting Regional Gains from Non-Renewable Resource Extraction: The Role of Sustainability-Based Cumulative Effects Assessment and Regional Planning for Mining Development in Canada' (2017) 4(1) *The Extractive Industries and Society* 36.

Azadi, M, Northey, SA, Ali, SH and Edraki, M, 'Transparency on Greenhouse Gas Emissions from Mining to Enable Climate Change Mitigation' (2020) 13(2) *Nature Geoscience* 100.

Bach, V, Finogenova, N, Berger, M, Winter, L and Finkbeiner, M, 'Enhancing the Assessment of Critical Resource Use at the Country Level with the SCARCE Method – Case Study of Germany' (2017) 53 *Resources Policy* 283.

Bah, MD, 'Mining for Peace: Diamonds, Bauxite, Iron Ore and Political Stability in Guinea' (2014) 41(142) *Review of African Political Economy* 500.

Bakamana, DB, 'Impacts of Political Dynamics and Implications to Development in the Democratic Republic of Congo (DRC)' (2021) 5(1) *Journal of African Interdisciplinary Studies* 32.

Barkemeyer, R, Holt, D, Preuss, L and Tsang, S, 'What Happened to the "Development" in Sustainable Development? Business Guidelines Two Decades After Brundtland' (2014) 22(1) *Sustainable Development* 15.

Bastida, AE, 'From Extractive to Transformative Industries: Paths for Linkages and Diversification for Resource-Driven Development' (2014) 27(2–3) *Mineral Economics* 73.

Baxter, R, 'The Global Economic Crisis and Its Impact on South Africa and the Country's Mining Industry' [2009] *Challenges for Monetary Policy-Makers in Emerging Markets* 105.

Bekessy, SA, Samson, K and Clarkson, RE, 'The Failure of Non-Binding Declarations to Achieve University Sustainability: A Need for Accountability' (2007) 8(3) *International Journal of Sustainability in Higher Education* 301.

Bell, MZ, 'Spatialising Procedural Justice: Fairness and Local Knowledge Mobilisation in Nuclear Waste Siting' (2021) 26(1) *Local Environment* 165.

Benegal, SD and Scruggs, LA, 'Correcting Misinformation About Climate Change: The Impact of Partisanship in an Experimental Setting' (2018) 148(1) *Climatic Change* 61.

Bersch, K and Koivumaeki, RI, 'Making Inroads: Infrastructure, State Capacity, and Chinese Dominance in Latin American Development' (2019) 54(3) *Studies in Comparative International Development* 323.

Beylot, A and Villeneuve, J, 'Assessing the National Economic Importance of Metals: An Input–Output Approach to the Case of Copper in France' (2015) 44 *Resources Policy* 161.

Bicaba, Z, Brixiová, Z and Ncube, M, 'Can Extreme Poverty in Sub-Saharan Africa Be Eliminated by 2030?' (2017) 19(2) *Journal of African Development* 93.

Blengini, GA, Nuss, P, Dewulf, J, Nita, V, Peirò, LT, Vidal-Legaz, B, Latunussa, C, Mancini, L, Blagoeva, D, Pennington, D and Pellegrini, M, 'EU Methodology for Critical Raw Materials Assessment: Policy Needs and Proposed Solutions for Incremental Improvements' (2017) 53 *Resources Policy* 12.

Blum, N, Nazir, J, Breiting, S, Goh, KC and Pedretti, E, 'Balancing the Tensions and Meeting the Conceptual Challenges of Education for Sustainable Development and Climate Change' (2013) 19(2) *Environmental Education Research* 206.

Bonnitcha, J and McCorquodale, R, 'The Concept of "Due Diligence" in the UN Guiding Principles on Business and Human Rights' (2017) 28(3) *European Journal of International Law* 899.

Bradshaw, S, Linneker, B and Overton, L, 'Extractive Industries as Sites of Supernormal Profits and Supernormal Patriarchy?' (2017) 25(3) *Gender & Development*, 439.

Burn, HS, 'Tim Marshall, Prisoners of Geography (UK: Elliott & Thomson Ltd, 2019)' (2019) 13(2) *CLAWS Journal* 228.

Byemba, GK, 'Formalisation of Artisanal and Small-Scale Mining in Eastern Democratic Republic of The Congo: An Opportunity for Women in the New Tin, Tantalum, Tungsten and Gold (3TG) Supply Chain?' [2020] *The Extractive Industries and Society* 420.

Cain, A, 'Alternatives to African Commodity-backed Urbanisation: The Case of China in Angola' (2017) 33(3) *Oxford Review of Economic Policy* 478.

Calvão, F, Mcdonald, CEA and Bolay, M, 'Cobalt Mining and the Corporate Outsourcing of Responsibility in the Democratic Republic of Congo' (2021) 8(4) *The Extractive Industries and Society* 100884.

Calvin, K, Pachauri, S, De Cian, E and Mouratiadou, I, 'The Effect of African Growth on Future Global Energy, Emissions, and Regional Development' (2016) 136(1) *Climatic Change* 109.

Calvo, G, Valero, A and Valero, A, 'Thermodynamic Approach to Evaluate the Criticality of Raw Materials and Its Application through a Material Flow Analysis in Europe' (2018) 22(4) *Journal of Industrial Ecology* 839.

Caramento, A, 'Cultivating Backward Linkages to Zambia's Copper Mines: Debating the Design of, and Obstacles To, Local Content' (2020) 7(2) *The Extractive Industries and Society* 310.

Carley, S and Konisky, DM, 'The Justice and Equity Implications of the Clean Energy Transition' (2020) 5(8) *Nature Energy* 569.
Carmody, P and Kragelund, P, 'Who Is in Charge – State Power and Agency in Sino-African Relations?' (2016) 49 *Cornell International Law Journal* 1.
Carrillo, I and Pellow, D, 'Critical Environmental Justice and the Nature of the Firm' (2021) *Agriculture and Human Values* 1.
Chen, Z, Zhang, L and Xu, Z, 'Analysis of Cobalt Flows in Mainland China: Exploring the Potential Opportunities for Improving Resource Efficiency and Supply Security' (2020) 275 *Journal of Cleaner Production* 122841.
Cherry, MA and Sneirson, JF, 'Chevron, Greenwashing, and the Myth of "Green Oil Companies"' (2012) 3 *Journal of Energy, Climate, and the Environment.*
Chien, F, Ngo, QT, Hsu, CC, Chau, KY and Iram, R, 'Assessing the Mechanism of Barriers Towards Green Finance and Public Spending in Small and Medium Enterprises from Developed Countries' (2021) *Environmental Science and Pollution Research* 1.
Childs, J, 'Geography and Resource Nationalism: A Critical Review and Reframing' (2016) 3(2) *The Extractive Industries and Society* 539.
Chirambo, D, 'Moving Past the Rhetoric: Policy Considerations That Can Make Sino-African Relations to Improve Africa's Climate Change Resilience and the Attainment of the Sustainable Development Goals' (2016) 7(4) *Advances in Climate Change Research* 253.
Chow, C, 'Blockchain for Good? Improving Supply Chain Transparency and Human Rights Management' (2018) 70(1) *Governance Directions* 39.
Collyer, FM, 'Global Patterns in the Publishing of Academic Knowledge: Global North, Global South' (2018) 66(1) *Current Sociology* 56.
Craig, RK, 'Water Law and Climate Change in the United States: A Review of the Legal Scholarship' (2020) 7(3) *Wiley Interdisciplinary Reviews: Water* e1423.
Craven, M, 'Between Law and History: The Berlin Conference of 1884–1885 and the Logic of Free Trade' (2015) 3(1) *London Review of International Law* 31.
Dados, N and Connell, R, 'The Global South' (2012) 11(1) *Contexts* 12.
Davies, AR, 'Environmental Justice as Subtext or Omission: Examining Discourses of Anti-Incineration Campaigning in Ireland' (2006) 37(5) *Geoforum* 708.
de Freitas Netto, SV, Sobral, MFF, Ribeiro, ARB and da Luz Soares, GR, 'Concepts and Forms of Greenwashing: A Systematic Review' (2020) 32(1) *Environmental Sciences Europe* 1.
DeGeorges, PA and Reilly, BK, 'The Realities of Community Based Natural Resource Management and Biodiversity Conservation in Sub-Saharan Africa' (2009) 1(3) *Sustainability* 734.
De Groot, R, Van der Perk, J, Chiesura, A and Van Vliet, A, 'Importance and Threat as Determining Factors for Criticality of Natural Capital' (2003) 44(2–3) *Ecological Economics* 187.
Destek, MA, 'Deindustrialization, Reindustrialization and Environmental Degradation: Evidence from Ecological Footprint of Turkey' (2021) 296 *Journal of Cleaner Production* 126612.
Deus, RM, Mele, FD, Bezerra, BS and Battistelle, RAG, 'A Municipal Solid Waste Indicator for Environmental Impact: Assessment and Identification of Best Management Practices' (2020) 242 *Journal of Cleaner Production* 118433.
Dioha, MO and Kumar, A, 'Exploring Sustainable Energy Transitions in Sub-Saharan Africa Residential Sector: The Case of Nigeria' (2020) 117 *Renewable and Sustainable Energy Reviews* 109510.
Dobler, G and Kesselring, R, 'Swiss Extractivism: Switzerland's Role in Zambia's Copper Sector' (2019) 57(2) *Journal of Modern African Studies* 223.
Dong, X, An, F, Dong, Z, Wang, Z, Jiang, M, Yang, P and An, H, 'Optimization of the International Nickel Ore Trade Network' (2021) 70 *Resources Policy* 101978.
Dos Santos, M, 'Power, Rights, Freedom, Technocracy and Postcolonialism in Sub-Saharan Africa' (2018) 50(3) *Acta Academica.*
Drobyazko, S, Okulich-Kazarin, V, Rogovyi, A, Goltvenko, O and Marova, S, 'Factors of Influence on the Sustainable Development in the Strategy Management of Corporations' (2019) 18 *Academy of Strategic Management Journal* 1.

Duclos, SJ, Otto, JP and Konitzer, DG, 'Swiss Extractivism: Switzerland's Role in Zambia's Copper Sector' (2019) 57(2) *Journal of Modern African Studies* 223.
Dumett, R, 'Africa's Strategic Minerals During the Second World War' (1985) 26(4) *Journal of African History* 381.
Dupont, C, 'The EU's Collective Securitisation of Climate Change' (2019) 42(2) *West European Politics* 369.
Eggert, RG, 'Minerals Go Critical' (2011) 3(9) *Nature Chemistry* 688.
Erdmann, L and Graedel, TE, 'Criticality of Non-Fuel Minerals: A Review of Major Approaches and Analyses' (2011) 45 *Environmental Science Technology* 7620.
Erickson, P, Lazarus, M and Piggot, G, 'Limiting Fossil Fuel Production as the Next Big Step in Climate Policy' (2018) 8(12) *Nature Climate Change* 1037.
Falchetta, G, Dagnachew, AG, Hof, AF and Milne, DJ, 'The Role of Regulatory, Market and Governance Risk for Electricity Access Investment in Sub-Saharan Africa' (2021) 62 *Energy for Sustainable Development* 136.
Famiyeh, S, Opoku, RA, Kwarteng, A and Asante-Darko, D, 'Driving Forces of Sustainability in the Mining Industry: Evidence from a Developing Country' (2021) 70 *Resources Policy* 101910.
Fent, A and Kojola, E, 'Political Ecologies of Time and Temporality in Resource Extraction' (2020) 27(1) *Journal of Political Ecology* 819.
Fessehaie, J and Morris, M, 'Value Chain Dynamics of Chinese Copper Mining in Zambia: Enclave or Linkage Development?' (2013) 25(4) *European Journal of Development Research* 537.
Feyaerts, H, Van den Broeck, G and Maertens, M, 'Global and Local Food Value Chains in Africa: A Review' (2020) 51(1) *Agricultural Economics* 143.
French, D, 'The Military Background to the "Shell Crisis" of May 1915' (1979) 2(2) *Journal of Strategic Studies* 192.
Frenzel, M, Kullik, J, Reuter, MA and Gutzmer, J, 'Raw Material "Criticality" – Sense or Nonsense?' (2017) 50(12) *Journal of Physics D: Applied Physics* 123002.
Freudenburg, WR and Gramling, R, 'Linked to What? Economic Linkages in an Extractive Economy' (1998) 11(6) *Society & Natural Resources* 569.
Gaustad, G, Krystofik, M, Bustamante, M and Badami, K, 'Circular Economy Strategies for Mitigating Critical Material Supply Issues' (2018) 135 *Resources, Conservation and Recycling* 24.
Geenen, S, 'Gold and Godfathers: Local Content, Politics, and Capitalism in Extractive Industries' (2019) 123 *World Development* 104605.
Geissdoerfer, M, Savaget, P, Bocken, NM and Hultink, EJ, 'The Circular Economy – A New Sustainability Paradigm?' (2017) 143 *Journal of Cleaner Production* 757.
Glöser, S, Espinoza, LT, Gandenberger, C and Faulstich, M, 'Raw Material Criticality in the Context of Classical Risk Assessment' (2015) 44 *Resources Policy* 35.
Gnassou, L, 'Tax Base Erosion: A Cautionary Tale of the DRC' (2020) *Africa Policy Journal* 27.
Graedel, TE and Reck, BK, 'Six Years of Criticality Assessments: What Have We Learned So Far?' (2016) 20(4) *Journal of Industrial Ecology* 692.
Graedel, TE, Allwood, J, Birat, JP, Buchert, M, Hagelüken, C, Reck, BK, Sibley, SF and Sonnemann, G, 'What Do We Know About Metal Recycling Rates?' (2011) 15(3) *Journal of Industrial Ecology* 355.
Graedel, TE, Harper, EM, Nassar, NT, Nuss, P and Reck, BK, 'Criticality of Metals and Metalloids' (2015) 112(1)4 *Proceedings of the National Academy of Sciences* 4257.
Grandell, L, Lehtilä, A, Kivinen, M, Koljonen, T, Kihlman, S and Lauri, LS, 'Role of Critical Metals in the Future Markets of Clean Energy Technologies' (2016) 95 *Renewable Energy* 53.
Gregory, J and Sovacool, BK, 'Rethinking the Governance of Energy Poverty in Sub-Saharan Africa: Reviewing Three Academic Perspectives on Electricity Infrastructure Investment' (2019) 111 *Renewable and Sustainable Energy Reviews* 344.
Gulley, AL, McCullough, EA and Shedd, KB, 'China's Domestic and Foreign Influence in The Global Cobalt Supply Chain' (2019) 62 *Resources Policy* 317.
Hache, E, Seck, GS, Simoen, M, Bonnet, C and Carcanague, S, 'Critical Raw Materials and Transportation Sector Electrification: A Detailed Bottom-Up Analysis in World Transport' (2019) 240 *Applied Energy* 6.

Haglund, DG, 'Strategic Minerals: A Conceptual Analysis' (1984) 10 *Resource Policy* 146.
Hailes, O, 'Lithium in International Law: Trade, Investment, and the Pursuit of Supply Chain Justice' (2022) 25(1) *Journal of International Economic Law* 148.
Hairong, Y and Sautman, B, 'The Beginning of a World Empire'? Contesting the Discourse of Chinese Copper Mining in Zambia' (2013) 39(2) *Modern China* 131.
Haites, E, 'A Dual-Track Transition to Global Carbon Pricing: Excellent Idea but Doomed to Fail' (2020) 20(10) *Climate Policy* 1344.
Hall, SM, 'Energy Justice and Ethical Consumption: Comparison, Synbook and Lesson Drawing' (2013) 18(4) *Local Environment* 422.
Hammett, D and Gough, KV, 'IDPR in 2016 and Beyond' (2016) 38(4) *International Development Planning Review* 347.
Hamzah, H, 'Legal Policy of Legislation in the Field of Natural Resources in Indonesia' (2016) 1(1) *Hasanuddin Law Review* 108.
Han, M, Lao, J, Yao, Q, Zhang, B and Meng, J, 'Carbon Inequality and Economic Development Across the Belt and Road Regions' (2020) 262 *Journal of Environmental Management* 110250.
Hatayama, H and Tahara, K, 'Adopting an Objective Approach to Criticality Assessment: Learning from the Past' (2018) 55 *Resources Policy* 96.
Hayes, SM and McCullough, EA, 'Critical Minerals: A Review of Elemental Trends in Comprehensive Criticality Studies' (2018) 59 *Resources Policy* 192.
Hazrati, M and Heffron, RJ, 'Conceptualising Restorative Justice in the Energy Transition: Changing the Perspectives of Fossil Fuels' (2021) 78 *Energy Research & Social Science* 102115.
He, Y, 'The Trade-Security Nexus and US Policy Making in Critical Minerals Resources Policy' (2028) 59 *Resources Policy* 238.
Heffron, RJ, 'The Role of Justice in Developing Critical Minerals' (2020) 7(3) *The Extractive Industries and Society* 855–863.
Heffron, RJ, 'Justice should Govern the New Momentum for COP26' (2021) 2(1) *Global Energy Law and Sustainability* 5.
Heffron, RJ and McCauley, D, 'The Concept of Energy Justice Across the Disciplines' (2017) 105 *Energy Policy* 658.
Heffron, RJ and Sheehan, J, 'Rethinking International Taxation and Energy Policy Post COVID-19 and the Financial Crisis for Developing Countries' (2020) 73 *Journal of Energy & Natural Resources Law* 465.
Heffron, RJ and Talus, K, 'The Evolution of Energy Law and Energy Jurisprudence: Insights for Energy Analysts and Researchers' (2016) 19 *Energy Research & Social Science* 1.
Heffron, RJ, Downes, L, Rodriguez, OMR and McCauley, D, 'The Emergence of the "Social Licence to Operate" in the Extractive Industries?' [2018] *Resources Policy* 101272.
Heffron, RJ, Rønne, A, Tomain, JP, Bradbrook, A and Talus, K, 'A Treatise for Energy Law' (2018) 11(1) *Journal of World Energy Law & Business* 34–48.
Heffron, RJ, Körner, MF, Schöpf, M, Wagner, J and Weibelzahl, M, 'The Role of Flexibility in the Light of the COVID-19 Pandemic and Beyond: Contributing to a Sustainable and Resilient Energy Future in Europe' (2021) 140 *Renewable and Sustainable Energy Reviews* 110743.
Helbig, C, Bradshaw, AM, Thorenz, A and Tuma, A, 'Supply Risk Considerations for the Elements in Nickel-Based Superalloys' (2020) 9(9) *Resources* 106.
Helbig, C, Schrijvers, D and Hool, A, 'Selecting and Prioritizing Material Resources by Criticality Assessments' (2021) 4(3) *One Earth* 339.
Hess, D, 'The Transparency Trap: Non-financial Disclosure and the Responsibility of Business to Respect Human Rights' (2019) 56(1) *American Business Law Journal* 5.
Hickel, J, 'The Contradiction of the Sustainable Development Goals: Growth versus Ecology on a Finite Planet' (2019) 27(5) *Sustainable Development* 873.
Hilson, AE and Ovadia, JS, 'Local Content in Developing and Middle-Income Countries: Towards a More Holistic Strategy' (2020) 7(2) *The Extractive Industries and Society* 253.

Hilson, G, 'The Africa Mining Vision: A Manifesto for More Inclusive Extractive Industry-Led Development?' (2020) 41(3) *Canadian Journal of Development Studies/Revue canadienne d'études du développement* 417.

Hilson, G, Hilson, A and McQuilken, J, 'Ethical Minerals: Fairer Trade for Whom?' (2016) 49 *Resources Policy* 232.

Hilson, G, Sauerwein, T and Owen, J, 'Large and Artisanal Scale Mine Development: The Case for Autonomous Co-Existence' (2020) 130 *World Development* 104919.

Hinton, J, Veiga, MM and Beinhoff, C, 'Women and Artisanal Mining: Gender Roles and the Road Ahead' [2003] *The Socio-Economic Impacts of Artisanal and Small-Scale Mining in Developing Countries* 149.

Hobson, K, 'Environmental Psychology and the Geographies of Ethical and Sustainable Consumption: Aligning, Triangulating, Challenging?' (2006) 38(3) *Area* 292.

Höök, M and Tang, X, 'Depletion of Fossil Fuels and Anthropogenic Climate Change – A Review' (2013) 52 *Energy Policy* 797.

Hu, X, Wang, C, Lim, MK and Chen, WQ, 'Characteristics of the Global Copper Raw Materials and Scrap Trade Systems and the Policy Impacts of China's Import Ban' (2020) 172 *Ecological Economics* 106626.

Huang, J, Zhang, G, Zhang, Y, Guan, X, Wei, Y and Guo, R, 'Global Desertification Vulnerability to Climate Change and Human Activities' (2020) 31(11) *Land Degradation & Development* 1380.

Humby, TL, 'The Thabametsi Case: Case No 65662/16 Earthlife Africa Johannesburg v Minister of Environmental Affairs' (2018) 30(1) *Journal of Environmental Law* 145.

Humprheys, D, 'Whatever Happened to Security of Supply? Mineral's Policy in the Post-Cold War World' (1995) 21(2) *Resources Policy* 91.

Hund, K, Schure, JM and van der Goes, A, 'Extractive Industries in Forest Landscapes: Options for Synergy with REDD+ and Development of Standards in the Democratic Republic of Congo' (2017) 54 *Resources Policy* 97.

Hunold, C and Young, IM, 'Justice, Democracy, and Hazardous Siting' (1998) 46(1) *Political Studies* 82.

Hurrell, A and Sengupta, S, 'Emerging Powers, North–South Relations and Global Climate Politics' (2012) 88(3) *International Affairs* 463.

Igbatayo, SA, 'Combating Illicit Financial Flows from Africa's Extractive Industries and Implications for Good Governance' (2019) 44(3) *Africa Development/Afrique et Développement* 55.

Ikeda, E, 'Renewable Energy Development, Export-Led Industrialisation, and Its Implications for Climate Strategies in Asian Developing Countries' [2021] *Renewable Energy Transition in Asia: Policies, Markets and Emerging Issues* 89.

Jacobson, DM, Turner, RK, Challis, AAL, 'A Reassessment of the Strategic Materials Question' (1988) 14 *Resource Policy* 74.

Jegede, AO, 'The Environmental and Economic Implications of the Climate Change and Extractive Industry Nexus in Africa' (2016) 7(4) *Environmental Economics* 95.

Jenkins, K, McCauley, D, Heffron, R, Stephan, H and Rehner, R, 'Energy Justice: A Conceptual Review' (2016) 11 *Energy Research & Social Science* 174.

Jenkins, KE, Sovacool, BK, Błachowicz, A and Lauer, A, 'Politicising the Just Transition: Linking Global Climate Policy, Nationally Determined Contributions and Targeted Research Agendas' (2020) 115 *Geoforum* 138.

Jiménez-Aceituno, A, Peterson, GD, Norström, AV, Wong, GY and Downing, AS, 'Local Lens for SDG Implementation: Lessons from Bottom-Up Approaches in Africa' (2020) 15(3) *Sustainability Science* 729.

Johnson, SM and Pratarelli, ME, 'The Intersection of Evolutionary Principles, Human Behavior and Environmental Sustainability' (2011) 3(2) *Journal of the Evolutionary Studies Consortium* 1.

Jones, B, Elliott, RJ and Nguyen-Tien, V, 'The EV Revolution: The Road Ahead for Critical Raw Materials Demand' (2020) 280 *Applied Energy* 115072.

Kabemba, C, 'China–Democratic Republic of Congo Relations: From a Beneficial to a Developmental Cooperation' [2016] *African Studies Quarterly* 16.

Kalantzakos, S, 'The Race for Critical Minerals in an Era of Geopolitical Realignments' (2020) 55(3) *The International Spectator* 1.

Kalonda, DM, Tshikongo, AK, Kule-koto, FK, Luboya, O, Numbi, CKB, Kalonda, DK, Bwalya, YK, Cansa, HM, Otshudi, AL and Kalala, ZL, 'Impact of Mining on Water of the Rivers Shinkolobwe, Lwisha and Kansonga in the Province of Katanga (DRC)' (2017) 3(2) *Journal of Medical Research* 71.

Kamenopoulos, SN and Agioutantis, Z, 'Geopolitical Risk Assessment of Countries with Rare Earth Element Deposits' (2020) 37(1) *Mining, Metallurgy & Exploration* 51.

Kaniki, AT and Tumba, K, 'Management of Mineral Processing Tailings and Metallurgical Slags of the Congolese Copperbelt: Environmental Stakes and Perspectives' (2019) 210 *Journal of Cleaner Production* 1406.

Kasperson, JX, Kasperson, RE and Turner, BL, 'Regions at Risk: Exploring Environmental Criticality' (1996) 38(10) *Environment: Science and Policy for Sustainable Development* 4.

Kastanaki, E and Giannis, A, 'Dynamic Estimation of Future Obsolete Laptop Flows and Embedded Critical Raw Materials: The Case Study of Greece' (2021) 132 *Waste Management* 74.

Katz, J and Pietrobelli, C, 'Natural Resource-Based Growth, Global Value Chains and Domestic Capabilities in the Mining Industry' (2018) 58 *Resources Policy* 11.

Kavlak, G, McNerney, J, Jaffe, RL and Trancik, JE, 'Metal Production Requirements for Rapid Photovoltaics Deployment' (2015) 8(6) *Energy & Environmental Science* 1651.

Kayika, P, Siachoono, SM, Kalinda, C and Kwenye, JM, 'An Investigation of Concentrations of Copper, Cobalt and Cadmium Minerals in Soils and Mango Fruits Growing on Konkola Copper Mine Tailings Dam in Chingola, Zambia' (2017) 1(10)3 *Archival Science* 2.

Kesselring, R, 'What Zambia and Switzerland Have in Common: Copper and Resistance to Extractivism' (2018) 43(172) *Afrika Bulletin* 3.

Khelifi, F, Melki, A, Hamed, Y, Adamo, P and Caporale, AG, 'Environmental and Human Health Risk Assessment of Potentially Toxic Elements in Soil, Sediments, and Ore-Processing Wastes from a Mining Area of Southwestern Tunisia' (2020) 42(12) *Environmental Geochemistry and Health* 4125.

Kisangani, EF, 'Conflict in the Democratic Republic of Congo: A Mosaic of Insurgent Groups' (2003) *International Journal on World Peace* 51.

Knoblauch, AM, Farnham, A, Zabré, HR, Owuor, M, Archer, C, Nduna, K, Chisanga, M, Zulu, L, Musunka, G, Utzinger, J and Divall, MJ, 'Community Health Impacts of the Trident Copper Mine Project in Northwestern Zambia: Results from Repeated Cross-Sectional Surveys' (2020) 17(10) *International Journal of Environmental Research and Public Health* 3633.

Koengkan, M and Fuinhas, JA, 'Exploring the Effect of the Renewable Energy Transition on CO_2 Emissions of Latin American & Caribbean Countries (2020) 39(6) *International Journal of Sustainable Energy* 515.

Koh, LP, Ghazoul, J, Butler, RA, Laurance, WF, Sodhi, NS, Mateo-Vega, J and Bradshaw, CJ, 'Wash and Spin Cycle Threats to Tropical Biodiversity' (2010) 42(1) *Biotropica* 67.

Koltun, P, 'Materials and Sustainable Development' (2010) 20 *Progress in Natural Science: Materials International* 16.

Kosai, S, Matsui, K, Matsubae, K, Yamasue, E and Nagasaka, T, 'Natural Resource Use of Gasoline, Hybrid, Electric and Fuel Cell Vehicles Considering Land Disturbances' (2021) 166 *Resources, Conservation and Recycling* 105256.

Krummel, D and Siegfried, P, 'The Dark Side of Samsung's Value Chain: The Human Costs of Cobalt Mining 'BLOOD, SWEAT AND COBALT' (2021) 90(2) *Journal of Geoscience and Environment Protection* 182.

Lall, S, 'Industrial Success and Failure in a Globalizing World' (2004) 3(3) *International Journal of Technology Management & Sustainable Development* 189.

Larmer, M, 'Nation-Making at the Border: Zambian Diplomacy in the Democratic Republic of Congo' (2019) 61(1) *Comparative Studies in Society and History* 145.

Le Billon, P, 'The Political Ecology of War: Natural Resources and Armed Conflicts' (2001) 20(5) *Political Geography* 561.
Lèbre, É, Corder, G and Golev, A, 'The Role of the Mining Industry in a Circular Economy: A Framework for Resource Management at the Mine Site Level' (2017) 21(3) *Journal of Industrial Ecology* 662.
Lee, J, Bazilian, M, Sovacool, B, Hund, K, Jowitt, SM, Nguyen, TP, Månberger, A, Kah, M, Greene, S, Galeazzi, C and Awuah-Offei, K, 'Reviewing the Material and Metal Security of Low-Carbon Energy Transitions' (2020) 124 *Renewable and Sustainable Energy Reviews* 109789.
Lei, Y, Cui, N and Pan, D, 'Economic and Social Effects Analysis of Mineral Development in China and Policy Implications' (2013) 38(4) *Resources Policy* 448.
Levenda, AM, Behrsin, I and Disano, F, 'Renewable Energy for Whom? A Global Systematic Review of the Environmental Justice Implications of Renewable Energy Technologies' (2021) 71 *Energy Research & Social Science* 101837.
Lewis, D, 'Contesting Parallel Worlds: Time to Abandon the Distinction between the "International" and "Domestic" Contexts of Third Sector Scholarship?' (2015) 26(5) *VOLUNTAS: International Journal of Voluntary and Nonprofit Organizations* 2084.
Liu, Y, Ma, R, Guan, C, Chen, B and Zhang, B, 'Global Trade Network and CH_4 Emission Outsourcing' (2021) *Science of The Total Environment* 150008.
Lokuwaduge, CSDS and Heenetigala, K, 'Integrating Environmental, Social and Governance (ESG) Disclosure for a Sustainable Development: An Australian Study' (2017) 26(4) *Business Strategy and the Environment* 438.
Lunde Seefeldt, J, 'Lessons from the Lithium Triangle: Considering Policy Explanations for the Variation in Lithium Industry Development in the "Lithium Triangle" Countries of Chile, Argentina, and Bolivia' (2020) 48(4) *Politics & Policy* 727.
Lungu, J, 'Copper Mining Agreements in Zambia: Renegotiation or Law Reform?' (2008) 35(117) *Review of African Political Economy* 403.
Lungu, J, 'Socio-economic Change and Natural Resource Exploitation: A Case Study of the Zambian Copper Mining Industry' (2008) 25(5) *Development Southern Africa* 543.
Maboloc, CR, 'Liberal Environmentalism and Global Climate Justice' (2020) 30(2) *Eubios Journal of Asian and International Bioethics*.
MacDonald, DV, Hanley, N and Moffatt, I, 'Applying the Concept of Natural Capital Criticality to Regional Resource Management' (1999) 29 *Ecological Economics* 73.
Machacek, E, 'Constructing Criticality by Classification: Expert Assessments of Mineral Raw Materials' (2017) 84 *Geoforum* 368.
Malin, SA, Ryder, S and Lyra, MG, 'Environmental Justice and Natural Resource Extraction: Intersections of Power, Equity and Access' (2019) 5(2) *Environmental Sociology* 109.
Mantalovas, K, Di Mino, G, Jimenez Del Barco Carrion, A, Keijzer, E, Kalman, B, Parry, T and Lo Presti, D, 'European National Road Authorities and Circular Economy: An Insight into Their Approaches' (2020) 12(17) *Sustainability* 7160.
Maponga, OP and Musa, C, 'Domestication of the Role of the Mining Sector in Southern Africa through Local Content Requirements' (2021) 8(1) *The Extractive Industries and Society* 195.
Martinez-Alier, J, 'Mapping Ecological Distribution Conflicts: The EJAtlas' (2021) 8(4) *The Extractive Industries and Society* 100883.
Martinez-Alier, J, Temper, L, Del Bene, D and Scheidel, A, 'Is there a Global Environmental Justice Movement?' (2016) 43(3) *Journal of Peasant Studies* 731.
Matisoff, DC, 'Different Rays of Sunlight: Understanding Information Disclosure and Carbon Transparency' (2013) 55 *Energy Policy* 579.
Mayer, A and Malin, S, 'How Should Unconventional Oil and Gas Be Regulated? The Role of Natural Resource Dependence and Economic Insecurity' (2019) 65 *Journal of Rural Studies* 79.
Mavhunga, CC, 'Africa's Move from Raw Material Exports Toward Mineral Value Addition: Historical Background and Implications' (2023) 48(4) *Materials Research Society Bulletin* 395.

McCauley, D and Heffron, R, 'Just Transition: Integrating Climate, Energy and Environmental Justice' (2018) 119 *Energy Policy* 1.

McCorquodale, R, Smit, L, Neely, S and Brooks, R, 'Human Rights Due Diligence in Law and Practice: Good Practices and Challenges for Business Enterprises' (2017) 2(2) *Business and Human Rights Journal* 195.

McLellan, BC, Yamasue, E, Tezuka, T, Corder, G, Golev, A and Giurco, D, 'Critical Minerals and Energy – Impacts and Limitations of Moving to Unconventional Resources' (2016) 5(2) *Resources* 19.

Menton, M, Larrea, C, Latorre, S, Martinez-Alier, J, Peck, M, Temper, L and Walter, M, 'Environmental Justice and the SDGs: From Synergies to Gaps and Contradictions' (2020) 15(6) *Sustainability Science* 1621.

Mitchell, L and Ramey, W, 'Look How Green I Am! An Individual-Level Explanation for Greenwashing' (2011) 12(6) *Journal of Applied Business and Economics* 40.

Molaei, F and Siavoshi, H, 'The Role of Nanofluids on Enhancing the Solar Energy Performance with Focusing on the Mining Industry' [2021] *International Journal of Energy Research.*

Morris, M and Fessehaie, J, 'The Industrialisation Challenge for Africa: Towards a Commodities-Based Industrialisation Path' (2014) 1(1) *Journal of African Trade* 25.

Mostert, H, Young, CL and Hassman, JL, 'Towards Extractive Justice: Europe, Africa and the Pressures of Resource Dependency' (2019) 26(2) *South African Journal of International Affairs* 233.

Motoori, R, McLellan, BC and Tezuka, T, 'Environmental Implications of Resource Security Strategies for Critical Minerals: A Case Study of Copper in Japan' (2018) 8(12) *Minerals* 558.

Mugume, R and Nattabi, KA, 'The Potential Trade Effects of Democratic Republic of Congo Joining the East African Community Bloc' (2021) 9(4) *African Journal of Economic Review* 291.

Müller, M, 'In Search of the Global East: Thinking Between North and South' (2020) 25(3) *Geopolitics* 734.

Murshed, M and Tanha, MM, 'Oil Price Shocks and Renewable Energy Transition: Empirical Evidence from Net Oil-Importing South Asian Economies' [2020] *Energy, Ecology & Environment* 1.

Nagtegaal, R, 'The Impact of Using Algorithms for Managerial Decisions on Public Employees' Procedural Justice' (2021) 38(1) *Government Information Quarterly* 101536.

Nakanwagi, S and Rukundo, AT, 'Covid-19 Pandemic Deranging Energy Transition in Uganda: Challenges and Prospects' (2020) 1(2) *Global Energy Law and Sustainability* 211.

Nakanwagi, S, 'Critical Minerals and the Global Energy Transition: Recognising Global South Perspectives' (2023) 4(1–2) *Global Energy Law and Sustainability* 115.

Nakazwe, M, 'Life Beyond the Glitz and Glamour of Mining: Strengthening the Mine Closure Regime in Zambia' (2017) 35(3) *Journal of Energy & Natural Resources Law* 325.

Nassar, NT, Graedel, TE and Harper, EM, 'By-Product Metals Are Technologically Essential but Have Problematic Supply' (2015) 1(3) *Science Advances* 1400180.

Ng'ambi, SP, 'Stabilisation Clauses and the Zambian Windfall Tax' (2010) 1(1) *Zambia Social Science Journal.*

Ngoasong, MZ, 'How International Oil and Gas Companies Respond to Local Content Policies in Petroleum-Producing Developing Countries: A Narrative Enquiry' (2014) 73 *Energy Policy* 471.

Nguyen, RT, Eggert, RG, Severson, MH and Anderson, CG, 'Global Electrification of Vehicles and Intertwined Material Supply Chains of Cobalt, Copper and Nickel' (2020) *Resources, Conservation and Recycling* 105198.

Njoh, AJ, 'Renewable Energy as a Determinant of Inter-Country Differentials in CO_2 Emissions in Africa' (2021) 172 *Renewable Energy* 1225.

Nkulu, CBL, Casas, L, Haufroid, V, De Putter, T, Saenen, ND, Kayembe-Kitenge, T, Obadia, PM, Mukoma, DKW, Ilunga, JML, Nawrot, TS and Numbi, OL, 'Sustainability of Artisanal Mining of Cobalt in DR Congo' (2018) 1(9) *Nature Sustainability* 495.

Nurmi, P, 'Green Mining – a Holistic Concept for Sustainable and Acceptable Mineral Production' [2017] *Annals of Geophysics* 60.

Obaya, M, 'The Evolution of Resource Nationalism: The Case of Bolivian Lithium' (2021) 8(3) *The Extractive Industries and Society* 100932.

Ojala, M, Cunsolo, A, Ogunbode, CA and Middleton, J, 'Anxiety, Worry, and Grief in a Time of Environmental and Climate Crisis: A Narrative Review' (2021) 46 *Annual Review of Environment and Resources* 35.

Olabisi, M and Sawyer, WC, 'The Demand for Imports and Exports in Africa: A Survey' (2020) 7(1–2) *Journal of African Trade* 45.

Olawuyi, DS, 'Can MENA Extractive Industries Support the Global Energy Transition? Current Opportunities and Future Directions' (2021) 8(2) *The Extractive Industries and Society* 100685.

Otamonga, JP and Poté, JW, 'Abandoned Mines and Artisanal and Small-Scale Mining in Democratic Republic of the Congo (DRC): Survey and Agenda for Future Research' (2020) 208 *Journal of Geochemical Exploration* 106394.

Owens, S and Driffill, L, 'How to Change Attitudes and Behaviours in the Context of Energy' (2008) 36(12) *Energy Policy* 4412.

Oyalowo, B and Lawanson, T, 'Housing and the SDGs in African Cities: Towards a Sustainable Future' [2021] *Housing and SDGs in Urban Africa* 321.

Palladino, N., 'The Role of Epistemic Communities in the "Constitutionalization" of Internet Governance: The Example of the European Commission High-Level Expert Group on Artificial Intelligence' (2021) 45(6) *Telecommunications Policy* 102149.

Papyrakis, E and Gerlagh, R, 'The Resource Curse Hypothesis and Its Transmission Channels' (2004) 32(1) *Journal of Comparative Economics* 181.

Patnaik, S, Temouri, Y, Tuffour, J, Tarba, S and Singh, SK, 'Corporate Social Responsibility and Multinational Enterprise Identity: Insights from a Mining Company's Attempt to Localise in Ghana' (2018) 24(5) *Social Identities* 604.

Paulick, H and Machacek, E, 'The Global Rare Earth Element Exploration Boom: An Analysis of Resources Outside of China and Discussion of Development Perspectives' (2017) 52 *Resources Policy* 134.

Peters, GP, Andrew, RM, Canadell, JG, Fuss, S, Jackson, RB, Korsbakken, JI, Le Quéré, C and Nakicenovic, N, 'Key Indicators to Track Current Progress and Future Ambition of the Paris Agreement' (2017) 7(2) *Nature Climate Change* 118.

Petrillo, A, De Felice, F, Cioffi, R and Zomparelli, F, 'Fourth Industrial Revolution: Current Practices, Challenges, and Opportunities' [2018] *Digital Transformation in Smart Manufacturing* 1.

Phelps, NA, Atienza, M and Arias, M, 'Encore for the Enclave: The Changing Nature of the Industry Enclave with Illustrations from the Mining Industry in Chile' (2015) 91(2) *Economic Geography* 119.

Pouresmaieli, M, Ataei, M, Qarahasanlou, AN and Barabadi, A, 'Integration of Renewable Energy and Sustainable Development with Strategic Planning in the Mining Industry' (2023) 20 *Results in Engineering* 101412.

Pratarelli, M.E., 'The Failure to Achieve Sustainability May Be in Our Genes' (2016) 27(2–4) *Global Bioethics* 61.

Quium, ASM, 'Transport Corridors for Wider Socio-economic Development' (2019) 11(19) *Sustainability* 5248.

Qurbani, ID, Heffron, RJ and Rifano, ATS, 'Justice and Critical Mineral Development in Indonesia and Across ASEAN' (2020) 8(1) *The Extractive Industries and Society* 355.

Rakner, L, 'Tax Bargains in Unlikely Places: The Politics of Zambian Mining Taxes' (2017) 4(3) *The Extractive Industries and Society* 525.

Ram, M, Aghahosseini, A and Breyer, 'Job Creation During the Global Energy Transition Towards a 100% Renewable Power System by 2050' (2020) 151 *Technological Forecasting and Social Change* 119682.

Rapanyane, MB, 'China's Involvement in the Democratic Republic of Congo's Resource Curse Mineral Driven Conflict: An Afrocentric Review' (2021) *Contemporary Social Science* 1.

Rees, WE, 'Human Nature, Eco-Footprints and Environmental Injustice' (2008) 13(8) *Local Environment* 685.

Renner, S and Wellmer, FW, 'Volatility Drivers on the Metal Market and Exposure of Producing Countries' (2020) 33(3) *Mineral Economics* 311.
Retief, FP, Fischer, TB, Alberts, RC, Roos, C and Cilliers, DP, 'An Administrative Justice Perspective on Improving EIA Effectiveness' (2020) 38(2) *Impact Assessment and Project Appraisal* 151.
Riddell, JB, 'Things Fall Apart Again: Structural Adjustment Programmes in Sub-Saharan Africa' (1992) 30(1) *Journal of Modern African Studies* 53.
Riddle, ME, Tatara, E, Olson, C, Smith, BJ, Irion, AB, Harker, B, Pineault, D, Alonso, E and Graziano, DJ, 'Agent-Based Modeling of Supply Disruptions in the Global Rare Earths Market' (2021) 164 *Resources, Conservation and Recycling* 105193.
Risberg, P, 'The Give-and-Take of BRI in Africa' (2019) 17 *New Perspectives in Foreign Policy* 43.
Roelich, K, Dawson, DA, Purnell, P, Knoeri, C, Revell, R, Busch, J and Steinberger, JK, 'Assessing the Dynamic Material Criticality of Infrastructure Transitions: A Case of Low Carbon Electricity' (2014) 123 *Applied Energy* 378.
Routledge, P, Cumbers, A and Derickson, KD, 'States of Just Transition: Realising Climate Justice Through and Against the State' (2018) 88 *Geoforum* 78.
Rubbers, B, 'Mining Boom, Labour Market Segmentation and Social Inequality in the Congolese Copperbelt' (2020) 51(6) *Development and Change* 1555.
Rudnick, RL, Gao, S, Holland, HD and Turekian, KK, 'Composition of the Continental Crust' (2003) 3 *The Crust* 1.
Ruggie, J, 'Report of the Special Representative of the Secretary-General on the Issue of Human Rights and Transnational Corporations and Other Business Enterprises: Guiding Principles on Business and Human Rights: Implementing the United Nations "Protect, Respect and Remedy" Framework' (2011) 29(2) *Netherlands Quarterly of Human Rights* 224.
Rutherford, B and Buss, D, 'Gendered Governance and Socio-Economic Differentiation Among Women Artisanal and Small-Scale Miners in Central and East Africa' (2019) 4(1) *Third World Thematics: A TWQ Journal* 63.
Ryder, SS, 'Developing an Inter-Sectionally-Informed, Multi-Sited, Critical Policy Ethnography to Examine Power and Procedural Justice in Multi-Scalar Energy and Climate Change Decision Making Processes' (2018) 45 *Energy Research & Social Science* 266.
Said, MY and Nurhayati, Y, 'A Review on Rawls Theory of Justice' (2021) 1(1) *International Journal of Law, Environment, and Natural Resources* 29.
Saguru, C, Ndlovu, S and Moropeng, D, 'A Review of Recent Studies into Hydrometallurgical Methods for Recovering PGMs from Used Catalytic Converters' (2018) 182 *Hydrometallurgy* 44.
Salmenperä, H, Pitkänen, K, Kautto, P and Saikku, L, 'Critical Factors for Enhancing the Circular Economy in Waste Management' (2021) 280 *Journal of Cleaner Production* 124339.
Schellens, MK and Gisladottir, J, 'Critical Natural Resources: Challenging the Current Discourse and Proposal for a Holistic Definition' (2018) 7(4) *Resources* 79.
Schlosberg, D, 'The Justice of Environmental Justice: Reconciling Equity, Recognition, and Participation in a Political Movement' (2003) 77 *Moral and Political Reasoning in Environmental Practice* 106.
Schlosberg, D, 'Theorising Environmental Justice: The Expanding Sphere of a Discourse' (2013) 22(1) *Environmental Politics* 37.
Schrijvers, D, Hool, A, Blengini, GA, Chen, WQ, Dewulf, J, Eggert, R, van Ellen, L, Gauss, R, Goddin, J, Habib, K and Hagelüken, C, 'A Review of Methods and Data to Determine Raw Material Criticality' (2020) 155 *Resources, Conservation and Recycling* 104617.
Schwanitz, VJ, Piontek, F, Bertram, C and Luderer, G, 'Long-term Climate Policy Implications of Phasing Out Fossil Fuel Subsidies' (2014) 67 *Energy Policy* 882.
Seck, GS, Hache, E, Bonnet, C, Simoën, M and Carcanague, S, 'Copper at the Crossroads: Assessment of the Interactions between Low-Carbon Energy Transition and Aupply Limitations' (2020) 163 *Resources, Conservation and Recycling* 105072.
Siegel, S and Veiga, MM, 'Artisanal and Small-Scale Mining as an Extralegal Economy: De Soto and the Redefinition of 'Formalization'' (2009) 34(1–2) *Resources Policy* 51.

Selmier II, WT and Newenham-Kahindi, A, 'Communities of Place, Mining Multinationals and Sustainable Development in Africa' [2020] *Journal of Cleaner Production* 125709.

Selwyn, B, 'Poverty Chains and Global Capitalism' (2019) 23(1) *Competition & Change* 71.

Shackleton, RT, 'Loss of Land and Livelihoods from Mining Operations: A Case in the Limpopo Province, South Africa' (2020) 99 *Land Use Policy* 104825.

Sharifi, A, 'Co-benefits and Synergies Between Urban Climate Change Mitigation and Adaptation Measures: A Literature Review' (2021) 750 *Science of the Total Environment* 141642.

Sharma, SS and Manthiram, A, 'Towards More Environmentally and Socially Responsible Batteries' (2020) 13(11) *Energy & Environmental Science* 4087.

Sikamo, J, Mwanza, A and Mweemba, C, 'Copper Mining in Zambia – History and Future' (2016) 116(6) *Journal of the Southern African Institute of Mining and Metallurgy* 491.

Slager, R, Gond, JP and Crilly, D, 'Reactivity to Sustainability Metrics: A Configurational Study of Motivation and Capacity' (2021) 31(2) *Business Ethics Quarterly* 275.

Smart, J, Nel, E and Binns, T, 'Economic Crisis and Food Security in Africa: Exploring the Significance of Urban Agriculture in Zambia's Copperbelt Province' (2015) 65 *Geoforum* 37.

Smith, T, 'The French Economic Stake in Colonial Algeria' (1975) 9(1) *French Historical Studies* 184.

Sonderegger, T, Berger, M, Alvarenga, R, Bach, V, Cimprich, A, Dewulf, J, Frischknecht, R, Guinée, J, Helbig, C, Huppertz, T and Jolliet, O, 'Mineral Resources in Life Cycle Impact Assessment – Part I: A Critical Review of Existing Methods' (2020) 25(4) *International Journal of Life Cycle Assessment* 784.

Sovacool, BK, 'The Precarious Political Economy of Cobalt: Balancing Prosperity, Poverty, and Brutality in Artisanal and Industrial Mining in the Democratic Republic of the Congo' (2019) 6(3) *The Extractive Industries and Society* 915.

Sovacool, BK, 'When Subterranean Slavery Supports Sustainability Transitions? Power, Patriarchy, and Child Labor in Artisanal Congolese Cobalt Mining' (2021) 8(1) *The Extractive Industries and Society* 271.

Sovacool, BK and Dworkin, MH, 'Energy Justice: Conceptual Insights and Practical Applications' (2015) 142 *Applied Energy* 435.

Sovacool, BK, Martiskainen, M, Hook, A and Baker, L, 'Decarbonization and Its Discontents: A Critical Energy Justice Perspective on Four Low-Carbon Transitions' (2019) 155(4) *Climatic Change* 581–619.

Sovacool, BK, Ali, SH, Bazilian, M, Radley, B, Nemery, B, Okatz, J and Mulvaney, D, 'Sustainable Minerals and Metals for a Low-Carbon Future' (2020) 367(6473) *Science* 30.

Sovacool, BK, Turnheim, B, Hook, A, Brock, A and Martiskainen, M, 'Dispossessed by Decarbonisation: Reducing Vulnerability, Injustice, and Inequality in the Lived Experience of Low-Carbon Pathways' (2021) 137 *World Development* 105116.

Svobodova, K, Owen, JR and Harris, J, 'The Global Energy Transition and Place Attachment in Coal Mining Communities: Implications for Heavily Industrialized Landscapes' (2021) 71 *Energy Research & Social Science* 101831.

Sze, J and London, JK, 'Environmental Justice at the Crossroads' (2008) 2(4) *Sociology Compass* 1331.

Taskinsoy, J, 'No Brainer, Tackle Climate Change by 2030 or Await the Doomsday by 2100: Tackle Climate Change by 2030' (2020) *SSRN Electronic Journal* 3532709.

Tayebi-Khorami, M, Edraki, M, Corder, G and Golev, A, 'Re-thinking Mining Waste Through an Integrative Approach Led by Circular Economy Aspirations' (2019) 9(5) *Minerals* 286.

Teng, JCY, Wang, JTY and Yang, CC, 'Justice, What Money Can Buy: A Lab Experiment on Primary Social Goods and The Rawlsian Difference Principle' (2020) 31(1) *Constitutional Political Economy* 45.

Têtu, PL and Lasserre, F, 'Chinese Investment in Greenland's Mining Industry: Toward a New Framework for Foreign Direct Investment' (2017) 4(3) *The Extractive Industries and Society* 661.

Thakker, U, Patel, R, Tanwar, S, Kumar, N and Song, H, 'Blockchain for Diamond Industry: Opportunities and Challenges' (2020) 8(11) *IEEE Internet of Things Journal* 8747.

Tobalagba, A and Vijeyarasa, R, 'Engendering Regulation of Artisanal and Small-Scale Mining: Participation, Protection and Access to Justice' (2020) 41(10) *Third World Quarterly* 1635.

Todd, H and Zografos, C, 'Justice for the Environment: Developing a Set of Indicators of Environmental Justice for Scotland' (2005) 14(4) *Environmental Values* 483.

Todd, I and McCauley, D, 'Assessing Policy Barriers to the Energy Transition in South Africa' (2021) 158 *Energy Policy* 112529.

Udoudom, MD and Bassey, SA, 'Plato and John Rawls on Social Justice' (2018) 9(3) *Researchers World* 110.

Unceta, RA, 'The Economic and Social Impact of Mining-Resources Exploitation in Zambia' (2021) 74 *Resources Policy* 102242.

van den Brink, S, Kleijn, R, Sprecher, B and Tukker, A, 'Identifying Supply Risks by Mapping the Cobalt Supply Chain' (2020) 156 *Resources, Conservation and Recycling* 104743.

Vandenhole, W, 'De-growth and Sustainable Development: Rethinking Human Rights Law and Poverty Alleviation' (2018) 11(2) *Law and Development Review* 647.

van Zanten, JA and van Tulder, R, 'Towards Nexus-Based Governance: Defining Interactions Between Economic Activities and Sustainable Development Goals (SDGs)' (2021) 28(3) *International Journal of Sustainable Development & World Ecology* 210.

Vasiljevic-Shikaleska, A, Gjozinska, B and Stojanovikj, M, 'The Circular Economy – a Pathway to Sustainable Future' (2017) 7(17) *Journal of Sustainable Development* 13.

Velenturf, AP and Purnell, P, 'Principles for a Sustainable Circular Economy' (2021) 27 *Sustainable Production and Consumption* 1437.

Velenturf, AP, Archer, SA, Gomes, HI, Christgen, B, Lag-Brotons, AJ and Purnell, P, 'Circular Economy and the Matter of Integrated Resources' (2019) 689 *Science of the Total Environment* 963.

Viebahn, P, Soukup, O, Samadi, S, Teubler, J, Wiesen, K and Ritthoff, M, 'Assessing the Need for Critical Minerals to Shift the German Energy System Towards a High Proportion of Renewables' (2015) 49 *Renewable and Sustainable Energy Reviews* 655.

Vrontisi, Z, Charalampidis, I and Paroussos, L, 'What Are the Impacts of Climate Policies on Trade? A Quantified Assessment of the Paris Agreement for the G20 Economies' (2020) 139 *Energy Policy* 111376.

Vural, G, 'How Do Output, Trade, Renewable Energy and Non-Renewable Energy Impact Carbon Emissions in Selected Sub-Saharan African Countries?' (2020) 69 *Resources Policy* 101840.

Wakenge, CI, Nyenyezi, MRB, Bergh, SI and Cuvelier, J, 'From "Conflict Minerals" to Peace? Reviewing Mining Reforms, Gender, and State Performance in Eastern Democratic Republic of Congo' (2021) 8(2) *The Extractive Industries and Society* 100894.

Walker, G and Day, R, 'Fuel Poverty as Injustice: Integrating Distribution, Recognition and Procedure in the Struggle for Affordable Warmth' (2012) 49 *Energy Policy* 69.

Walker, G, 'Beyond Distribution and Proximity: Exploring the Multiple Spatialities of Environmental Justice' (2009) 41(4) *Antipode* 614.

Walker, G, 'Globalizing Environmental Justice: The Geography and Politics of Frame Contextualization and Evolution' (2009) 9(3) *Global Social Policy* 355.

Wallerstein, I, 'The Rise and Future Demise of the World Capitalist System: Concepts for Comparative Analysis' (1974) 16(4) *Comparative Studies in Society and History* 387.

Wang, J, Yang, L, Lin, J and Bentley, Y, 'The Availability of Critical Minerals for China's Renewable Energy Development: An Analysis of Physical Supply' (2020) *Natural Resources Research* 1.

Watari, T, Nansai, K and Nakajima, K, 'Review of Critical Metal Dynamics to 2050 for 48 Elements Resources' (2020) 155 *Conservation and Recycling* 104669.

Watson, B, 'The Troubling Evolution of Corporate Greenwashing' (2017) 129 *Chain Reaction* 38.

Weldegiorgis, FS, Dietsche, E and Franks, DM, 'Building Mining's Economic Linkages: A Critical Review of Local Content Policy Theory' (2021) 74 *Resources Policy* 102312.

Werthmann, K, 'Gold Rush in West Africa: The Appropriation of "Natural" Resources: Non-industrial Gold Mining in South-Western Burkina Faso' (2000) *Sociologus* 90.

White, R, Hallinan, J and Rayment, B, 'Environmental Law: Climate Change Takes Centre Stage in Land and Environment Court' (2019) 54 *Law Society Journal: Law Society of New South Wales Journal* 80.

Willis, CP, 'Sexual Violence by the State: The Role of Political Institutions in Sexual Violence Perpetration' (2021) 65(3) *International Studies Quarterly* 768.

Witt, MT, 'Book Review: Kwame Anthony Appiah. Cosmopolitanism: Ethics in a World of Strangers. New York: WW Norton & Company, 2006' (2006) 28(4) *Administrative Theory & Praxis* 646.

Xun, D, Hao, H, Sun, X, Liu, Z and Zhao, F, 'End-of-life Recycling Rates of Platinum Group Metals in the Automotive Industry: Insight into Regional Disparities' (2020) 266 *Journal of Cleaner Production* 121942.

Yan, W, Wang, Z, Cao, H, Zhang, Y and Sun, Z, 'Criticality Assessment of Metal Resources in China' (2021) 24(6) *iScience* 102524.

Yang, T, 'The Emergence of the Environmental Impact Assessment Duty as a Global Legal Norm and General Principle of Law' (2018) 70 *Hastings Law Journal* 525.

Yu, JK and Wang, HX, 'Evolution of Distant Water Fisheries Policies in China: Overview, Characteristics and Proposals' (2021) 207 *Ocean & Coastal Management* 105592.

Yu, Y, 'Assessing the Criticality of Minerals Used in Emerging Technologies in China' [2020] *Gospodarka Surowcami Mineralnymi-Mineral Resources Management* 5.

Yuan, Y, Yellishetty, M, Muñoz, MA and Northey, SA, 'Toward a Dynamic Evaluation of Mineral Criticality: Introducing the Framework of Criticality Systems' (2019) 23(5) *Journal of Industrial Ecology* 1264.

Zhang, HB, Dai, HC, Lai, HX and Wang, WT, 'US Withdrawal from the Paris Agreement: Reasons, Impacts, and China's Response' (2017) 8(4) *Advances in Climate Change Research* 220.

Zhang, YX, Chao, QC, Zheng, QH and Huang, L, 'The Withdrawal of the US from the Paris Agreement and Its Impact on Global Climate Change Governance (2017) 8(4) *Advances in Climate Change Research* 213.

Institutional Reports, Working Papers and Papers

AFRODAD, 'Impacts of Fluctuating Commodity Prices on Government Revenue in the SADC Region: The Case of Copper for Zambia' (African Forum and Network on Debt and Development, 2016).

Alsweilem, KA, Cummine, A, Rietveld, M and Tweedie, K, 'A Comparative Study of Sovereign Investor Models: Sovereign Fund Profiles' (Harvard Kennedy School, Belfer Center for Science and International Affairs and Center for International Development at Harvard University, 2015).

Amnesty International, 'Chinese Mining Industry Contributes to Abuses in Democratic Republic of the Congo' (2021).

Amnesty International, 'Profits and Loss: Mining and Human Rights in Katanga, Democratic Republic of Congo' (2013).

Amnesty International, 'Democratic Republic of Congo: "This Is What We Die For": Human Rights Abuses in the Democratic Republic of the Congo Power the Global Trade in Cobalt' (2016).

Anderson, CS, *Selenium and Tellurium Minerals Yearbook: Volume I. Metals and Minerals* (US Geological Survey, 2018).

Banda, W, 'Zambia's Domestication of the Africa Mining Vision: A Gap Analysis' (Centre for Trade Policy and Development Lusaka, 2019).

Barteková, E and Kemp, R, 'Critical Raw Material Strategies in Different World Regions' (The United Nations University–Maastricht Economic and Social Research Institute on Innovation and Technology (UNU-MERIT), 2016) Working Paper 5.

Bebbington, A, Abdulai, AG, Hinfelaar, M, Humphreys Bebbington, D and Sanborn, C, 'Political Settlements and the Governance of Extractive Industry: A Comparative Analysis of the Longue

Durée in Africa and Latin America' (Effective States and Inclusive Development Research Centre, 2017) SID Working Paper No 81.

Beckerman, W, 'A Poverty of Reason: Sustainable Development' (Independent Institute, 2002) No 338.9 B393p.

British Geological Survey World Mineral Production 2014–2018.

Business and Human Rights Centre, '"Going Out" Responsibly: The Human Rights Impact of China's Global Investments (2021).

Caritas Zambia, 'Bringing Agenda 2030 to Life: Zambia Sustainable Development Report' (2019).

Church, C, 'Sustainability and Second Life: The Case for Cobalt and Lithium Recycling' (International Institute for Sustainable Development, 2019).

Coulomb, R, Dietz, S, Godunova, M and Nielsen, TB, 'Critical Minerals Today and in 2030: An Analysis for OECD Countries' (OECD Publishing, 2015) OECD Environment Working Papers No 91.

Esteves AM, Coyne, B and Moreno, A, 'Local Content Initiatives: Enhancing the Subnational Benefits of the Oil, Gas and Mining Sectors' (National Resource Governance Institute, 2013).

European Commission, 'Methodology for Establishing the EU List of Critical Raw Materials' (2017).

European Commission, '2020 Study on the Review of the EU's list of Critical Raw Materials' (2020).

European Commission, 'The Update of the NDC of the European Union and its Member States' (2020).

European Commission, 'Closing the Loop – An EU Action Plan for the Circular Economy' (2015).

European Commission, *Critical Materials for Strategic Technologies and Sectors in the EU – A Foresight Study* (Luxembourg: Publications Office of the European Union, 2020).

European Commission, Directorate-General for Internal Market, Industry, Entrepreneurship and SMEs, Bobba, S, Claudiu, P, Huygens, D et al, *Report on Critical Raw Materials and the Circular Economy* (Publications Office, 2018).

European Commission, *Study on the Review of the List of Critical Raw Materials: Criticality Assessments – Final Report* (EU Publications, 2017).

European Commission, *Study on the EU's List of Critical Raw Materials (2020) Final Report* (2020).

Fortier, SM, Nassar, NT, Lederer, GW, Brainard, J, Gambogi, J and McCullough, EA, 'Draft Critical Mineral List – Summary of Methodology and Background Information' (US Geological Survey, 2018) US Geological Survey technical input document in response to Secretarial Order No 3359 (No 2018-1021).

Gu, X, Dinkelbach, C, Heidbrink, C, Huang, Y, Ke, X, Mayer, M and Ohnesorge, HW, *China's Engagement in Africa: Activities, Effects and Trends* (Centre for Global Studies, 2022).

Hallegatte, S, Vogt-Schilb A, Bangalore, M, and Rozenberg, J, 'Unbreakable: Building the Resilience of the Poor in the Face of Natural Disasters. Climate Change and Development Series' (World Bank, 2017).

Hund, K, La Porta, D, Fabregas, TP, Laing, T and Drexhage, J, *Minerals for Climate Action: The Mineral Intensity of the Clean Energy Transition* (World Bank, 2020) 73.

ICSG, *The World Copper Factbook 2018* (International Copper Study Group, 2018).

IEA, 'Global Energy Review 2020' (International Energy Agency, 2020).

IEA, 'The Role of Critical Minerals in Clean Energy Transitions. World Energy Outlook Special Report' (International Energy Agency, 2021).

ILO, 'Child Labour in Mining and Global Supply Chains' (International Labour Organisation, 2019).

Impact Facility, 'Digging for Change Report – Towards a Responsible Cobalt Supply Chain' (Impact Facility, 2020).

IPCC, 'Climate Change 2014: Synthesis Report' (Contribution of Working Groups I, II and III to the Fifth Assessment Report of the Intergovernmental Panel on Climate Change, 2014).

IRENA, 'Renewable Energy and Climate Pledges: Five Years After the Paris Agreement' (International Renewable Energy Agency, 2019).

IRENA, 'Geopolitics of the Energy Transition: Critical Materials' (International Renewable Energy Agency, 2023).

Kabandula, A and Seekings, J, 'Donor Influence, the Minister of Finance and Welfare Policy Reform in Zambia, 2003–11' (2016) CSSR Working Paper 395.

Kahn, ME, Mohaddes, K, Ng, RN, Pesaran, MH, Raissi, M and Yang, JC, 'Long-Term Macroeconomic Effects of Climate Change: A Cross-Country Analysis' (National Bureau of Economic Research, 2019) No w26167.

Knoepfel, I, 'Who Cares Wins: Connecting Financial Markets to a Changing World?' (UN Environment Programme, 2004).

Ladislaw, S and Tsafos N, 'Energy Spheres of Influence' (Center for Strategic and International Studies, 2019).

Lee, H, Calvin, K, Dasgupta, D, Krinner, G, Mukherji, A, Thorne, P, Trisos, C, Romero, J, Aldunce, P, Barret, K and Blanco, G, 'IPCC, 2023: Climate Change 2023: Synthesis Report, Summary for Policymakers' (Contribution of Working Groups I, II and III to the Sixth Assessment Report of the Intergovernmental Panel on Climate Change, 2023).

Liebenthal, R and Cheelo, C, 'Understanding the Implications of the Boom–Bust Cycle of Global Copper Prices for Natural Resources, Structural Change, and Industrial Development in Zambia' (UNU-WIDER, 2018) WIDER Working Paper No 2018/166.

Lokanathan, V, 'China's Belt and Road Initiative: Implications in Africa' (Observer Research Foundation, 2020) ORF Issue Brief No 395.

Lundstøl, O and Isaksen, J, 'Zambia's Mining Windfall Tax' (UNU-WIDER, 2018) WIDER Working Paper 2018/51.

Manley, D, 'Ninth Time Lucky: Is Zambia's Mining Tax the Best Approach to an Uncertain Future?' (NRGI Briefing, October 2017).

McCarthy, A, Dellink, and R Bibas, R, 'The Macroeconomics of the Circular Economy Transition: A Critical Review of Modelling Approaches' (OECD, 2018) Environment Working Paper No 130.

Mostert, H and Young, C, 'From Promise to Practice: South Africa's Legal Framework for Mineral Resources and the Sustainable Development Goals' (South African Institute of International Affairs, 2018).

National Research Council, *Minerals, Critical Minerals, and the US Economy* (National Academies Press, 2008).

Natural Resources Governance Institute, 'The Resource Curse, The Political and Economic Challenges of Natural Resource Wealth' (NGRI Reader, 2015).

NSTC, 'Critical and Strategic Mineral Supply Chains Assessment of Critical Minerals' (National Science and Technology Council, 2016) Report 2016-03-16 FINAL.

OECD, 'The Changing Face of Fragility and Its Implications Post-2015' in *States of Fragility 2015: Meeting Post-2015 Ambitions* (OECD Publishing, 2015) 29–54.

OECD, *International Trade and the Transition to a Circular Economy* (OECD Publishing, 2018).

OECD, 'Interconnected Supply Chains: A Comprehensive Look at Due Diligence Challenges and Opportunities Sourcing Cobalt and Copper from the Democratic Republic of the Congo' (2019).

OECD, *Mining and Green Growth in the EECCA Region*, OECD Green Growth Studies (OECD Publishing, 2019).

OECD, 'Responsible Business Conduct. Interconnected Supply Chains: A Comprehensive Look at Due Diligence Challenges and Opportunities' (2019).

Office of the Historian, '260. Study Prepared by the Ad Hoc Inter-Agency Group on Critical Imported Materials' (Foreign Relations of the United States, 1969–1976, Volume XXXI, Foreign Economic Policy, 1973–1976).

Parrique, T, Barth, J, Briens, F, Kerschner, C, Kraus-Polk, A, Kuokkanen, A and Spangenberg, JH, 'Decoupling Debunked. Evidence and Arguments Against Green Growth as a Sole Strategy for Sustainability' (European Environment Bureau, 2019).

Parthemore, C, 'Elements of Security: Mitigating the Risks of US Dependence on Critical Minerals' (Center for a New American Security, 2011).

Peyer, C, Feeney, P and Mercier, F, 'PR or Progress? Glencore's Corporate Responsibility in the Democratic Republic of the Congo' (Rights and Accountability in Development, 2014).

POLINARES, 'Framework for Understanding the Sources of Conflict and Tension'. Work Package 1, Internal Project document, April 2010.

Ramdoo, I, 'Making Global Supply Chains Sustainable: The Case of the Gold Sector' (European Centre for Development Policy Management, 2015) Briefing Note 83.
Roskill, 'Cobalt Sustainability Monitor Report' (2011).
Schnebele, EK, 'Silicon. Mineral Commodity Summaries' (US Geological Survey, 2018).
Schröder, P, 'Promoting a Just Transition to an Inclusive Circular Economy' (Royal Institute of International Affairs, 2020).
Schulz, KJ, DeYoung, JH, Jr, Seal, RR, II and Bradley, DC (eds), *US Geological Survey, 'Critical Mineral Resources of the United States – Economic and Environmental Geology and Prospects for Future Supply'* (2017) US Geological Survey Professional Paper 1802, F1–F40.
STRADE, 'China's Mineral Sector and the Belt & Road Initiative' (Strategic Dialogue on Sustainable Raw Materials for Europe, March 2018) European Policy Brief No 2/2018.
Sumner, A, C Hoy and E Ortiz-Juarez, 'Estimates of the Impact of Covid-19 on Global Poverty' (UNU-WIDER, 2020) WIDER Working Paper 2020/43.
Sutton, P, 'A Perspective on Environmental Sustainability?' (2004) Paper for the Victorian Commissioner for Environmental Sustainability1-32.
Umicore, 'Sustainable Procurement Framework for Cobalt'.
UNFCCC, Nationally Determined Contributions under the Paris Agreement: Synthesis Report by the secretariat. United Nations Convention on Climate Change FCCC/PA/CMA/2021/8, Conference of the Parties serving as the meeting of the Parties to the Paris Agreement, Third Session, Glasgow, 31 November 2021.
US Department of Labor, '2019 Findings on the Worst Forms of Child Labor'.
US Geological Survey, *Mineral Commodity Summaries 2021* (2021).
WBCSD, 'Collaboration, Innovation, Transformation: Ideas and Inspiration to Accelerate Sustainable Growth – a Value Chain Approach' (World Business Council for Sustainable Development, 2011).
WEF, 'Making Mining Safe and Fair: Artisanal Cobalt Extraction in the Democratic Republic of the Congo', White Paper (World Economic Forum, 2020).
Wissenbach, U and Wang, Y, 'African Politics Meets Chinese Engineers: The Chinese-Built Standard Gauge Railway Project in Kenya and East Africa' (Johns Hopkins University-SAIS, 2017) Working Paper 13.
World Bank, 'Democratic Republic of Congo: Growth with Governance in the Mining Sector' (2008).
World Bank, *World Development Report 2010: Development and Climate Change* (2008).
World Bank, 'World Development Indicators 2011' (2011).
World Bank, 'Action Plan on Climate Change Adaptation and Resilience' (2019).
Thomason, JS, Atwell, RJ, Bajraktari, Y, Bell, JP, Barnett, DS, Karvonides, NS, Niles, MF and Schwartz, EL, 'From National Defense Stockpile (NDS) to Strategic Materials Security Program (SMSP): Evidence and Analytic Support' (Institute for Defense Analyses, 2010) IDA Paper P-4593.

Conference Papers

Florestal, M, 'On the Origin of Fear in the World Trade System: Excavating the Roots of the Berlin Conference 2 of 1884–1885' in *Proceedings of the ASIL Annual Meeting* (Cambridge University Press, 2007) 143–46.
Genc, B, Mlangena, T and Onifade, M, 'Safety Towards Zero Harm in the South African Platinum Sector' in *Proceedings of the 27th International Symposium on Mine Planning and Equipment Selection – MPES* (Springer, 2018) 535–44.
Gulley, AL, Nassar, NT and Xun, S, 'China, the United States, and Competition for Resources that Enable Emerging Technologies' (2018) 115(16) *Proceedings of the National Academy of Sciences* 4111.
Mutua, M, 'What Is TWAIL?' in *Proceedings of the ASIL Annual Meeting* (Cambridge University Press, 2000 94) 31–38.

Purnell, P, Dawson, D, Roelich, KE, Steinberger, JK and Busch, J, 'Critical Materials for Infrastructure: Local vs Global Properties' (2013) 166(5) *Proceedings of the Institution of Civil Engineers – Engineering Sustainability* 272.

Sinkala, P, Fujii, Y, Kodama, JI and Fukuda, D, 'An Overview of Copper Mining in Zambia's Copperbelt Province' in *Proceedings of Spring Meeting of MMIJ Hokkaido Branch* (MMIJ-Hokkaido Branch, 2018) 35–36.

Triatmanto, B and Natsir, M, 'A Descriptive Analysis of Sustainability Development Goals (SDGs), Community Empowerment, and the Participatory Rural Appraisal Approach' in *Proceedings of the 6th International Conference on Community Development* (ICCD, 2019).

Dissertations and Theses

Mukwasa, M, 'When Is Compensation Payable for Breach of a Stabilisation Clause? The Case for the Cancelled Mining Development Agreements in Zambia' (Doctoral Dissertation, University of Pretoria, 2010).

Sbert Carlsson, C, 'Mining from the Lens of Ecological Law: Obstacles and Opportunities for Re-formation' (Doctoral Dissertation, Université d'Ottawa/University of Ottawa, 2019).

Blogs, Websites, Internet Sources

Ambrosio, N, 'COVID-19 and Climate: Multifaceted Impacts' (*PreventionWeb*, 2020).

Brady, J, 'NPR Cookie Consent and Choices' (NPR, 2022).

Business and Human Resource Centre, Zambia, 'Court Fines Glencore's Mopani Copper $13 Million for Tax Avoidance (27 May 2021).

Chadha, R, 'Skewed Critical Minerals Global Supply Chains Post COVID-19: Reforms for Making India Self-reliant (Brookings, 10 June 2020).

Creamer Media, 'Zambia's Refined Copper Outlook Positive' (*Mining Weekly*, 2018).

Daly, T, 'China Moly to Spend $2.5 Billion to Double Copper, Cobalt Output at Congo Mine' (Reuters, 6 August 2021).

Doherty, B, Blum, P and Zihlmann, O, 'The Inside Story of Glencore's Hidden Dealings in DRC' *The Guardian* (5 November 2017).

Dunn, K, 'Does ESG Investing Actually Make a Difference? (*Fortune*, 2021).

Environmental-expert.com, 'Nord-Schrott Profile' (2021).

Environmental-expert.com, 'Regulator-Cetrisa Profile' (2021).

Environmental-expert.com, 'Umicore S.A. Profile' (2021).

European Commission, 'Sustainable Corporate Governance' (nd).

Fair Cobalt Alliance (FCA), *The Impact Facility.*

Farand, C, 'EU 2020 Budget Boosts Climate Action Spending' (*Climate Home News*, 19 November 2019).

Farchy, J and Warren H, 'China Has a Secret Weapon in the Race to Dominate Electric Cars' (Bloomberg, 2 December 2018).

Ferris, N, 'Why Critical Mineral Supplies Won't Scupper the Energy Transition (*Energy Monitor*, 2021).

First-quantum.com, 'First Quantum Minerals Ltd – Our Operations'.

FutureLearn, 'Are the Sustainable Development Goals the Best Approach to Sustainability?' (Trinity College Dublin, 2021).

Galvez, L, 'Your Smartphone Could Have Contributed to Devastation in the DRC' (*Impakter*, 10 July 2021)).

GBR, 'Is Zambia Losing Its Shine?' (Global Business Reports, 2021).
Home, A, 'Column: Cobalt, Congo and a Mass Artisanal Mining Experiment' (Reuters, 2021).
Homes, A, 'Europe Joins Global Scramble for Critical Minerals (MINING.COM, 2020).
Human Rights Watch, 'World Report 2019. Our Annual Review of Human Rights Around the Globe' (2019).
Hume, N, 'Death Toll at DRC Mine Rises to 43' *Financial Times* (2019).
Imahashi, R and Nagumo J, 'China and Green Energy Drive Copper Prices to Record High: Shares in Asian Miners and Nonferrous Producers Surge Despite Supply Concerns' (NIKKEI Asia, 24 May 2021).
Jaeger, J, Banaji, F and Calnek-Sugin, T, 'By the Numbers: How Business Benefits from the Sustainable Development Goals' (World Resources Institute, 2017).
Jinchuan Group International Resources, 'Business Overview' (*Jinchuan-intl.com*, 2021).
Kell, G, 'The Remarkable Rise of ESG' (Forbes, 2018).
Kelly, A, 'Apple and Google Named in US lawsuit Over Congolese Child Cobalt Mining Deaths' *The Guardian* (16 December 2019).
Keraval, G, 'Mining the Future: How China Is Set to Dominate the Next Industrial Revolution' (*FP*, 1 May 2019).
Kettle, J, 'Mining Sector Faces Energy Transition Conundrum: Can the Industry Balance Decarbonisation, ESG Rules and Mining Asset Investments?' *Financial Times* (2020).
Khokhar, T and Serajuddin, U, 'Should We Continue to Use the Term "Developing World"?' (World Bank, 2015).
Klovig Skelton, S, 'Major US Tech Companies Named in Lawsuit over Mining Deaths of Congolese Children (*Computer Weekly*, 2020).
Konkola Copper Mines, 'Copper'.
Lavietes, M, 'Tesla, Apple among Firms Accused of Aiding Child Labor in Congo' (2019).
Lin, X, 'China Takes Extraordinary Initiatives in South–South Cooperation' (United Nations Office for South–South Cooperation, 2019).
LME, 'LME Partners with Charities Pact and The Impact Facility to Fund Two Responsible Sourcing Projects' (London Metal Exchange, 2021).
Mapila, K, 'Copper Can Save Zambia – Capitalizing on Rising Demand Will Have Long-Term Benefits if Handled Properly' (*The World Today*, 2021).
MINING.COM, 'CO_2 Emissions from Cobalt Production Expected to Soar – Report' (2021).
Mining for Zambia, 'Zambia's Mines – A Concentrated Mining Sector: Four Big Mines and Several Important Smaller Operations Make Up Zambia's Copper-Mining Landscape' (2016).
Nakanwagi, S, 'Mine Closure and Justice Implications' (*IJPIEL*, 13 August 2021).
Natural Resource Governance Institute, '2017 Resource Governance Index Democratic Republic of Congo (Mining)'.
Ngounou, B, 'Africa: The Impact of Mining on the Environment' (*Afrik21*, 10 June 2021).
Odea, S, 'Smartphone Users 2026' (Statista, 2021).
OEC, 'Raw Copper in Zambia' (Observatory of Economic Complexity).
Okeowo, A, 'China, Zambia, and a Clash in a Coal Mine' (*The New Yorker*, 9 October 2013).
Olson, S, '9 Biggest Chinese Mining Companies' (Investopedia, 2021).
Roston, E, 'Climate Changed: The Massive Cost of Not Adapting to Climate Change' (Bloomberg, 2019).
Simon, F, 'EU to Push New Standards for "Greenest" Car Batteries on Earth' (EURACTIV, 2020).
Siwale, T, 'The Current State of Artisanal and Small-Scale Mining in Zambia' (International Growth Centre, 2019).
Thimmiah, S, 'Where Are Miners and Metals in the Circular Economy?' *The Guardian* (20 February 2024).
Turner, A, 'Number of Smartphone Users Worldwide (Billions)' (BankMyCell.com, 2024).
UN Department of Economic and Social Affairs, 'United Nations Declaration on the Rights of Indigenous Peoples' (2021).

UNDP, 'COVID-19: Looming Crisis in Developing Countries Threatens to Devastate Economies and Ramp Up Inequality' (2020).

UNICEF, 'Ground-breaking Multi-stakeholder Initiative to Address Child Labour in DRC Mining Communities' (Press Release, 16 November 2020).

Warwick, F, 'Zambia 2019 Copper Output Drop Due to New Mining Taxes' (Spglobal.com, 2019).

Watson, B, 'The Troubling Evolution of Corporate Greenwashing' *The Guardian* (20 August 2016).

White Paper on China's Policy on Mineral Resources of 2003.

World Bank, 'Worldwide Governance Indicators' (2019).

World Resources Institute, 'Historical GHG Emissions' (*Climate Watch*, 2021).

Xinhua, 'Roundup: Expectations Remain High among Zambians as Copper Prices Rise' (*Xinhuanet*, 2021).

INDEX

www.ingramcontent.com/pod-product-compliance
Ingram Content Group UK Ltd.
Pitfield, Milton Keynes, MK11 3LW, UK
UKHW020815290926
15470UKWH00003B/1181

9 781509 976706